FANTASTIKA
AT THE EDGE OF REALITY
YET MORE BEST OF SCIENCE FICTION

ALSO AVAILABLE

Chained to the Alien: The Best of Australian Science Fiction Review (Second Series)

Skiffy and Mimesis: More Best of ASFR: Australian SF Review (Second Series)

Unleashing the Strange: Twenty-First Century Science Fiction Literature

Warriors of the Tao: The Best of Science Fiction: A Review of Speculative Literature

Xeno Fiction: More Best of Science Fiction: A Review of Speculative Fiction

FANTASTIKA
AT THE EDGE OF REALITY
YET MORE BEST OF SCIENCE FICTION

EDITED BY
DAMIEN BRODERICK AND VAN IKIN

WILDSIDE PRESS

*For Dane Ikin and Nick Stathopoulos
and for all the sercon writers and readers
who keep sf criticism alive and flourishing*

The editors gratefully acknowledge the Faculty of Arts at the University of Western Australia for support and encouragement toward the publication of *Warriors of the Tao,* *Xeno Fiction,* and *Fantastika at the Edge of Reality.*

Copyright © 2014 by Damien Broderick and Van Ikin.

Please see "Chapter Sources in Chronological Order" at the end of this volume for information on original publication dates and sources for the works contained herein.

Published by Wildside Press LLC.
www.wildsidebooks.com

CONTENTS

Introduction I, by Damien Broderick 7

Introduction II, by Van Ikin 10

An Interview with Stanislaw Lem, by Anne Brewster. 12

Peter Weir: Master of Unease, Interviewed by Terry Dowling
       and George Mannix 15

Patterns of Epic: The Re-Affirmation of Western Values in *Star
       Wars* and *The Lord of The Rings*, by Hal Colebatch. 37

Gaia in Isaac Asimov's *Foundation* Novels: Ecological
       Hypothesis as Fictional Terminus, by Jacob George C. 51

Women of Darkness, edited by Kathryn Ptacek: Original Horror
       and Dark Fantasy by Contemporary Women Writers,
       by Yvonne Rousseau. 58

Women of Wonder, edited by Pamela Sargent, by Marilyn
       Walters. 62

Wordlust and Wild, Wild Womyn, by Russell Blackford 69

Sara Douglass' *Battleaxe* and *Enchanter*, by Tess Williams 73

Doris Lessing: An Overview, by Caroline Flynn 77

The Eighteenth Century and Science Fiction: A Symbiosis?,
       by Donald M. Hassler 84

The Island of Doctor Moreau, or the Case of Devolution,
       by Pascale Krumm. 90

Deus ex Machina: *Red Dwarf, Better Than Life, Last Human*,
       by Doug Naylor, by Marian Foster 104

Analogues of Anomie: Lee Harding's Novels, by Russell
       Blackford 107

Fantasy Fiction and Terry Pratchett's Discworld,
    by Kevin Smith 116

A Conversation with Roger Zelazny: 8th April, 1978, Talking
    with Terry Dowling and Keith Curtis 152

Roger Zelazny's Form and Chaos Philosophy, by Carl P. Yoke . . .163

"Wake Up, You Lot!" John Foyster as SF Critic, by Bruce
    Gillespie. 182

Chapter Sources in Chronological Order 195

Contributors 197

Index 201

INTRODUCTION I

DAMIEN BRODERICK

Why *Fantastika*?

Although the journal from which these essays are drawn is named *Science Fiction: A Review of Speculative Literature,* its remit has always been broader than just science fiction (sf). While editor Van Ikin's central focus has remained on science fiction as such—that is, stories about imagined worlds beyond our reality, yet wrought by the empirical, mimetic tools of reasoned science—there has always been a place, as well, for other kinds of wildly imaginary or transgressive fantastical writing.

Borrowing from European usage, the superb critic and theorist John Clute has recently started to call this larger zone *Fantastika,* and we have adopted his term to characterize the pieces in this third volume of the best from Ikin's *Science Fiction.*

"Fantastika" might seem at first glance just a highfalutin dress-up of what most people call "sci fi," but it's much more than that. It records an epochal shift in the way the European mind viewed the world, and narrated what it saw. Here is Clute's own motivation for this term (abbreviated from his 2007 address at the Center for the Future in Prague):[1]

> Up until about 1700... we did not categorize works of art according to their use of (or failure to use) material that might be deemed unreal. After that point, in English literature... a fault line was drawn between mimetic work, which accorded with the rational Enlightenment values then beginning to dominate, and the great cauldron of irrational myth and story...

Fantastika, then, are those abundant modes of telling the world that escape the strictures of polite, measurable functionality. They revert to, and expand upon, the narrative possibilities caught in earlier days by myth, legend, prophecy and tales of horror.

---

1 John Clute, "Fantastika in the World Storm." http://www.johnclute.co.uk/word/?p=15

There is a beauty in the eighteenth century Enlightenment, but it is an Apollonian beauty, the beauty of the intensely described, a beauty achieved through refusal and exclusion and measure and argument. It... engineers the rise of Western Civilization over the past four centuries, but it also blueprints the gulag. And after 1750 or so, as might be expected, a consciously subversive reaction sets in.

Stories begin to surface which subvert the ordered world above; which contradict the closed mundanity of the work produced during the Apollonian Ascendancy; which say there is more to the world than the dressage of proper measure. These stories re-import all the old material, the irrational, the impossible, the nightmare, the inevitable, the haunted, the storyable...

In these terms, it's plausible to regard science fiction of the 20th and early 21st century as the natural voice of a persistent Apollonian pressure to conform, reshape the unruly into spandex, aspire to cool godlike knowledge and power. It's not that Dionysian fuming and glee fail to burst into this rationalized sf world, but when they do it is usually in opposition to the main narrative trajectory. Heinlein's competent men and women, Asimov's psychohistorians and robopsychologists, van Vogt's Nexialist polymaths, Clarke's spaceship dreamers laid down templates that most sf embodied into ten thousand stories of planetary exploration, invasion and resistance, uncanny powers mastered by sheer grit and disciplined thinking. At the same time, in satire directed against McCarthyism in the 1950s, a new breed of sf writers made amused, sardonic, satirical sport of barbarities, decade by decade showing the poverty and stupidity of racism, sexism, other bigotries—not by preaching, but through entertaining drama.

Meanwhile, suppressed aspects of the human experience were seething against the cauldron's lid, bursting up in the form of horror tales and fantasies that exposed more directly the lure and fear of cruelty, of desire, of wish—of the unconscious that powers the Apollonian dream.

In the essays in this book, a range of responses is offered to fictions at the boundaries of reality—the fences abutting these landscapes of fantastika. Some explicitly survey examples of the fantastic, the utopian, the dystopian. Others look at the architecture of fiction that twists the mimetic to the breaking point: Terry Pratchett's teeming Discworld, moving through space on the back of an immense turtle, A'Tuin; Asimov's hyper-rational Foundation universe caving in under the pressure of mind-readers and the planetary consciousness Gaia; Roger Zelazny's worlds always halfway between light and dark, reason and unreason; Doris Lessing's Sufiesque hidden histories of this world and others; the "sci fi" of *Star Wars* set against the rich fantasy of Tolkien's *Lord of the Rings*. And much more, some of it apparently domestic but bursting free of the ordinary in moments of shock or epiphany, some exploring the response of fantastika to the condition of women, still the aliens in the heart of the Enlightenment world. Several even directly address the nature of sf criticism (from quite different standpoints), and how fantastika is most rewardingly read.

All these chapters, as noted above, are drawn from Professor Van Ikin's long-running journal. This is our third selection, a companion to *Warriors of the Tao* (Borgo/Wildside, 2011) and *Xeno Fiction* (Borgo/Wildside, 2013). Van is a connoisseur of all the odd flavors of fantastika's menus. His first anthology, *Australian Science Fiction*, in 1982, was an early and exemplary sampling of the best sf from the island continent. Published by University of Queensland Press, it delved back into the roots of fantastika in Australia in 1845, and forward to brilliant writers such as Peter Carey who were opening out literary fiction in this formerly despised direction. In 1990 he edited the anthology *Glass Reptile Breakout*, published by the Centre for Studies in Australian Literature, and two years later he and Terry Dowling compiled the excellent anthology *Mortal Fire: Best Australian SF.*

This background of knowledgeable scholarship is the basis for the most important historical study to date of Aussie sf: *Strange Constellations: A History of Australian Science Fiction*, from Greenwood Press in 1998, co-written by Van with Dr. Russell Blackford and Dr. Sean McMullen. The Australian contribution to criticism of fantastika is represented here especially in a tribute to a great amateur critical scholar, the late John Foyster.

Van's chief contribution to the study of fantastika is his distinctive and long-running critical magazine, familiarly known by the iconic initials *SF*. With its cleanly printed pages and a trademark yellow or white stiff cover, always a cut above the traditional mimeograph-copied sf fanzines, *SF* is not quite an academic literary review nor a wildly anything-goes celebratory or controversy-fuming fanzine. The voices in Van's magazine have engaged in a long conversation, with no stuffily imposed tone beyond civility and a willingness to cite sources, usually good-humored, sometimes naive, sometimes hair-raisingly hieratic. All those sampled here, we hope, will provide guidance (both insightful and entertaining) in the long trek through the exotic cosmos of 20th and 21st century fantastika.

INTRODUCTION II

VAN IKIN

It was back in 1975 that we came up with the name for *Science Fiction: A Review of Speculative Literature.* I've never been able to recall the exact comment that triggered everything, but I remember capping a long discussion with the suggestion that we simply call the journal "Science Fiction"—and George Mannix instinctively said "Science Fiction *what?*" I hastened to explain that it was my devious plan that readers would have to peer inside each issue to answer that question, and that they would find it to be a journal containing artwork and images, and even the occasional short sf story, as well as plenty of critical voices covering the spectrum from academics to interviewed authors.

On top of that, they were to find that the contents *challenged* their notions of what constituted "science fiction".... That led to more discussion (I remember it as a long but exciting night) and eventually we added the sub-title so that "Science Fiction" was somewhat contrarily played off against "Speculative Literature." Looking back to that moment, I can see that the folk at that gathering—Terry Dowling, Keith Curtis, Bradley Wynne, Geoff Pollard, and I—were enthused with the idea of *fantastika...* but we didn't think to coin a term for it. (I wonder what the sales might have been if we had?)

A number of essays in this book stirred strong responses from readers when originally published. In "Patterns of Epic: The Re-Affirmation of Western Values in *Star Wars* and *The Lord of the Rings*," Australian sf author Hal Colebatch vigorously defends the observation that "the *Star Wars* trilogy is not merely profoundly religious, but... it is more centrally in the Western religious tradition than perhaps any other popular film that has ever been made. Certainly it is a far more religious film than any Hollywood Biblical epic." Readers of today, being more attuned to the possibilities of fantastika, would probably nod general agreement before going into a huddle to determine if they agree that it is *far more* religious than any Hollywood Biblical epic... but back in 1992, Colebatch struck a nerve, for he had articulated a new (and somewhat unsettling) way of viewing a familiar work from the canon. He had drawn attention to the way the concerns of *Star Wars* reached beyond the boundaries of simple sf frolics.

Carl Yoke's essay on "Roger Zelazny's Form and Chaos Philosophy" also opened new frontiers, though in a different way. Taking Zelazny's acknowledgement that his work is broadly guided by a philosophy of "form and chaos," Yoke as critic teases this out, carefully identifying what Zelazny has added to literary thinking and thoughtfully reflecting upon the ideas that readers are imbibing. To my mind it has always been a central function of literary criticism to identify the covert ideologies and agendas of fiction, and it has always been particularly important for critics to name (and if necessary shame) the hidden assumptions underlying works that are supposedly "mere entertainments." In this case, happily, the process is reversed, for the critic is able to tease out nuances and subtleties coded into Zelazny's works, demonstrating their function as intellectual explorations. As it happens, Yoke shows Zelazny to have grasped one of the central facets of fantastika and to have produced narratives to challenge what Clute describes as "the closed mundanity of the work produced during the Apollonian Ascendancy."

Zelazny speaks for himself in this volume, interviewed in Sydney in 1978 by Terry Dowling and Keith Curtis. The interview strongly reflects our editorial enthusiasm for what we meant by "speculative literature," for Zelazny reaches out to discuss comics, films, mythology, and even sf poetry—effortlessly weaving the tapestry of what we can now call fantastika. (His comments on literary collaboration also stand up well after thirty-five years: it's high time some bright-eyed postgrad explored his claim that collaboration is "a kind of Stanislavskyan method of writing"…)

Damien has graciously described me as "a connoisseur of all the odd flavors of fantastika's menus." I'll accept that compliment any day, so don't take what follows as any kind of demur—but it's possibly more true to say that I strongly believed we should be doing as much as we could to let all manner of voices be heard and to keep readers informed of the growing diversity of the field. The idea was to encourage readers to sample the odd flavors of the menu. History can already show that we could have done much more in that respect—but I would still like to think that the things we *did* accomplish were well worth the struggle. In particular, I will always be pleased to have published with the kind of "randomness" that gave prominence to Zelazny in one issue, H.G. Wells in the next, and Lee Harding after that, with book reviews in their shorter space trying to reflect yet other flavors from the menu.

AN INTERVIEW WITH STANISLAW LEM

ANNE BREWSTER

Brewster: *Of your early novels,* The Invincible *might suggest that humanity has an innate tendency for wisdom, whereas* Memoirs Found in a Bathtub *depicts human beings as fickle creatures locked in a power struggle and subject to paranoia and angst. How is this conflict resolved in your later writing?*

Lem: I doubt if *The Invincible* can be taken for a good case of human wisdom in action. The crew of the rocketship will revenge the comrades from another ship which was attacked by non-living mechanisms and only the hero of the novel understands fully the futility of any such undertaking. (And *this* too only at the end of the story.) Because I see no contradiction between the first and the second novel, I do not think I should try to resolve this dilemma.

Your concept of man as self-evolver as developed in The Star Diaries *and* A Perfect Vacuum *places great faith in the rational being. Do you envisage* future man *as a product both of rational and a-rational (or non rational) thinking?*

I am again somewhat amazed by your point of view. The self-evolving beings in *The Star Diaries,* as, say, the inhabitants of the planet Dichotica, are fools and slaves of their "autoevolutionary technology" and have from its use nothing but a lot of misery. This is my opinion: the wisest technology is applied in the stupidest way, and because of this, causes the opposite of what was intended. I will say: man *should* be rational, but he *is not*.

Do you see the role of philosophic or abstract thinking in A Perfect Vacuum *as an extension of logic or a celebration of pure fantasy?*

I was playing with logic, to produce some paradoxes; perhaps superficially their appearance—their content—seems to be fantastic, but I think that the *core* was very serious indeed. There is no contradiction between irony and/or the sardonic mode of seeing things and what we call truth or *adaequatio rei et intellectus.*

What is the role of fantasy in the contemporary world? Do you think the world of today places specific demands on writers, for example to encourage them to delve into the fantastic as alternative to mundane values?

But again, the fantastic does not in my eyes exclude the mundane values; they can come and work together. There exists what one names "pure fantasy" with witches, sorcerers etc., but I think this kind of literature is a feeble surrogate of narcotic drugs (this is the way I see the work of Tolkien for example). I am not interested in pure fantasy—not in the least. I use some of these forms as a *vehiculum* of parables, even jokes, but everywhere there *must* be some hard core (of things, of problems) related to our real world.

Your robot and pilot tales often follow the structure of fairy tales and folktales. Do you feel your prominent role as one of the world's leading science fiction writers has anything in common with the village bard or perhaps the soothsayer of old? Do you feel you have been influenced by these forms?

Sure, I have been in a way influenced by these forms, but I would rather state it another way: I did use some of these classic forms "with malice aforethought," to make a trivial point in a non trivial way. There can develop a very original tension of high literary value if one puts together forms and contents taken from some distant genres, if one violates this way some old convention/tradition, the result is then ironical or monstrous or simply comical. The tension develops between the form and the content which never appeared united—I could call this method the method of breeding—*cross-breeding* perhaps—some stagnant old forms and some new developing problems or themes. I am no bard and no soothsayer, but only a fellow who likes to laugh at human stupidity and madness. I am, in a word, malicious as reporter of human follies.

Science and technology offer man a greater freedom and have thus liberated the imagination. Yet in practice they may have the opposite effect and may encourage consumerism and conformism rather than fostering good art. Can you comment on this?

There I am agreeing with your standpoint fully. This greater freedom serves as amplification of human shameless desires of the lowest kind. The computer used for astrological forecasting is therefore a symbol of this abuse of technical fruits in my eyes. The imagination is not especially splendid these days; we are rather locked in a little vicious circle of scenarios coined by futurology (and sf too). The only driving force is today (for our imagination) natural science; the artistic imagination is in a shabby state indeed. And I do not see a trace of *social* imagination in the whole intellectual world.

What, in your view, is the future of robotics? How do you think the development of ultra-intelligent machines will alter humanity's perspective on itself?

I doubt if there shall be this ultra-intelligent machine soon, even if its construction were technically possible, because there is no *need* for it on the Market, our Ruler and God. I think there will be, rather, military robots, automates to fight wars *for* rich countries, since the welfare state mollifies the human spirit and then no-one will hear a word about conscription… And *if* such a mechanical genius should be built, this will not alter the state of things; this will be a sensation for a day or two. The mass culture can undertake nothing and can have nothing (for consumption) from such a synthetic genius.

You have often remarked on the improbability of making contact with extraterrestrial civilizations. Are you becoming more optimistic?

No, I am becoming more pessimistic there. I think we (that is the human race) must have a totally false image of the Universe: because from the whole of our natural science, from this knowledge follows necessarily the *existence* of the "Others," and we do *not* see a trace of them in the sky, even though a lot of observatories have worked and searched after them (signals) for some decades. So there must be hidden some big misunderstanding—we do not see the Universe the way it *is* and the way we *should* see it. That is mystery wrapped in an enigma. I would be glad to hear the answer, to live to learn the solution of this riddle.

—1982

PETER WEIR: MASTER OF UNEASE

INTERVIEWED BY

TERRY DOWLING AND GEORGE MANNIX

Peter Weir is Australia's most provocative and original film-maker. His work would not be conventionally regarded as science fiction, but it does often rest in the broad area of imaginative and speculative work that tends to be pigeonholed under that name. Peter Nicholls' *Encyclopedia of Science Fiction*, for instance, has an entry for *The Cars That Ate Paris*, describing it as a film that "does not readily fit into any traditional category," and later revised editions will undoubtedly mention other Weir films with equal caution. *Picnic at Hanging Rock* invites a similar classification, especially since it presents the audience with what one reviewer, Scott Murray, has called a "time zone":

> Given the rock's ability to warp time around its perimeters, one can view the monolith as a kind of time zone, one that absorbs people into a fourth dimension.(*Cinema Papers*, Nov.-Dec., 1975)

While, fortunately, there is no such heavy-handedness in the film itself, this potential is not to be ignored. On the other hand, one could say that *The Last Wave* is quite openly a "science fiction" film. It tells the story of a mysterious lost race called the Mulkurul whose tribal remains are found beneath the streets of Sydney and whose spirit has "possessed" a young lawyer. His prophetic "big dreams" (to note a pertinent connection with Jungian psychoanalytic theory) foretell of an impending disaster—part of an ancient cycle being fulfilled. Weir's other major films—the formative early piece, *Homesdale*, and the telemovie, *The Plumber*—by their suggestion of breakdowns in what could be called orthodox reality, their challenging of our assumptions about what is normal, fit easily into the same broad traditions established by everything from *The Twilight Zone* to Guy Green's *The Magus* or Polanski's *The Tenant*. The following is an interview with a writer/producer/director who, regardless of whatever departures from the genre he might undertake, will always remain a "natural" within the field of speculative and imaginative film-making.

§

Dowling/Mannix: *You have said that you would like to be known as the "master of unease." This seems to suggest a conscious program on your part—a definite role for yourself as film-maker almost as if you were meeting a particular need. Could you say something about what led to this preferred role?*

Weir: Well, I think it was probably a phrase I plucked out of the air to answer another question or in reply to another kind of categorizing. I would like to be a master film-maker, I think—if you see it in the craft sense. It seems to me one of the things I enjoy from film to film, even doing television commercials in fact, is the pleasure in mastering that craft. To some extent I still think of myself as an apprentice learning the craft of film-making or of story-telling. "Unease" is an interesting word, and I prefer it to other words that have been suggested. That's why I say it was possibly a reply to another type of statement, like the famous Hitchcock "master of suspense"—obviously it's a play off that. Though I've used a little suspense, I'm still learning about it. Unease is something that has come naturally to me, I think, from my earliest films.

Has there always been this interest in unease in your own background?

Not consciously, although it crosses over into a view of life, I think. I became uneasy very quickly. (Laughs) To give an example: I was in a hotel room in America a couple of months ago, and heard a strange sound in the middle of the night and couldn't work out what it was. I went through all the normal things, you know—it's a rat in the ceiling or it's somebody in the room upstairs, yes, that's it. But what would they be doing that would make that strange sound? It was a kind of scraping sound with almost a breath—something like the sound a possum can make in this country. That's impossible in a thirty-storey hotel in New York. But I couldn't work it out, and somewhere in there I had a fraction of a second of deep unease, of not really knowing, of touching something that later on is still very interesting and exciting. That area—somewhere inside that fraction of a second—is where I work.

Without wishing to force you into any categories, the very fact that you have permitted yourself to be interviewed in a journal like Science

Fiction *suggests that you see your work as having certain connections with what is popularly regarded as fantasy and science fiction. How do you see this connection?*

Well, firstly, I was no good at science at school. (Laughs) To me, fiction and non-fiction are essentially the same thing. I mean, who draws the line anyway? I remember when I worked for Film Australia and did a couple of documentaries, I was fascinated by this word "documentary" because it implied that there was some kind of truth behind it—you know, actual documents, this sort of thing. Yet I saw in the cutting-room how one could twist the truth into whichever direction one wanted. And cutting into another area, in my own case I don't have television. I don't buy newspapers, except, say, the Saturday papers, just to keep up with what's happening in movies or secondhand cars or something. But I'd reached a point where I frankly did not believe what was coming through the television or through newspapers. But I'm just being cute about the term "science fiction." There is an area of science fiction I've grown up with. Probably there's a lot of my generation that was into Saturday afternoon pictures. You had lots of westerns and occasionally crime thrillers and, of course, *Flash Gordon* and the science fiction films which were generally not well done but were always interesting to see. They were something I grew up with. But it wasn't, I guess, as for many, until *2001* that suddenly that whole category was elevated and placed in a new perspective. Your imaginings as a cinema-goer could be opened up into new areas. guess I owe it to that film that I began to look elsewhere into this category called science fiction for subjects.

Do you read science fiction or fantasy?

No. I've picked up a couple of things but have somehow found it more accessible on the screen than on the printed page.

I was just wondering about certain authors—like J.G. Ballard and Philip K. Dick....

Well, Ballard, I know the name; but no. I've been tempted. Asimov is another famous one, isn't he? I've seen them on the bookshelves and been tempted to go towards them, but for whatever reason I've drawn back.

If you were asked to list influences from film, literature, painting, etc., what artists or works would you name?

I'd just take a stab. It would be just like compiling a "best of" thing. In fiction it would certainly be Charles Dickens' work that I've been able to go back to over the years—that has been consistent. Otherwise I've just gone through vogues—you know, I read all of Aldous Huxley's or all of Fitzgerald's at some point. But I've lost interest in those now.

That was a rather unfair sort of question, really. When someone like yourself has been responsible for so many strong images, it seems very churlish to then try to pin you down about those images. For us it is just a general background question, to get some idea of what you've been exposed to.

It would be haphazard really, you know, including films and film-makers, so it would be an incredibly strange collection of different things that I've loved and enjoyed. I could throw you on a wrong track by saying, for example, that I've loved Hieronymus Bosch's paintings, because I have. They've struck chords. But I guess my own source of images and stories has come out of me, is something within me... personal observation, not strong literary or film influences. I might say, for the record, being in the film area, it has certainly been Kubrick who has been my inspiration. In fact, generally, not European film-makers. It's been Hitchcock and above all Kubrick that inspire me. But just recently, by the way, I think that *Alien* is a fantastic piece of work. I love that of all the current science fiction films. *Star Wars* I enjoyed and found fantastically clever, but it was *Alien* that really swept me away.

Because of what, in particular?

It was a curious situation because I had in fact been offered a very similar story not long before *Alien* was made. It was an old science fiction film which was to be a re-make.... The original title of the short story was "Who Goes There?" Howard Hawks did it, I think. It was set in the polar ice regions, in the Antarctic or somewhere, and there's an American base there....

That was The Thing, *wasn't it? And the original story was by John W. Campbell.*

The Thing was the movie, right! John Carpenter's doing it now. He did *Dark Star*, *Halloween* and *The Fog*. He'll do a great job. Anyway, I had this storyline sent to me by my agent, but I couldn't crack it. I loved the setting of the story and the finding of this alien vegetable matter. In fact, it's frighteningly close to the *Alien* idea. They take it into their camp, it begins to thaw out, and then it starts slowly killing off all those in the base. And the question is: how to destroy it? I would enjoy the setting-up of it, but the minute the creature took on life of some kind, I found I dropped out and found it silly. But I really came back to it like a dog with a bone, trying to find a way to do it. I couldn't and eventually turned the project down. When I saw *Alien* I realized there was a way to do it and Ridley Scott and his scriptwriters had found it.

A project like that would now be pretty pointless, wouldn't it?

My agent asked if I wanted to go back to it and I said, No, I think Scott's done it. He's just turned what was for me a B picture area into an A area. These terms sound so funny but, in other words, something done well enough transcends its form. But, of course, as soon as you mention Scott, you mention Giger, and since then I've chased round for all the drawings of his I could get hold of. He is dazzling. He's plugged in to some area of the unconscious, and for me that film, as well as looking up and out into space, is looking back inside. He's touched some archetype, some ancient fear there.

On this theme of looking inwards, even as you look out, we should mention surrealism. Your films all build on and reflect the sort of anxiety and sense of imminence which the French Surrealists called inquietude. *Your "obsession with rocks"—recalling for a moment the stone Roman head found in Tunisia which you said "became the starting point for* The Last Wave*"—reminds me very much of the* objets trouvés—*the found objects—which inspired and motivated the Surrealists. Your attention to details of light and landscape, the tension you create around commonplace objects being made suddenly outré, all reinforce this connection. To what extent have you been motivated by the Surrealists? The illusionist Surrealist painters perhaps?*

I was absolutely overwhelmed by my first contact with Surrealism. I can't recall specifically where it was, but I was at Sydney University. It was back in about '63, and there was a period of some considerable creative energy. There was Albie Thoms running the theater group. Bruce Beresford was just starting in movies with Dick Brennan and a number of others who went on to do feature work. Germaine Greer was creating storms in the English Department. And all of them were drawn towards SUDS—the Sydney University Dramatic Society. I was just on the fringe of that—a fresher—and not really involved. It was very cliquey. But I went to their productions. They had a great drama festival there and brought out Arrabal with his Theater of Cruelty, and what have you. I don't know how I'd feel about it today, but the play *Fando and Lis* of his, which was bizarre, and Boris Vian's *The Apartment* (I think it was called that) were the two most powerful. Among them were a number of other plays that were similar in feeling, all belonging, as I say, to the Theater of the Absurd or whatever, and all obviously drawing off the post-First World War turmoil and so on.

And around then I guess I was looking at the painting of Dali's which I still love very much. Dali remains the strongest of that group for me, and influenced my earliest films and revue sketches, I think.

I was involved in a lot of comedy, a lot of university fringe theater as an actor and performer with Grahame Bond. He and I formed a little team in the late sixties there, making films and doing revues. And glancing back through that material I am embarrassed because they are, in a sense, so self-consciously "surreal." But this was, of course, part of a Western World movement that was going on possibly in reaction to the Vietnam War, I think, or part of the dust cloud raised by that.

There was a new movement of Pop Art, Andy Warhol's soup cans, and so on, which I always felt was a distant cousin of Surrealism and rather paler beside the outrage and cry of agony that is reflected in creative work after the First World War. For me, these sorts of movements in art are locked into great social upheavals and particularly war. That's not to exclude what was happening in Europe, particularly France, at the end of the nineteenth century; you know, that fantasy and melancholy or whatever.

Anyway, there I was firmly done up in that, and so my earliest films reflect this "rather infantile surrealism" as a critic described one film. And it was, too. Ever since then I have tried to divest myself of any tricks or devices, because I began to see that apparently I could be clever by simply being obscure. Then, of course, these films were only reaching a small audience. They had a lot of other things going for them anyway, but I thought, I must strip myself of these props and find the real energy and power within the images, from as realistic a setting as possible. By doing so, I would double the impact and reach a lot of other people....

Which is what Dali does with his essentially realistic settings. I'll just throw a number of quotes at you, not for you to comment on necessarily, but just to show you how amazing and inevitable we found these connections between your own work and certain key ideas of the Surrealists. For instance, we have Dali saying that:

Geology has an oppressive melancholy, which it will never be able to brush from its back. This melancholy has its source in the idea that time is working against it.

Or again, his remarking that: "Geology is a state of the landscape. / The soul is a state of the landscape...." There is a reference to the

Surrealist drive to explore "the mystique of chance encounter," and to Chirico's desire to "rehabilitate the object," and so put things into new situations which alarm your audience. And lastly, we have Ernst speaking of the need for "the cultivation of... a systematic bewildering."...

That's a good one.

It's close to what you have done.

Yes.

Quite often your own audiences don't know what to do with an experience you have given them. They're fascinated, but when it's in their laps, it's easier for them to dismiss it, even criticize it, which is a point we'll come back to in a moment if we may. But all these references are just obvious points for us to mention.

It reminds me, actually, that when we were talking earlier about literature and influences, I should have mentioned that in the last few years it is definitely Carl Jung who has excited me more than any other writer, though I've read very little. A friend gave me *Memories, Dreams, Reflections*, which impressed me immensely. I re-read the book because I didn't understand so much of it on the first reading; it's so extraordinarily personal, in such code—it takes some time, I think, to crack it. But he gave a kind of framework to a lot of the ideas I've had which I thought were a bit eccentric or just plain odd. He showed me that other people think this way about certain things....

It has a more general application?

That's right. His famous archetypal images, and the studies he conducted of primitive tribal groups in Africa when he was there, and how these people possessed a different perception of the world. All of this came together for me around the time I was finishing the script of *The Last Wave*, and a lot of that material, I found, could be looked at from a Jungian perspective. But let me add that I am in no sense an academic or a student of all his work. What I really mean is that I was just looking through that doorway that he really entered, and where he went I don't really know. But I'm still peering after him.

This brings me back to Hitchcock and later on, Stanley Kubrick. You've said that you have a great admiration for the work of Alfred Hitchcock who has been acclaimed as the "master of suspense." It would appear that you have gone beyond what Hitchcock set out to do. You are far more—it's a bad word but—"poetic" perhaps. Hitchcock seems to be making entertainment more directly; whereas you don't seem to be doing just that. What similarities would you see your work as having to this, and what differences?

I think it's vastly different. When you say that I am more poetic or whatever, I think that, in some areas, this would simply be the fact that I had not mastered the narrative to the extent that he had. I think I would love to make a film finally that was totally accessible to a very broad public, that was as pregnant as some of his mass-entertainment films were, with ideas and mysteries and possibilities. In a sense, there is no similarity. He's from another tradition. But you can just learn from him, I think. You can put yourself through a kind of Hitchcock film-school. Mind you, I didn't do that until... in fact, it was only two years ago. Right through to the end of *The Last Wave*—to that point—I would not look at any classics. It began as a kind of joke. Back in the late sixties, friends would say: "You must come to the AFI [Australian Film Institute] and see the great Renoirs and Kurosawas and Howard Hawks," whatever. And I said I didn't want to. In actual fact, the reason was, I think, that I thought that if I realized how far I had to go, I really might hesitate. Somehow it was... well, in those days, as film-makers, we were like streetfighters (and still are to a degree) or guerillas, working from the hills with very small arms against a powerful military junta of some kind. And I thought, God, if I knew how small we were and what a great tradition there was....

And I think I was right. Because having finished *The Last Wave*, I was living in Adelaide, and there was a very good film library there—the State film library—which had all these classics. So I bought a projector and week in and week out for a year I would borrow four or five films a week. I worked my way through from the Russians to the Germans of the twenties; the silent films, the Chaplins, right through. I've still got a long way to go. But my breath was just taken away as I watched some of these things, the early Hitchcocks and so on. And I think I was in a position to understand or to work out what they'd been up to or doing and learn from them, which I don't think I would have all those years ago.

It didn't discourage you, obviously.

No! No! It's also given me a kind of confidence to think that I've reached some of those points on my own in fact, without influence. In other words, as film-makers we're dealing essentially with ideas and with stories which are common to all people. The film is simply a system of recording and transmitting the ideas.

Which is that Jungian notion again—the idea of things being common to all people. We come back to certain basics.

Very much so.

I believe you tell a story of how Hitchcock characterizes suspense in its classic form—a story involving a chair in a locked room. Obviously it did something for you, so would you like to re-tell it for us here?

Well, I think it locks back into that stripping away of gimmicks and tricks in the early surrealist type of films that I did, where I wanted to reduce the amount of games that I was playing with the audience—to simplify, in other words. Hitchcock was asked in one interview what the essence of suspense was and could he give an example? And he gave this fabulous example in which there was a small bare room with one chair in it, that was all. The chair was placed in the centre of the room and clearly marked in a certain position. There was only one way into the room—a door which was locked and bolted. No other way to get in, no windows, nothing. And the room was guarded all night so that nobody could get in. The next morning, the room was opened and the chair examined, and it had moved two inches. When I read that, I felt the back of my neck tingle, a distinct movement of hair.

On this same subject, you yourself have said that: "Within the ordinary lies the greatest possibilities for things to happen." With the Hitchcock story in mind, do you ever feel that there are only so many ways of exploring such moments of strangeness, of encounter, of possibility? Is there any limitation to the number of ways you could use to provoke your audience, tease them and give them that "back of the neck" feeling?

No. I think it's unlimited. But it depends on the elements that you put together. In Hitchcock's story, he was dealing with no people, for example. It was just a chair. But the possibilities occur, I think, by the way, as you are making the film more frequently with different things. You've got certain key images that are part of your story, dealing with this kind of moment, and you write them in. As you would, say, for that scene with the chair, if you knew this was pivotal and the story went on from there about why this chair moved or whatever. That's one kind of planned example. But, in actual fact, I think some of the greatest moments of electricity occur during the shooting and sometimes during the cutting. Going back to the principles of montage of Eisenstein, of the actual editing process, you can get some electric moments in the cutting-room that were never planned by putting one image with another. Or one sound with an image. I've done this frequently in fairly ordinary scenes;

laid in very strange sounds from all sorts of sources and they've created a particular effect as you view the film. Also, during the shooting, I've sometimes slowed the film down so I've shot in slow motion, though you wouldn't know. For example, sometimes with Chamberlain when he was talking with the Aborigines or vice versa, I would shoot the scene in the standard way, at standard speed, which is twenty-four frames a second. And during a conversation there are times, naturally, where one party's just listening. So, if it's appropriate, I'll bring in a special camera which shoots at super-slow motion, ask the actor not to blink or move his hands or face at all, and film just a quick burst in slow motion. Then, when I've cut the scene at the normal speed and someone's talking, we'll cut to the person being spoken to and I'll cut in a couple of seconds of his face listening. And then back to our original party who's speaking. Sometimes, as people have watched the scene, they've said there was something odd in that face. That's a case of using a particular means....

In your films to date you are, in a sense, beguiling your audience into crisis—into a "reality crisis" or a crisis of perception. There are unexpected, intruding causes and effects so that the viewer has to re-examine reality. What would you like to think this crisis does for the individual? What benefit does he get from being in such a state of unease?

Well, I suppose something I simply enjoy when I come out from seeing a film is that you carry the experience outside the theater with you—you get in a sense something money can't buy, something which comes to mind time and again after viewing the film. It stays with you. And that, of course, ties in with the entertainment value of the piece. I mean, apart from unease or anything else, I see myself primarily as a storyteller, telling stories in my own particular way. My tradition is that—the greatest tradition of entertainment.

In presenting the Hanging Rock *experience, for example, or the excessive "it can't be happening" realities of* The Cars That Ate Paris *or* The Plumber *or even* Homesdale, *you are in fact isolating the viewer—stranding him—in much the same way as Kubrick does at the end of* 2001; *forcing him to work out what is going on here. Is this a fair assessment of what you're doing as well?*

Yes. To forget you are in the theater, too. It's a lovely feeling when a film really works and you are isolated. The same thing can happen in live theater and in opera; a lack of awareness of doors and exits and seats. The experience is all around you.

It's interesting how that affects some of your audience. It sends them scrambling for comfortable explanations. They resent being put in a situation where you are provoking them....

(Laughs) The more pragmatic of them, anyway.

Yes. Some viewers and even critics feel cheated or resent the absence of easy solutions in what they would see as unnecessary mystery mongering on your part. As such, your films can almost be seen as provocations. You do seem to be provoking your audience to re-assess the nature of the reality around them, to question the basic shared assumptions that hold society together. Is this a fair statement of intention?

Yes, I think so. Again, sometimes it's a lack of understanding of the craft. Sometimes I've not known what to do with the atmosphere that I've created. It's like making a Chinese meal without any recipe and you really don't know how to do it again or exactly what it was you did. To take another quote of Hitchcock's talking on what could be called rules of audience, you can be mysterious but never mystify. He has a point. Sometimes I've wanted to tell the audience more, to share it more with them, but I've not really known how to. As you go on, you really want to master these things so you can make the decision yourself as to which way you will go.

In this same area, you seem to have a lot of respect for the actual editing of a film. You do regard that as being a definite creative part?

Oh, absolutely. If you cut the whole film-making process into three parts, it's script, shooting, and editing. And who's to say which is more important? They're all part of the whole.

Do you do your own editing?

Not physically, no. But I sit with the editor. I prefer to have an editor than do it myself.

In a recent article in Cinema Papers *on your "themes and preoccupations," Brian McFarlane speaks of you as "an artist with a vision and a growing understanding of how this vision may be realized in terms of film." Later in the same article, McFarlane suggests that "horror" is at the heart of your vision. Others would suggest that it involves more the moment of hesitation that a character and a viewer feels when he is caught—suspended—between the moment of disorientation and his placing of it, his explaining it away. Would you like to encapsulate for us, what you see your vision as being?*

Well, I certainly have never had a plan of action, no overall view. Perhaps one of the roles of critic is to find that, if they so choose. But I've certainly never thought of it in that way. My films are just me at that point in time; the themes and obsessions that recur are part of me. I think that possibly a lot of these areas are to do with something else entirely—quite possibly with a fascination with death or with the fact that we all must die. It's an area that's very difficult to talk about and unfortunately it's not an area that we seem to be able to discuss in our western society. I think that behind a lot of my themes and obsessions is a skirting around the edges of the great final adventure (laughs), the great leap....

Given your recent exposure to Jung, you may no longer find that death is the great final adversary most people would see it as being.

No, I'd like to find that.

Without wishing to pin this on you, do you think there will be Jungian overtones appearing in your films? Are you impressed enough with the ideas and ways of thinking you've discovered to make that a conscious facet of what you will do in the future?

No. No. I start off firstly with stories that come to me through the mail, if you like, or through agents or friends who bring them to me. And through my own processes of creativity. The beginnings of a story occur and then you get another clue and eventually you write something down.

But you do feel you impose something of your own onto a story that you are given?

Oh, absolutely. But that happens later. I think the initial thing I'm looking for is a good story—the "once upon a time" that is full of characters and events and moments. When the material is coming from elsewhere as happened of course with *Picnic* and with my next film, *The Year of Living Dangerously* (which is from an Australian novel), I have to get inside these stories and make them mine—cannibalize them and swallow them and digest them and become part of the pages and part of the process of thinking that the novelists used to write them. I must totally absorb them in order to bring them back to something of my own. Which of course makes it difficult to find suitable material.

I approach film-making as a story-teller. There is no conscious planning. I mean, things do just happen, and sometimes it's very odd how they do. For example, last year I did a documentary on a potter who lives locally—a fine craftsman, a marvelous man who had been a teacher at East Sydney Tech, and had just retired from that position. Anyway, it was a very little subject to deal with; the man was not flamboyant, as you would imagine, a quiet craftsman working away at home, teaching a little, but a man of enormous calm and almost Zen-like qualities without putting him into the hippie set. I found it fascinating that he'd been in a Japanese prisoner-of-war camp and yet, after the war, had found his way back to Japan and a love of the Japanese aesthetic, had many Japanese friends, and so on. That was the starting point. Anyway, it made a very simple documentary, showing him working in his house at night with a Japanese friend, another potter; shots of his pots, etc. Very simple, about twenty minutes long. Anyway, end of story. I delivered the film to the Crafts Council and that was it. A couple of friends have since seen it and said it's spooky; some of those shots when he's lighting his kiln, and so on. And they commented on the strange music we found and used. I had another look at the film and—yes—you can see these things in it. There are some eerie moments. Yet it just came along with me; how could I impose it?

I think you've made the next question regarding reality crisis as a theme rather redundant. One could say that your themes look like being (I have to put it this way because with your storytelling priority this is probably no longer a conscious thing) the isolation and alienation that leads on to a possibility of revelation and hopefully a transformation. But sometimes it just seems to be provocation. I don't see this as being a fair comment any longer because all this is incidental to what you're doing first of all, which is telling a story. But on our viewing of your films, these things recur, whether by accident or unconsciously, and there does seem to be a strong case for saying that these are Peter Weir themes.

I think Bergman put it very well when he was asked about conscious themes and signs in his films, and he said how much he worked off intuition. He was being quoted various examples that fitted someone's theory and he used the image of an archer firing an arrow high and then down into a forest. Like the archer, Bergman said he too just fires. Then, after the film is complete, he makes his way through the forest and tries to find where the arrow fell and then wonders why it fell in such a way and why it fell where it did. It was an elaborate way of saying that one just works by intuition and does it. That's my approach, I think.

Also, going back to that film history thing, I feel I don't have a burden of film history. I'm not a film buff. I don't reproduce other people's images and approaches. That must be a curse—knowing too much. Sometimes I think that education in any area can, in fact, inhibit that intuition. Because you do tend to say: I don't think it can be done, or else it's been done too well before—I must simply follow in the path of. Going further on this point, I have kept myself a primitive; I am to some extent like the primitive painter who has just picked up a brush and done it—to the amazement of those who have said that you've got to learn how to apply the brush properly, and so on. I think it was, for me, the right thing to do. It kept me free. But, of course, I then had a hard road learning the craft as I went along. Hence my emphasis on the number of times I did not know how to tell a story well enough, and have sometimes hidden in a mist of flashiness.

The films you have made to date, creating these moments of confrontation and encounter, are really quite fragile things....

Yes, very.

They seem to be easily overbalanced and seen as just black comedy, mere psychological thrillers or even portentous posturing. In trying to make images "resonate" within a film, do you feel that as director you are treading a particularly dangerous line?

Oh, absolutely, yes. Very thin ice. And again, I think it's by further developing the craft that you can be a little more certain where you put your foot each time and not take so many risks.

Your line doesn't become any narrower, you just become more adept at keeping on it?

I think so. I mean, there is a danger. I remember what an eighteenth-century French pianist once said; a very famous virtuoso pianist whose name is no longer a part of the history of music. But as a young man he did have a great talent as a composer, and he said that in the mastering of the craft, he lost the art. And so part of the thing, I think, is to develop further your craft and your control of where you want to take the audience, but not to lose that precious desperation of the art—that madness, that willingness to experiment which to a degree I've kept in all my films. In other words, one could become too safe. So the real line you're walking, I think, is between craft and art.

It's interesting that you're going to observe these convictions within your storytelling priority. In finding this balance between art and craft, concept and execution, which of your films do you think is the most successful so far?

I think the last one, *The Plumber*, given what I wanted to do and the extent to which I achieved it. I don't think it was one hundred per cent in any sense of what I wanted to do, but it was significantly higher than with some of the other films. I got a better control of rhythm and structure in that film. Mind you, it was a simpler piece, made for television. It was a short story, if you like, as against a novel. I tried a different system with that film, too, in the cutting. I videotaped it all, each cut. As you cut a film, you start with what's called the rough cut—which is just what it is—and you then go through the various refining processes, which might be three or four, maybe more. It's much the same as going through the draft of a screenplay, honing it down, changing scenes in relation to each other, emphasizing characters and de-emphasizing others, whatever. And I kept copies of all the cuts here at home on television, and would just re-run it, late at night or early in the morning, sometimes for friends, sometimes for myself. So I think I got to know the material better. There's a curious ritual about going into the cutting-room and looking at what the editor has done the day or night before. This demystified that cutting-room.

Would you tell us, in retrospect, how you view each of your major films?

I think I have an inevitable relationship with most of them. There's a kind of moratorium period where you simply have to stay away from them. It seems to take about three or four years before I can even look at one again. Except for *The Plumber*, which is less painful, I should say. I've heard this of other filmmakers. It's like looking at yourself several years ago. Of course by the time you finish a film, you're involved with ideas you've probably been working with for at least two years anyway, if it's gone fast. So in a sense you're already two years on from those particular views in some areas. And you change constantly. I think it comes down to liking bunches of scenes and sounds and scraps of music and someone's face, that sort of thing. It's like a family snapshot album—you can feel a curious mixture of sentiment and embarrassment and regret.

With the exception of Picnic at Hanging Rock, *and your new film, all your films are based on your own story ideas. Do you ever see filmmaking as your only medium? Or do you see yourself moving into any other, like writing? I am reminded of J.G. Ballard and, I think, Patrick White saying they would like to have been painters.*

No, I don't think so. If for some reason I couldn't work in films, then I think I would find some other outlet—possibly writing. I've done a little bit of sculpting. I have a natural affinity for stone. In fact, I made my own little sarcophagus. Ever since my grandfather died, and the funeral parlor people came with their brochures about coffins and things,

I decided I would beat them by having my own. So I've almost finished a little sarcophagus for my ashes which I cut out of a block of sandstone. (Laughs) I had it written in my will. I remember a very Dickensian lawyer with one eyebrow raised as I described it. He said, "Would one describe it as a stone box, would you say? I see. Fine." He put: one stone box. Then he said, "Where are they to place it?," and I said, "Well, I don't want to put them to any trouble. Some appropriate quiet spot." (Laughs) I've carved other things, you know, faces and stone blocks in a vaguely Graeco-Roman style or Coptic designs of one kind or another. And that's been another natural outlet for me, rather than, say, painting or something like that.

The Cars That Ate Paris is often cited as being from a short story by Peter Weir. Was that published as a short story?

No, but I have written most of my films as short stories first not to be published but just as a way of feeling the ideas out. It's a case of taking on a discipline almost as if you were going to publish.

But you'd never consider publishing them as stories?

No. I don't think they're really good enough. It's just not my forté. But I write them up like that, then I tape record them, often like a little play reading which I'll just play in my car. I'll do that with scripts, too. I'll do all the voices and sound effects. I've got a tape of *Picnic* somewhere with (drums fingers on table) horses galloping like that. (Laughs) I'll do all the voices, everything I can. For wind, I'll go (blows). Anything, so you can make it live in another form. It's great playing it in the car as if it was a radio show. You can listen and think, oh God, that's bad and I'd better fix that, or that scene's got more potential…

You start to build the visual behind it?

Yes, absolutely. Hearing it in all sorts of other ways. And the related way, I think, is music. I'm a great cassette freak. I find that music begins to gather round a story, anything from rock-and-roll to classical music to folk, or all three, which seems to have threads connected to the ideas you're working with. It becomes part of the whole process of getting a film out. I think music is undoubtedly the greatest key to those hidden passageways in your mind. When you're highly charged as in the process of making a film, the light is in a sense switched on throughout the labyrinth of your mind (using that image) and music can take you through many doors, find many things, unlock images. It will often, of course, have nothing to do with the music that's finally put on the soundtrack.

In fact, in most cases, I find that at the end of production you'll go in a completely different direction with the music. But it helps you get somewhere. I always carry a cassette when I'm shooting. I don't play it every day but I'll often play it for the cast or myself. My bag of tapes is like a doctor's bag—there's everything from African music to rock-and-roll. I play them on the way to the set or on the way home at night.

The soundtrack of The Plumber, *for instance, is a brilliant use of native music to set up the contrasting images. That certainly contributed to the feeling on the back of the neck.*

Yes, that's a great piece of music—from the Barundi tribe. A friend, Jim McElroy, found it and gave it to me.

Hearkening back to the Surrealist notion of "found objects" for a moment, and inspiration from what you've seen and heard, would you care to describe the particular images—the conceptual starting points—that led you to make your five major films: Homesdale, The Cars That Ate Paris, Picnic at Hanging Rock, The Last Wave *and* The Plumber?

Well, going back to *Homesdale*, it was the house we were renting at Church Point. It was a very old colonial home that just had mystery about it and which later in fact became the guest house, Homesdale, in the film. It seemed to have a story attached to it. People would come and see it and say: "This reminds me of something," or: "There's something about this house." It was like a house on a plantation or in the Crimea, and I wonder if it was ever a hospital or if someone had died there. So, the house became the inspiration, in a sense.

The Cars That Ate Paris came from driving through France and being diverted by a man in a yellow jacket with a little barrier, who pointed to a side road. So that was an actual experience that happened. Why did I take the road? Simply because he had on a day-glo jacket and had a little barrier? And later in England I was reading about road accidents and noticed a tiny little column talking about ten or fifteen dead on the British roads and then a big article about a shotgun shooting. So I got to thinking that if you wanted to kill someone, you do it in a road accident.

So you're synthesizing from everywhere really, aren't you?

Yes. And the automobile was, if you like, the "object" there. *Picnic*, of course, came through the novel itself, but it brought a whole collection of these other things. *The Last Wave* was that Roman head I found in Tunisia. Knowing I was going to find it: it was the most demonstrably psychic experience I've ever had—that foreknowledge... a definite premonition. But as I say, I've always had this great affinity for stone, and ever since I first went to Europe in '65, a love of ruins. I never wanted to buy the guide-book and know who built it or who lived there. That was always dull for me. I just liked all that falling-down marble. So it was appropriate in a sense that I found that Roman head.

The Plumber was a different thing altogether. It was an anecdote told to me at dinner by the very woman who'd lived through it. So it was a different experience, really.

Could you tell us something about your recent project, The Year of Living Dangerously? *Do you see it as a departure from your usual role at all?*

Yes. It's from a novel of the same title by Chris Koch, whose brother, Phillip Koch, was a journalist with the ABC. A large part of the inspiration and background research has come through his brother's experience. It's a story set in southeast Asia, centering on one of a group of journalists who are covering a collapsing Asian regime. The story opens with one particular journalist, Hamilton, arriving as a replacement, meeting his cameraman there, and the subsequent events leading down to the collapse of this regime. It's just a very fine story. I've recently been up in Asia and will go again researching it. It's just so exciting to walk through the bazaars and markets experiencing the new light and the new sounds with this story in mind. I don't know where it will take me. It's a fascinating feeling with a film, I think. Each time you start, you really set sail into unknown waters. You leave at midnight in a fog, not quite sure of where you're going. You've got some rough course, but what you'll see along the way, you don't know.

*We've heard about some other projects—*The Thorn Birds *and even* Gallipoli *involving David Williamson. Is this latter project something you were approached about or were you working on it?*

No. No. I thought of it years ago. I've always been fascinated with the First World War and as far back as '75 I was thinking that I might do something on the trenches in France. Then it occurred to me that perhaps I should tackle Gallipoli, but thought it too obvious. And then in '76 I was on my way to the opening of *Picnic* in London and thought I'd detour and visit the battlefields and make a decision after visiting that. That was such a curious experience—as anyone will tell you who's been there—and I thought, yes, I'll make a film about this in one way or another. So I left it there and then wrote a short story—or storyline, if you like—which I gave to David Williamson. And we drove on through umpteen drafts trying to find the right way to handle this material so it wouldn't be too expensive and not too documentary. I think we've found that, and Pat Lovell's to produce it. She's looking for money at the moment.

That would be after The Year of Living Dangerously?

It would appear that way at the moment, yes.

What about The Thorn Birds *project?*

Well, I spent five months with that project, working with a screenwriter trying to bring the material closer to my own style and simply failed. I thought I could do it even though I knew it was going to be tough. I had full support from the Warner Brothers studio people. They gave me creative freedom, given that I couldn't change the actual building blocks of the story—key characters had to remain, and so on. But I simply could not do it and reluctantly gave it up. It was exciting in that people had loved it and there was a large audience waiting for it. But I couldn't make it fit me; couldn't digest it.

It's now being done by Arthur Hiller who did Love Story....

I think he'll do a fine film. It probably should have gone to him in the first place. It's appropriate. I was the wrong man for it.

That means you're pulling it back down to a local production again, aren't you? The Year of Living Dangerously *is Australian-produced, isn't it?*

Yes, with Jim McElroy. He's been the co-producer on all the other films, with the exception of *The Plumber*. *The Thorn Birds* was also in a period in which I was opening myself up. I wanted to widen the choice of material, widen my possibilities and not always be locked into this obsessive sort of storytelling. And I found I couldn't do it. (Laughs)

As a general question, how do you see the imaginative scene at the moment—in writing, in film-making, here in Australia, throughout the world? Do you still think it's a healthy industry you're working in?

The current generation of film-makers is interesting. I'm glad that the strict division between the art-house and the commercial world which existed in the sixties has collapsed. I think that's a very healthy thing. There are those, of course, who still religiously believe that the two types of films are incompatible. I don't. I have too much respect for audiences, anyway. Then again, there are those who will criticize *Alien* and not even go to see it because it's too popular. I've heard people say that, and it's so limiting. It's truly elitist to despise what the general public like. Often I'm quite mystified by what films the public have loved and that I thought were poor films or silly. But they make the decision to go. I don't believe that people's minds are manipulated to the extent that they go because of advertising. I think that you can do that for the first couple of weeks with a film, but the kind of repeat business the big films do is usually because people have loved them.

There are many "big" films that have failed in spite of advertising.

Yes, exactly. People won't go.

You talked earlier about the fact that you don't watch television or read newspapers as a day to day activity, and seemed to suggest that there was a sort of skepticism on your part towards the kind of information that comes through those media....

I got that out of order. That's probably reason number two. As for number one... well, when I was in my late teens, my grandfather, Archie, was living with us. He was a marvelous man, the boy's ideal grandfather; a bit of a pirate really. He would let you climb trees and throw rocks and he was always watching you with a cheeky smile. But he had one period in the day when you kept away from him—when the morning newspaper arrived.

Like a lot of older people, he got up very early to get the paper, and you'd find him in the kitchen there having read it for an hour from cover to cover, in a very cranky mood about some revolution in South America or something. And I remember saying to him once: "Why read this? What use is it your knowing about what's happening in Paraguay, Grandfather? It's pointless." And he'd say that they should do this or they should do that. And I thought, this is information you shouldn't have. It's not necessary to know about it.

So whether that stayed in my mind or not, I don't know. But in sophisticated western living, I think you do try to keep anxieties at arms' length. It's part of the reason that I would live here, apart from the great beauty and the fact that it's my own country. I would resist the logic of living in Los Angeles, which is really a reasonable point of view which my agent puts to me. Why not move over here?—simply because of all the possibilities of getting films going just through chatting like we are now, you know, from an idea or chance remark.

But it does make one anxious. I've read Kubrick saying the same thing of his living in England. And I've found the same with newspapers and television—they're really just creating and promoting anxiety. And you get to hear of the key issues anyway. During the Iran crisis I bought the newspapers to keep up to date with that; it obviously seemed to have relevance to all of us. So it's not: number one—skepticism.

But secondly, I do doubt it. You might as well imagine what's going on in the White House or anywhere else. You'll probably have a chance through fiction to reach something of the truth. (Laughs) Look at *Dr. Strangelove*.

It's interesting to note that the "master of unease" is also subject to bouts of it.

(Laughs) Yes. As far as television went, I think I watched too much of it at home, and couldn't afford one when I left home and got married. Then I just thought: if I get one I'll never do anything. When I go to motels, shooting films or researching something, I tend to watch a lot of it and catch up with casting. Obviously with Australian shows, it's of benefit to know who's doing what. And I'll go out to see the new *Fawlty Towers* or whatever. I have a strong interest in humor.

Yes, that goes right back to your work with Grahame Bond and the Architecture Revues, and things like that, doesn't it? Do you intend to follow it through in film-making?

I'd like to very much. I just did a batch of commercials with John Cleese. He and I got on well. We've exchanged letters since then and are looking for something to do together.

Just to finish up by directing conversation back into our vested interest pocket for a moment.... Having noted such themes as isolation and reality crisis, your respect for the work of Kubrick and Hitchcock, and most especially your own major "fantasy" works—notably The Last Wave—*would you ever consider making a science fiction film as a means of exploring your interests?*

Oh, absolutely. I think that's why I brought up the example of *Alien* in some detail. And I think it has been others who have led the way for me in that area—as I say, Kubrick and Lucas and to some extent Spielberg with his *Close Encounters*. And certainly Ridley Scott. He's a fabulous film-maker. He really uses light well and knows how to put power behind the images which is something you can't learn at any of the film schools. You've got to find it or know it.

—Sydney, 1st May 1980

PATTERNS OF EPIC

THE RE-AFFIRMATION OF WESTERN VALUES IN *STAR WARS* AND *THE LORD OF THE RINGS*

HAL COLEBATCH

The Lord of The Rings and *Star Wars* are on different levels as works of art, *The Lord of The Rings* being much the more complex and profound of the two. But the similarities are more striking than the differences.

Each is a large work whose existence breaks the rules of commercial success, and whose backers took great risks with their investments in fields where failures far outnumber successes. Each, when it went into the world, was seen as being in opposition to the spirit of its times and was attacked with considerable hostility by progressive intellectuals. Yet each has been stupendously successful.

Starting from a humdrum environment, each work moves into a series of strange, sometimes beautiful, sometimes terrifying settings where an apparently ordinary character, finding himself in exile, must fight both armies and monsters as well as temptations to seize Totalitarian power for himself, and is finally pitted against a supreme Enemy, a destroyer who would devour all.

In each, the ordinary central character grows to heroic stature as a result of consciously choosing to take a hard part, though this choice is initially made almost light-heartedly from longing for adventure and in ignorance of what the quest will really entail. Later, more than once, the choice to go on has to be made again, each time with fewer illusions and more grim determination.

With the help, at first, of an old guide possessed of great wisdom and (limited) magical powers as well as formidable fighting abilities in a crisis, and accompanied by good but somewhat comic assistants, each hero thus embarks on a series of adventures in fulfilment of a mission which seems more hopeless as time goes on. But each guide, it turns out, has long watched the hero who, unknown to himself, is the repository of great and perilous hopes. Early in each story, the guide dies fighting a superior enemy in order to buy time to allow the hero and his party to escape from an enemy fortress, but undergoes a sort of resurrection to return later as a transmogrified, more spiritual being.

Each hero becomes aware of the bad news, what Frodo calls "terrible," and worse than anything he had imagined. There have always been dangers beyond the border of the safe mundane little worlds in which the respective heroes lived—like the barrow-wights in the sinister green burial-mounds beyond the Hobbits' Shire and the sand-people in the wastelands beyond Luke's father's farm—but the supreme Enemy has been only a far shadow. Then each hero finds this supreme Enemy's malice, bad enough when perceived only as a distant generalized threat to the natural order of things, is also directed at him *personally* and *individually.* He cannot even hope that he may be too unimportant to be spared the personal attention of the Annihilator. But each hero also learns that forces and hopes for good are also focused on him personally too. In each case the supreme Enemy is robed in black, like Death.

In each tale a subsidiary enemy, deeply wicked but less powerful than the ultimate Enemy, and once himself a champion of the "good" side, has ambitions of overthrowing the ultimate Enemy. He offers uncorrupted champions of good the temptation of bringing peace and order if they will join him ("…knowledge, rule, order…," Sarumen offers Gandalf; "Together we can end this destructive conflict and bring order to the Galaxy," Darth Vader offers Luke Skywalker). But this temptation to exercise coercive power is rejected. Each hero also meets a lonely wandering warrior who, after a period of initial mistrust, becomes a firm friend and leader of the forces of good in a climactic battle simultaneous with each principal hero's eventual confrontation with the supreme Enemy. The principal heroes are by that time partly outside the organized military forces of the "good side." Their personal confrontation with the enemy is of a different type.

In each tale the heroes and their friends undergo a series of adventures divided into three parts *(The Lord of The Rings* is actually six books, but was released in three volumes and is now generally regarded as a trilogy). The mood and flavor of the parts change as the heroes grow in maturity and nobility. Unlike many formless and even deliberately random modernist works, there is a definite shift in atmosphere as the conflict moves onto higher planes. The two tales begin small, close to home, with a single individual about whom little is known. They then move to take in a larger vision of great deeds and a far wider existence. New lands are entered, and new complexities and depths behind the original issues are revealed. Important enemies (Gollum and Darth Vader) are found to have more to them than was at first apparent, and the ultimate Enemies are seen briefly for the first time. In the third part of each tale, the individual hero is again the center, but he has grown in stature and his destiny is combined with the wider sweep of events.

The initial exile leads to eventual greatness. The central characters become aware not merely of the great political and military issues into which they have entered, but also of their own moral responsibilities. A major theme in each case is the contrast between the ordinariness of the heroes and the destinies to which they are called.

Each hero is in a world in ruins. The society on Tatooine, Luke Skywalker's home planet, is obviously decaying under the dead hands of the Empire, while in *The Lord of The Rings* the description of the young hobbits coming to Bree, the village nearest their little shire, where all seems well-ordered, prosperous, placid and contented, has a subtly chilling undertone:

> Bree was the chief village of the Bree-land, a small inhabited region, like an island in the empty lands about.... Down the Road, where it swept to the right to go round the foot of the hill, there was a large inn, it had been built long ago when traffic on the roads had been far greater.... But the North Road was now seldom used: it was grass-grown, and the Bree-folk called it the Greenway.

The peace and contentment which the hobbits take for granted, and have even become bored with, comes to be seen as a local and temporary accident. There is a gradual realization that only the dwindling strength of old guardians still keeps these pockets of humdrum happiness in existence.

Both tales place value on physical competence; their heroes are people who do things. However, they also take ideas seriously. Unlike the case in much modem drama, each hero gradually becomes a better and "higher" person. As a result of making a series of brave difficult choices, each grows gradually in stature, responsibility and authority as well as moral sense, a process Tolkien described as ennoblement. The last and hardest temptation which each hero faces is to "do the right deed for the wrong reason"—Frodo to end the realm of Sauron by claiming the Ring, Luke to defeat the Emperor and Darth Vader by using the dark side of the Force. When at last each confronts the Enemy, he fails in the penultimate moment but makes it possible for one of the Enemy's own creatures to rebel and a general deliverance is brought about just when the last armies of "good," fighting against hopeless odds, seems about to be destroyed.

Each hero's friends grow, too, from immature adventurers into figures of responsibility and authority. Both heroes are physically maimed in their battles, and in the end they do not marry princesses (though their friends do). They end spiritually comforted but alone. There are other similarities: both works are enjoyed by children and adults, though they are frequently described by hostile critics as being "childish." They can be judged by criteria appropriate to both juvenile and adult art.

Each hero, in his wanderings, as well as gathering friends, encounters various secondary and subsidiary enemies and monsters, some of these being direct agents and subordinates of the ultimate Enemy, and some (Shelob and Jabba the Hutt) being allowed a degree of independence by the ultimate Enemies because of their usefulness and because their altogether "lower," physical appetites (symbolized by their bloated bodies) pose no threat of competition to the ultimate Enemies' own spiritual appetites. On the spiritual plane the ultimate Enemies can tolerate no rivals.

The friends each hero makes are diverse in attitudes, and some are not human. The "good" army is in each case a mixed force, apparently accepting military discipline and hierarchy voluntarily. The "bad" army is disciplined by terror, with death the explicit punishment for mishaps and mistakes.

The "good" side, in each case, is, *in toto,* quite powerful, but apparently hopelessly outmatched when pitted against the apparently limitless power the Enemies command. The "good" are just "strong enough to fail" and to indulge in fools' hopes.

Both tales, while dealing with battles and wars against cruel enemies, generally avoid depictions of extreme brutality. Their outlook is ultimately optimistic, but not in the socially progressive sense, and they look to individual rather than social salvations. Their "happy endings" promise no everlasting Utopias.

Each work seems hard to translate into the medium of the other, but many of the situations are strikingly similar. The dive in Mos Eisely where Luke Skywalker and the robots meet Han Solo while an enemy circles and searches outside is not exactly like the Inn at Bree where Frodo and the other young Hobbits meet Strider, but there are similarities. The description of Gandalf's sacrificial battle with the Balrog in *The Lord of The Rings* would serve well for the similar battle in *Star Wars.*

> His enemy halted again, facing him, and the shadow about it reached out.... But Gandalf stood firm. "You cannot pass," he said.... "The dark fire shall not avail you...." From out of the shadow a red sword leapt gleaming.
>
> Glamdring glimmered white in answer.

There was a ringing clash and a stab of white fire.

Both stories are set in societies where a religion exists that has some similarities to a Christless Christianity but which is in decline and out of step with the temper of the times. Indeed the old religion seems only a vestige, but a new, evil demi-god, wielding supernatural power, seems to be growing towards god-like strength. Presumably if the religion that was once the common property of good people had remained a potent force, a healthier state of society would have endured. In each tale an unhonored, almost extinct, remnant of an ancient knightly order preserves a spiritual as well as a military heritage in wild and forgotten places.

Specifically religious issues are mentioned little, and doctrinal matters not at all, but in each story the struggle between good and evil causes the whole structure to be permeated with spiritual issues and questions. By the end of *Return of the Jedi* it becomes plain that the *Star Wars* trilogy is not merely profoundly religious, but that it is more centrally in the Western religious tradition than perhaps any other popular film that has ever been made. Certainly it is a far more religious film than any Hollywood Biblical epic.

In both stories some form of life after death, the immortality of the individual soul, and some form of judgment are accepted. This gives the stories a mental atmosphere at once both classically "Western" and at odds with much of the atmosphere of modern secular society, art and culture.

Family heritages of honor and tradition are also very important. On solemn and "perilous" occasions, in moments of great challenge or great portent, characters in *The Lord of The Rings* are addressed by patronymics, such as "Frodo Son of Drogo." It is a sort of stiffening of the spine, an injunction to "remember who you are," and to remember both individual and family honor. The individual is seen at such moments as being enriched by being connected to, and being the product of, the traditions and heroisms of the past

The fact of "ancientry" has its own significance. When, in Tolkien's posthumously-published *Unfinished Tales,* Aragorn retrieves the original and most splendid jewel of his household, the Elendilmir, from Isengard, he says of the later (imitation and inferior) Elendilmir, which he has worn until then, that it is also a "thing of reverence" and beyond his worth, since "heads have worn it before."

Early in the first *Star Wars* film, it is a solemn and portentous moment when Luke Skywalker is given his father's old lightsaber. In *Return of the Jedi,* Luke rejects the seductive blandishments of the evil Emperor with the words: "I am a Jedi, like my father before me." This emphasis on honor, the worth of the individual, and the individual's links with the past, is quite at variance with ideas of salvation by social engineering or the creation of a New Order. The integrity of the individual is aided by tradition. (In the modern world the opposition of collectivists to hereditary titles, even when such titles confer no privileges, is because they reinforce a feeling of identity with something other than the State.) Ultimately both stories are concerned with the salvation of individual souls—in the case of *Star Wars* in a rather surprising way.

The fundamental outlook behind both is traditional and conservative. However, they deal with challenge, change and active response to violent upheavals in the established order. It is a basically Burkean conservatism.

In both, "conservative" figures who do not meet challenge but deny it are doomed. In *The Lord of The Rings* the Elves and the men of Gondor decline because they hunger for "endless life unchanging," attempting nothing new, and trying instead to arrest time and cling to the past. In the War of the Ring the good side only begins to gain its first small victories when Gandalf spurs the mazed King of Rohan, and Pippin and Merry spur the Ents, into taking the strategic initiative. In *Star Wars* Luke's uncle dies because he cannot face the fact that a passive, hardworking life is no longer enough. He clings to his old way of farming until the Imperial storm-troopers come.

The values of these works may be "reactionary" in that they deal with the desirability of restoring a better past that has been usurped, but they also show the necessity for active reaction. They are about rebellion and counter-rebellion and, either directly or by implication, about natural order and natural law. In both, the good side are seen and named by the Enemies as rebels, and indeed they are in rebellion against the domination of evil empires. They are, however, counter-revolutionaries, fighting to preserve the natural order against usurpers.

They are thus in the tradition of Edmund Burke, whose thought is central to the Western, or at least the English-speaking, tradition of legitimate rather than arbitrary authority. Burke opposed the French Revolution even before the Terror (which he predicted) because he believed it was caused principally by the teachings of metaphysicians such as Rousseau who lacked experience of political reality and who held false and dangerous ideas. He argued that "enduring rights can only emerge within the protective environment of a well-ordered society." He regarded the social order as an organic whole, whose faults were to be approached like the wounds of a father "with pious awe and trembling solicitude." According to Burke, radical and arbitrary restructuring of the social order to cure its faults was as much a matter of horror as would be chopping one's own wounded father to pieces and throwing the bits in a witch-doctor's cauldron in hopes of a cure. Yet Burke endured great political odium in Britain for supporting the American rebellion and better treatment for Ireland, both in the name of ancient rights. A necessary part of Burkean conservatism is rebellion as a last resort to protect the permanent things. Thus it is not a doctrine of subservience to the State.

The "rebels" in *The Lord of The Rings* and *Star Wars* are actually rebels against a greater rebel who has overturned the natural order (the religious implications of this regarding the place of man in a Fallen world are obvious). The theme is perhaps the oldest in Western literature.

Tolkien made his own position quite explicit. Sauron aspired to Divine honors, and given that:

> [E]ven if in desperation "The West" had bred or hired hordes of orcs and had cruelly ravaged the lands of other men as allies of Sauron, or merely to prevent them from aiding him, their cause would still have remained indefeasibly right. As does the cause of those who now oppose the State-God and Marshal This or That as its High Priest, even if it were true (as it unfortunately is) that many of their deeds were wrong, even if it were true (as it is not) that the inhabitants of "The West," except for a minority of wealthy bosses, live in fear and squalor, while the worshippers of the State-God live in peace and abundance and mutual esteem and trust....[1]

He continued that:

> Some critics seem determined to represent me as a simple-minded adolescent, inspired with, say, a with-the-flag-to-Pretoria spirit, and willfully distort what is said in my tale. I have not that spirit... but I have not made any of the people on the "right" side, Hobbits, Rohirrim, Men of Dale or Gondor, any better than men have been or are, or can be. Mine is not an "imaginary" world, but an imaginary historical moment on Middle Earth—which is our habitation.

The rebels are not inspired by dreams of Utopia. It is more than once said in *The Lord of The Rings*—even or especially at the grimmest times when the good side might be looking to dreams to sustain its morale—that even if the Ring is destroyed, this will not bring Utopia. Other evils will certainly come, for Sauron himself is no more than a "servant or emissary" of the ultimate source of evil, the Satanic Morgoth. However, there is still absolute morality, which does not change. These moral absolutes, an intrinsic part of traditional Western Christianity, are the opposite of doctrines of moral relativism or positivism. In *The Two Towers* Eomer asks:

> The world is all grown strange.... How shall a man judge what to do in such times?

Aragorn replies:

> As ever he has judged, Good and evil have not changed since yesteryear; nor are they one thing among Elves and Dwarves and another among Men, it is a man's part to discern them as much in the Golden Wood as in his own house.

Given the absolute demands of morality, no cosmic, yin-yang unity of good and evil is possible. C.S. Lewis, reviewing *The Lord of The Rings,* wrote that:

> [T]he text itself teaches us that Sauron is eternal: the War of The Ring is only one of a thousand wars against him. Every time we shall be wise to fear his ultimate victory, after which there will be "no more songs." Again and again we shall have good evidence that "the wind is setting East, and the withering of all woods may be drawing near." Every time we win we shall know that our victory is impermanent, if we insist on asking for a moral for the story, that is its moral: a recall from facile optimism and waiting pessimism alike, to that hard, yet not quite desperate, insight into Man's unchanging predicament by which heroic ages have lived.

Neither work is "progressive" in the Wellsian sense of containing a vision of continuing scientific improvement. Nor does it look, like the strain of progressive thought associated with Frazer's *The Golden Bough,* to a happy future in which science will displace religion. "What," asked H.G. Wells as scientific and socialist prophet, "is the culminating effect of a survey of history, of the science of life, and of existing condition?" He answered himself, with full-blown if temporary confidence, that:

> It is an effect of steadily accentuating power, rage and understanding.... Progress continues in spite of every human fear and folly.

The phenomenally successful *Star Wars* shows a milieu of faster-than-light spaceships in which the implications of good and evil, heroism and cowardice, loyalty and treachery, kindness and cruelty, have not changed at all. This is nothing less than a rejection of the whole heritage of Nineteenth Century progressivism. In 1864 Victor Hugo, one of the most powerful "progressive" minds of his day, hailed the development of ballooning with a prediction that aircraft would make war impossible, and would instantly abolish armies and frontiers and liberate mankind.[2] Dickens delighted to see telegraph wires pierce the cruel old heart of the Coliseum. Cruelty, he felt, would hardly survive electricity. (He died the day the Ems telegram triggered the Franco-Prussian War.) Macauley believed railways and steamships symbolized not only progress but a heartening advance towards universal peace.

The "unprogressive" nature of both *The Lord of The Rings* and *Star Wars* is plain. In *The Lord of The Rings,* beauty, glory and wonder have roots in the past. One angry progressive critic *of Star Wars* saw "the sting" (the confidence trick) in it as being the fact that it was set "a long time ago," implying that progress was not necessarily progressive. In *Star Wars* there is no suggestion that the overthrow of the Empire and the destruction of the Emperor will bring Utopia. The dark side of the Force, with its power to corrupt, will still exist. In both tales the "rebels" fight to prevent the victory of absolute darkness and to preserve the best society possible. There will still be troubles, tragedy, social and personal inequalities, threats of new ills, and there will still be Death and whatever lies beyond it. These themes run quite counter to Nineteenth-Century progressivism and Utopianism and their Twentieth-Century legacies.

The Utopian revolutionary is, ultimately, inspired by a quasi-religious eschatology, holding that the end of the Revolution will be the setting up of a New Jerusalem, or Kingdom of Heaven on Earth. The conservative rebel believes he is fighting against the setting up of a Hell on earth—against the Auschwitzes and Gulags that Utopian revolutionaries bring—and believes that the ultimate progressive dream of abolishing traditional good and evil will succeed only in the first part of that program. As Joseph Conrad put it in 1885:

> [T]o pass through robbery, equality, anarchy and misery under the iron rule of military despotism. Such is the lesson of common-sense logic. Socialism must inevitably end in Caesarism.

Since *Star Wars* was made primarily for an American audience, it had no need to spell out that the good republic recently usurped by the Emperor was a free-enterprise, commercial republic. That is in the background of American culture. Things like spaceships are private property, as was Uncle Olwen's farm. When Luke sells his land-speeder he complains: "Since the XP-38 came out, they just aren't in demand." There is still something left of a market economy. In the fourth draft of the script, omitted from the film but published in *The Art of Star Wars,* Luke's friend Biggs says to him:

> What good is all your uncle's work if it's taken over by the Empire?... You know they're starting to nationalize commerce in the central systems [and] it won't be long before your uncle's merely a tenant.

Plainly the old republic was not collectivist or socialist. It is interesting that even without this information the implications and atmosphere of *Star Wars* were sufficiently plain for progressive and collectivist-minded intellectuals to give it a most hostile reception on its release.

Though the rebels in these two tales have no belief in Utopia, they are still prepared to sacrifice their own lives to overthrow tyranny and restore an order which, though intrinsically imperfect, is immeasurably less bad than that of the Enemy. This is not a conceit of romantic fiction, of course: it is no more than people have been prepared to do in fact for centuries. But it is opposed to the progressive and "liberalistic" slogan: "Nothing is worth dying for!" Good characters in both tales accept death both by sacrificing their lives in battle for others (Gandalf, Obe-Wan and various other fighters) and by old age at the end of long lives (Aragon, Yoda). Implicit here is a religious and specifically Christian belief that earthly life is a preparation for death—or rather for what lies beyond death. The evil characters, however, are circumscribed by a purely Earthly consciousness. They are at last withered hideous creatures clutching power at all costs because this is the only form their desire for deathlessness can take.

The good people in both tales are led by aristocrats, among others, but there are aristocrats on the evil side as well, and we hardly need to be told that aristocrats, like all other leaders, can be evil. The potential of power to corrupt is a major theme of both works. So is lack of power. Some of the lesser villains (Gollum, Salacious Crumb) have been corrupted by their own littleness. Again, such notions are at odds with Utopian doctrines which see the solutions to human problems as being in better planning and the control of social systems.

In both tales the good uphold orders of hierarchy and some ritual splendor. They utilize science and/or magic (in short, power) but do not regard it as an end in itself. Institutionalized ugliness, drabness, and the exultation of perverted science are the province of the Enemies. While the Enemies have imposed brutal discipline on their own forces, the good people accept hierarchy, but an organic hierarchy and one in which individuals can quite properly rise. Good characters grow when they do noble deeds of their own initiative and volition. The young hobbits in *The Lord of The Rings* and Han Solo and Lando in *Star Wars* grow from immature adventurers to responsible leaders, though their bravery does not diminish but increases with responsibility and their acceptance of a moral dimension to their actions. In *The Lord of The Rings* Merry takes the first step towards "ennoblement" when he goes to help Eorwyn in the apparently hopeless fight against the Lord of the Nazgul. In *Star Wars* Han Solo begins the same journey when he turns back to help in the apparently hopeless attack on the first Death Star. Lando, in *The Empire Strikes Back,* throws away everything he has built up to thwart Darth Vader's plans rather than collaborate in the final betrayal of his friend.

The attitude to power and to politics and social organization in these tales is also at odds with progressivism. It is taken for granted that a hierarchical structure which is accepted as legitimate rather than arbitrary, in which values depend on something more than the caprice of the rulers, is the only structure in which justice, and therefore freedom, are possible. As Shakespeare put it in *Troilus and Cressida,* "Take but degree away, untune that string, and hark what discord follows!" Much the same notion is summed up in those five short words of most unprogressive injunction: "Fear God. Honor the King" (1 Peter, 2:17).

In both tales, the great Enemies, like Totalitarians today, make hierarchy dependent on their own power. Their own lieutenants, however terrifying they appear to those below, themselves lead the precarious lives of a Roehm, a Yagoda, a Yezhov or a Beria. In the evil empires, not the State but society has withered. The tyrants will kill their own subordinates for failures not their fault, without pity, whereas the good people would regard the deaths of any of their subordinates as a tragedy. This is part of the difference between an organically healthy, and therefore just, hierarchy, and one ruled by arbitrary terror.

Part of the predictable consequence of this is that the tyrants find themselves surrounded by sycophants, afraid to disagree with them or bring them bad news. Yet, as in the real world, this is not an immediately crippling handicap. The real problem for them is that Evil is smaller than Good in that Evil cannot understand Good in the way Good can understand Evil. This is far more a Christian than a dualistic or a "New Age" religious view.

The enemy vision turns naturally to the idea of dethroning a leader as soon as any rising subordinate has the power to do so, recapitulating the social arrangements of some animals such as wolves. In *Star Wars* the Emperor assumes Luke Skywalker is corruptible by the temptations of the dark side, as he assumes Darth Vader is totally and irretrievably overcome by it (as does Vader himself. He says, when Luke first asks him to remember his heritage and rebel against the Emperor: "It is too late for me, Son.") In *The Lord of The Rings* Sauron never conceives that anyone else holding the Great Ring will try to destroy it, or do anything but trample down rivals to wield it. In both cases their failure to understand anyone having a goal beyond seizing power proves fatal to them. Part of the heterogeneity, and the humanity, of the good sides in these tales is that the beings making them up have diverse interests, emphases and gifts. Even the non-human characters are recognizable as having certain individual human characteristics. We see little of these aspects of the regimented forces on the enemies' sides, but some of them at least display courage and self-sacrifice. In *The Empire Strikes Back* Captain Nida of the destroyer *Avenger*, which loses the *Millennium Falcon* outside the asteroid belt, sacrifices himself to Darth Vader's wrath, assuming "full responsibility," apparently to protect his subordinates. Even an orc in *The Two Towers* returns to a foredoomed battle rather than forsake some "stout lads." It is a conservative and individualistic rather than a progressive or collectivist belief that it is possible to be a good person fighting in a bad cause. (In *The Last Battle* C.S. Lewis made the point, on the religious aspect of this, that a good god will accept good things done in the name of an evil cause, not because Good and Evil are one but precisely because they are utterly apart).

Star Wars' Emperor can hardly have built a star fleet of his own from nothing in a fairly short time, and presumably when gaining power he took over the old Republic's existing fleet, as Caesar took over the Legions, Hitler took over the German Reichswehr and Lenin forced ex-Czarist officers to serve the Soviets. One can imagine in *Star Wars* an old guard of ex-Republican officers in the Imperial star fleet (Admiral Ousel and Captain Nida—both killed by Darth Vader for failure—might well be among them), doing their duty with increasing reluctance, never trusted by the new regime, and doomed to liquidation as soon as their services can be replaced. (One may wonder if Admiral Ousel deliberately bungled the star fleet's approach to the Hoth base to allow the rebels time to escape?) In both tales (and again, as in real life) the evil principle's power depends on its abilities to put good qualities such as bravery and selflessness to evil uses.

In both stories women do little fighting, though some of the leaders on the "good" side are women. This is an integral part of the chivalrous tradition. In *The Lord of The Rings* (the question does not arise much explicitly one way or the other in *Star Wars)* the "good" side are chivalrous fighters. They spare the lives of their enemies if they can. This is in marked contrast to many sadistic books and films of the last decade or so, including a rash of films in the 1960s and 1970s—*Shout at the Devil, Play Dirty, The Dirty Dozen, The Guns of Navarone, etc.*—which took an indulgent or approving attitude to torture or other terror practiced by the "right side" or scorned the idea of "civilized" (that is, chivalrous) war.

Tolkien's own general attitude to this is made plain in a letter written to his son on January 20, 1945:

> I have just heard the news.... Russians 60 miles from Berlin. It does look as if something decisive might happen soon. The appalling destruction and misery of this war mount hourly: destruction of what should be (indeed is) the common wealth of Europe, and the world, if mankind were not so besotted.... Yet people gloat over the endless lines, 40 miles long of miserable refugees, women and children passing West, dying on the way. They seem to have no bowels of mercy or compassion, no imagination, left in this dark diabolic hour. By which I do not mean it may not all, in the present situation, mainly (not solely) created by Germany, be necessary and inevitable. But why gloat? We are supposed to have reached a stage of civilization in which it might still be necessary to execute a criminal, but not to gloat, or hang his wife and child by him while the orc-crowd hooted.... Well, well, you and I can do nothing about it. *And that [should] be a measure of the amount of guilt that can justly be attached to any member of a country who is not a member of its actual government.* [emphasis added][3]

In both tales the enemy armies are conscripted, and many of their members are, in a sense, victims too. At one point in *The Lord of The Rings*, Sam contemplates the body of a dead enemy invader:

> He was glad he could not see the dead face. He wondered what the man's name was and where he came from; and if he was really evil at heart, or what lies or threats had led him on the long march from his home; and if he would not really rather have stayed there in peace.

In the fourth draft of the first *Star Wars* script (the scene was finally omitted from the film) Luke's friend Biggs tells him: "I'm not going to wait for the Empire to draft me into service." Luke agrees: "I won't be drafted into the Imperial Starfleet." The Imperial forces depend on conscription. The "good" side may conscript, but one gets the impression in both tales that the armies of good are formed of men who have voluntarily chosen to submit to military discipline.

Again, it is an important part of the tradition of Western chivalry that the enemy be seen as something other than a collectively evil and guilty mass of sub-humans. A collectivist ideology, followed to its logical conclusion, makes the possible goodness or human worth of individual enemies a practically meaningless concept. It is notable that Soviet writings on the Second World War usually refer to German soldiers simply as "the Fascists," despite the fact that the German armies were made up overwhelmingly of conscripted workers. To the Totalitarian, the defeated enemy must go to "the rubbish-heap of history" (that is: die).

It is explicitly stated at the end of *The Lord of The Rings* and it is possible to assume at the end of *Star Wars* that, with the destruction of Sauron and the Emperor, most of the personnel of the defeated armies were set free and also recovered liberty and dignity (as happened after World War II with the West German, Italian and Japanese populations). This is the Western, conservative, and chivalrous, as distinct from the ideological or Totalitarian, end. It is connected with Christianity, but does not necessarily imply some eschatology of Universalism, Apocatastasis or Pelagianism. Not all are necessarily saved, least of all by their own unaided efforts, though Tolkien did write that he saw everything in the World created by God as being ultimately good.

"Patterns of Epic" is an extract from *Return of the Heroes*, by Hal Colebatch (Australian Institute for Public Policy, Perth, 1990; 103pp).

NOTES

1. Humphrey Carpenter, ed: *The Letters of J.R.R. Tolkien* (Allen & Unwin, 1981), p.224.

2. Francois Mallet, *La conquete de l'air et la paix universelle*, (1910), p.73, quoted in I.F. Clarke, *Voices Prophesying War 1763-1984* (Oxford University Press, 1966), p.3.

3. Humphrey Carpenter, p. 111.

GAIA IN ISAAC ASIMOV'S *FOUNDATION* NOVELS

ECOLOGICAL HYPOTHESIS AS FICTIONAL TERMINUS

JACOB GEORGE C.

Science fiction, generally seen as a literary ghetto during the pre-Second World War phase, emerges in the American literary scene of the 1940s as a significant genre which exhibits many of the characteristics of American literature and experience. The close alignment between science fiction and American literature perhaps stems from the fact that both have "romance" as their basic form. American science fiction takes wing with the vast space-epics written in the true spirit of romances, full of optimism for the future of the human race. The writer with affirmative aspirations who finds himself in an indifferent and even hostile intellectual environment in post-Second World War America opts for science fiction since, like all romances, it provides space for conflicts and resolutions which fulfill logical and aesthetic expectations. The American writer, who in Hawthorne's terms had been searching for "a neutral territory somewhere between the real world and the fairy land" (38), apparently sees science fiction as one of the surviving literary terrains where human essence is discussed without highbrow abstractions.

Among the American science fiction writers who exploit the potential of science fiction to hold and manipulate a considerable quantum of ethical and imaginative burden, Isaac Asimov ranks supreme. He takes advantage of science fiction's plasticity, versatility and currency of appeal, and makes it an important mode to expose contemporary problems. While in science writing and other non-fiction Asimov merely analyses and exposes contemporary reality, in science fiction he extrapolates the present-day problems working out rational solutions which are logically convincing and scientifically plausible. Asimov's faith in science and technology and his tendency to find scientific and rational solutions to human problems is most obvious in the *Foundation* novels. Inaugurated at the height of the Second World War, these novels draw the extrapolated picture of a world in crisis and reflect Asimov's own fear that a new Dark Age is about to commence. Yet the *Foundation* novels argue, with the underlying optimism of "the American Way of Life," that if the causes for the decline can be analyzed and their course predicted through the application of science to history, then perhaps it may be possible to control the events to some extent and contain the harm.

The time-frame of Asimov's fictional canvas in the *Foundation* series extends up to twenty thousand years into the future. Humanity, by then, has spread out into the whole of the galaxy and has forgotten its planet of origin, which has become uninhabitable. Hari Seldon, a psychologist, formulates a new science for predicting mass behavior (psychohistory) and proves that the Galactic Empire, which has ruled twenty five million planets for twelve thousand years bringing peace and prosperity, is on the verge of disintegration. Using psychohistory, Seldon predicts thirty thousand years of misery and barbarity after the fall of the Galactic Empire. The attempt to limit the Galactic dark phase to one thousand years is initiated with the establishing of two Foundations (one led by the physical scientists and the other by the psychologists) at opposite ends of the Galaxy. The seven *Foundation* novels (the first three written in the 1940s and the next four between 1982-92) built around this core problem discuss the different possibilities and solutions for the preservation of knowledge and culture in the face of a decline to barbarism.

Foundation (1951) and *Foundation and Empire* (1952), the first two of the novels, discuss at length the process of stabilization of the First Foundation, a scientifically advanced, militaristic state which is seen as a possible solution to check the Galactic stagnation and disintegration. Established on a metal-poor planet (Terminus) with few resources, the First Foundation is nevertheless very much reminiscent of America. It becomes a dynamic world in which individual initiative counts. The guidance of efficient political leaders and talented physical scientists help the First Foundation in its fast growth. Advanced technology, spiritual powers and shrewd strategies of economic warfare enable the First Foundation (like the United States) to defeat the old Galactic Empire (obviously the extrapolated British Empire) and become the most powerful state in the Galaxy. Ironically the First Foundation is soon plagued by the inertia of ruling classes, despotism, and maldistribution of wealth—the ills which brought down the Galactic Empire. Asimov's near disillusionment with the idea of a scientifically advanced state as a bringer of Utopia coincides with the dominant attitude of the 1950s to negate the false and dangerous claims of science. Yet Asimovian science fiction does not turn to skepticism or pessimism like the other science fiction of the times and retains the optimistic zeal to search for alternatives.

The third *Foundation* novel, *Second Foundation* (1953), discusses such an alternate solution which privileges the powers of the mind over those of science, technology, religion and commerce. The "mentalists" or psychohistorians of the Second Foundation guide the society through subtle mind-control activities done diplomatically and secretly. What the Second Foundation ultimately offers is "a benevolent dictatorship of the mentally best" *(Second Foundation* 126), where the mentalists inevitably become "a ready-made ruling class" (127).

The changed environment of the 1980s sees the disappearance of Asimov's faith in mental science and technology so prevalent in the first three volumes of *Foundation.* The Cold War and the resultant nuclear anxiety, environmental problems, overpopulation, and the various other negative impacts of scientific advancements wipe off the feeling that science and technology can bring peace.

In Foundation's Edge (1982) the "mentalists" of the Second Foundation can no longer maintain the Galactic Empire's rate of progress. The knowledge that there is a force to protect and guard the state, irrespective of the nature of the crisis, drives away all initiative and precipitates a decadent and hedonistic culture. In addition, the superhuman Second Foundationers begin to bicker among themselves and play "power games" in their competition to gain political power and leadership. Asimov, through these simulation games, establishes the impracticability of two social systems towards which America inevitably moves. Thus Asimov's third solution—which he calls Gaia—does not merely solve the fictional crisis posed in *Foundation* novels but reaches out to the heart of the world's present conflicts, transforming them into fictional problems with plausible resolutions.

The new system is generally seen as one invented under the influence of B.F. Skinner and other behaviorists, according to whom everything supposedly can fit harmoniously together in a coexistence satisfying all needs, in perfect, controlled, peaceful balance. But a striking similarity between Asimov's thesis and James E. Lovelock's Gaia hypothesis prompts the argument that Asimov has perhaps drawn more from the ecological hypothesis than from the theories of the behavioral scientists.

Lovelock's hypothesis attempts to establish that "Earth's living matter, air, oceans, and land surface form a complex system which can be seen as a single organism and which has the capacity to keep our planet a fit place for life" (*Gaia*, preface vii). He names the planet-sized entity Gaia, after the Greek Earth-goddess, and argues with conviction that "the entire range of living matter on Earth... could be regarded as constituting a single living entity, capable of manipulating the Earth's atmosphere to suit its overall needs and endowed with faculties and powers far beyond those of its constituent parts" (*Gaia*, 9). Lovelock's hypothesis contradicts the conventional wisdom which holds that life adapted to the planetary conditions as it and they evolved their separate ways. He points out the irrationality and danger in remaining at odds with nature and feels that Gaia will change the pessimistic view which sees nature as a primitive force to be subdued and conquered. Lovelock's notion of Gaia not only offers an alternative to the depressing picture of our planet as a demented spaceship (forever travelling driverless and purposeless, around an inner circle of the sun), but also visualizes a future in which *homo sapiens* "become a truly collective species, corralled and tamed as an integral part of the biosphere... the destiny of mankind is to become tamed, so that the fierce, destructive and greedy forces of tribalism and nationalism are fused into a compulsive urge to belong to the commonwealth of all creatures which constitute Gaia" *(Gaia* 148). Lovelock argues that the loss of tribal and individual freedom in Gaia gains sufficient compensation "in the form of an increased sense of wellbeing and fulfillment, in knowing ourselves to be a dynamic part of a far greater entity" (148).

Asimov perhaps recognizes in Lovelock's hypothesis an analogous vision with fictional potential. Gaia offers him a new equation which conforms with his belief that nation-states are an outmoded form of government, ill-equipped to meet the global problems. He thinks that if we are to survive as a species, we must "begin to look for ways of attaining a rational disarmament and a reasonable form of world government" *(Asimov's Galaxy* 175). Asimov, through fictional simulations, proposes that while militaristic states get destroyed by strife, paternalistic states established by calculation and diplomacy end up as a hell of individual egos struggling for dominance. The invalidation of these possible resolutions leads Asimov to the Gaia hypothesis, which offers the inspiration to chalk out a progressive and rational basis for an ideal future state.

Ironically, in the story the plan is designed and piloted not by a human being but by a robot (R. Daneel Olivaw) with the capacity for mental telepathy. The possibility of machines "taking over" in future is a recurrent idea in Asimov's fictional as well as non-fictional writings. He believes that robots "are sufficiently intelligent to replace us... In the course of human evolution and the vast evolution of life before that... one species replaces another [when] the replacing species is in one way or another more efficient than the species replaced.... *Homo sapiens* [do not] possess any divine right to the top rung" *(A Conversation with Isaac Asimov* 69). Incidentally, Asimov's prediction echoes Lovelock's observation that "we are not the first species destined to fulfill [a lead] role, nor possibly the last" *(Gaia* 149). Gaia in *Foundation's Edge* (1982) and *Foundation and Earth* (1986) is obviously a replacement of this sort. In the fictional world of Asimov, Gaia has grown into a single sentient world in rational ecological balance, from the stones in the mountains to its human inhabitants. The humans and robots in Gaia, under Daneel's guidance, work to create a Utopia which offers life in the form of Galaxia, a living, remembering Galaxy—"a way of life fundamentally different from all that has gone before and repeating none of the old mistakes" *(Foundation's Edge* 345).

The ingenuity of Asimov in extrapolating Lovelock's hypothesis becomes apparent in the elaborate descriptive and argumentative passages in *Foundation's Edge* and *Foundation and Empire*. The passage which introduces Gaia to Golan Trevize, the protagonist, is typical:

> The whole planet and everything on it is Gaia. We're all individuals—we're all separate organisms—but we share an overall consciousness.... [The Planet] runs itself. Those trees grow in rank and file of their own accord. They multiply only to the extent that is needed to replace those that for any reason die... It rains when it is necessary and occasionally it rains hard when *that* is necessary—and occasionally there's a siege of dry weather when *that* is necessary.... I remain a human being—but above us is a group consciousness as far beyond my grasp as my consciousness is beyond that of one of the muscle cells of my biceps. *(Foundation's Edge* 300-01)

The fictional Gaia projected here is shown to accommodate all the three principal characteristics of the hypothetical Gaia. According to Lovelock, Gaia has:

> 1. The tendency to optimize conditions for all terrestrial life as long as the optimizing capacity is not seriously interfered with.
> 2. The tendency to keep vital organs or aspects at the core while keeping expendable or redundant ones on the periphery.
> 3. The tendency to maintain relatively constant conditions by active control or homeostasis. *(Gaia,* 127*)*

Asimov adds further credibility to his fictional restatement of Lovelock's vision by incorporating an elaborate debate, on the three paths before mankind, from which Gaia emerges as the only rational alternative. The First Foundation, which represents the most commonly taken path, allows free will but, like all worlds of "Isolates," offers only misery, bloodshed and anarchy, and can never have decency, kindness and mutual concern—the distinguishing marks of Gaia. The Second Foundation, which depends on the guidance of the mentally best, allows limited free will, stops bloodshed and brings peace, but has self-destructive competitions, hatreds and betrayals amongst the ruling class. Gaia, the hitherto unknown path in human history, draws its strength from collective existence. Asimov emphatically outlines Gaia in *Foundation and Earth* as "a superorganism; a whole planet with a mind and personality in common... [which is to] become Galaxia, a super-superorganism embracing all the swarm of the Milky Way" (13-14). It is "a new society, a new scheme of life, a frightening revolution that would be greater than any since the development of multicellular life" (32). Thus, what qualifies Gaia above the other paths in Asimov is its offer of a new dynamic "Life." This offer which makes the Asimovian Utopia attractive and plausible draws its rationale from Lovelock who finds in the Second Law of Thermodynamics the unequivocal statement that "the entropy of a closed system must increase. Since we are all closed systems, this means that all of us are doomed to die.... The death sentence of the Second Law applies only to identities, to closed systems, and could be rephrased: 'Mortality is the price of identity'" *(Gaia* 125). Hence Lovelock points out that greater chance of survival and durability remains not with the individual but with the family, the tribe, the species, and finally in a still greater measure, with Gaia. What ultimately is crystallized in both Lovelock and Asimov is the aspiration to go beyond the limits of the individual existence.

The Gaian configuration in the Asimovian fictional cyberspace marks a deviation and abandonment of the familiar fictional constituents of individuality, creativity, variety and spontaneity. These generative principles of fiction are valorized in the first three novels of *Foundation,* but the second set of *Foundation* novels manifests a realization that these elements cannot be taken any further. This recognition is compounded by the political and ecological imperatives and the aesthetic considerations that demanded a definite change in the fictional direction. The factionalized Gaia systematically discards each of the generative principles and claims the terrain for itself by remaining an overarching category. But in the absence of constituent identities, fiction reaches the point of exhaustion. The controlled, programmed and systematized fictional space and categories of *Foundation's Edge* and *Foundation and Earth* signify a pronounced departure in a writer who rarely ventures into formal and technical experimentation.

—2002

WORKS CITED

Asimov, Isaac. *Asimov's Galaxy: Reflections on Science Fiction.* New York: Doubleday, 1989.

— *Foundation.* New York: Gnome Press, 1951.

— *Foundation and Empire.* New York: Gnome Press, 1952.

— *Second Foundation.* New York: Gnome Press, 1953.

— *Foundation's Edge.* New York: Doubleday, 1982.

— *Foundation and Earth.* New York: Doubleday, 1986.

Hawthorne, Nathaniel. *The Scarlet Letter.* Ed. Harry Levin. Cambridge: Riverside Press, 1960.

Ingersoll, Earl G. "A Conversation with Isaac Asimov." *Science-Fiction Studies.* 14:1 (1987): 68-77.

Lovelock, James E. *Gaia: A New Look at Life on Earth.* New York: OUP, 1979.

WOMEN OF DARKNESS, EDITED BY KATHRYN PTACEK

ORIGINAL HORROR AND DARK FANTASY BY CONTEMPORARY WOMEN WRITERS

YVONNE ROUSSEAU

Kathryn Ptacek's anthology, *Women of Darkness*, contains twenty "dark fantasy and horror" stories by "contemporary women writers." Of these, the most successful stories are by the anthology's two best-known authors: Lisa Tuttle and Tanith Lee.

The horror in Lisa Tuttle's "The Spirit Cabinet" derives not from the séances described in it but from a violation of the laws of the physical universe, producing a death that police can account for only by "an explosion of the most tremendous force"—although the surrounding room and neighborhood are undisturbed. The result may remind some readers of Sandra Orgel's artwork, "Sheet Closet," in the "Womanhouse" created by Judy Chicago and others in 1972. Orgel's and Tuttle's women are palpably closeted in domesticity, and the psychological horror of Tuttle's story is that its outcome results from a kind of irresponsibility typical in women's domestic lives: the heroine Katy's propensity to submit her own judgment to masculine will, especially where an issue seems too trivial to warrant the discord involved in her insisting.

Tanith Lee's "The Devil's Rose" involves another psychological weakness—thinking of evil as merely picturesque (the way that the undeclared Elizabethan war on Spanish treasure-ships encouraged British readers to regard pirates as glamorous and romantic—in contrast to the sordid reality depicted in Voltaire's *Candide*, or suffered by present-day Vietnamese and Cambodian boat people). In Lee's story, a scholar, recounting the ancient tale of a girl who danced with the Devil, observes: "young girls do sometimes... embrace such morbid fancies—the love of death, or the Dark Angel, the Devil." Unfortunately, a young girl (especially in the nineteenth-century provincial society of the small

Eastern European town described in "The Devil's Rose") is likely, in her ignorance, to see no more than warm-blooded freedom in the "wickedness" that her elders warn her against, and to expect even so extreme a social outlaw as the Devil to cherish her daringness if she aligns herself with his censured glamour. But true evil, as unfolded in the hauntingly Pushkinesque prose of "The Devil's Rose," is mean and cold-hearted callousness.

In both these stories, to admit desire (however trivial) is to lay oneself open to horror. In Lee's story, the desire is to find love; in Tuttle's, to ease a cramp in one leg. Acting upon these desires brings disaster. Indeed, unease about desire is everywhere in this anthology—reflecting a world where a woman's simple desire to walk alone in the moonlight is considered so presumptuous that if she is raped and murdered while carrying it out a great number of people will claim that she only got what she deserved. The underlying fear is expressed in Carol Orlock's "Nobody Lives There Now. Nothing Happens," where townsfolk react with paranoia to gifts that fulfill their desires. The ghostly newcomers, Mr. and Mrs. Marquette, are suspected; and are eagerly blamed for the "cruel tricks" that follow.

The expression of uncontrolled desire is regarded, in polite society, as childish—and six of these stories involve violent children. In Nancy Holder's "Cannibal Cats Come Out Tonight" and Melissa Mia Hall's "The Unloved," they are abused children who have grown up with bizarre notions and none of the expected sympathies. Holder's monsters are male—Hall's, female. Holder's story resembles Theater of the Absurd, its two "blood brothers" solemnly changing their minds about which pop idols are good enough to eat, as their tastes (with experience) become increasingly fastidious. In Hall's more Gothic story, beautiful blonde identical twins have grown to adulthood with the question: are all men like daddy? From the small sample they are provided with, the answer they perceive is yes—and the "mirror" twin's last chance for a baby (to be borne by the "real" twin) is wrecked by a man using psychological violence instead of the physical violence that "daddy" favored.

Holder's and Hall's monsters are handsome or beautiful; the adolescent girls of Elizabeth Massie's "Hooked on Buzzer" and Rachel Cosgrove Payes's "Mother Calls But I Do Not Answer" are shunned for their ugliness, and have developed correspondingly monstrous inner desires. Both are in some sense abused children—as are the more normal young girls of Wennicke Eide Cox's "Sister," who are the prey of a rapist stepfather. In Cox's story, the murdered sister is transformed into a nixie who rises from the lake to save her younger sister and revenge herself. But achievement of revenge brings unease. The survivor's relief is tainted with fear, lest the lake be haunted as well now by her sister's male equivalent.

The only unabused violent child in this anthology is the demonic infant of Kit Reed's "Baby." This story (which I find too absurd to be effective) plays on fears about the way parenthood warps one's judgment: as Fay Weldon expresses it, in *The Cloning of Joanna May*: "Women without children are smarter, tougher and more decisive than women who have children. Women with children are torn in so many directions they become kind, nice and hopeless in their own interests in the effort to understand themselves, let alone their children."

In this anthology, the theme of love gone wrong is even more pervasive than that of violent children. It involves the same fear that Reed's "Baby" exploits—that one's moral character will become unfixed. This is expressed most vividly in the only deadly new virus story: Sharon Epperson's "Slide Number Seven," where misguided love for the whole world inspires the heroine to free the "yearning souls inescapably trapped in dirty, sweating, traitorous flesh." Similarly, in the only zombie-possession story—Nancy Varian Berberick's "Ransom Cowl Walks the Road"—the law will judge the husband-killer to be morally deranged. (The killer's consciousness is presented too shallowly, however, for anxiety about mistaken identity to engage the reader's emotions.)

When love goes wrong, rejection arouses anger. Contemporary women often confess to fear and guilt about feeling anger; and two of these stories describe grisly retribution for angrily desiring revenge. Both involve recourse to another society's ancient magic: Japanese myth in Lucy Taylor's "The Baku," Brazilian voodoo in Karen Haber's "Sambo Sentado." In these stories, magic from more primitive states of society works like a metaphor for primitive feelings—viewed as dangerous. Even the idea of producing harmless catharsis through crowd spectacles such as professional wrestling is given short shrift in Cary G. Osborne's unconvincing "Monster McGill" (where the audience takes things much too seriously).

In two stories about rejecting rejection, the discarded lovers find that killing the objects of their desire makes them much more obliging. Like Cox's nixie "Sister" story, Joan Vander Putten's "In the Shadows of My Fear" involves an underwater female corpse, put there by a man who is subsequently bitten to death. But the man in Putten's tale is not merely wicked but insane: a necrophiliac Bluebeard. Similarly insane, but immensely practical, the heroine of Patricia Russo's "True Love" succeeds for years in deriving macabre "light and joy and support" from her lover, after he refuses to yield these things through affection. Apart from the warping of her personality, she incurs no retribution.

Elsewhere, however, much more trivial desires bring drastic retribution. Shopping guilt inspires both Wendy Webb's "Midnight Madness" (an oddly effective senseless nightmare, set in a supermarket) and Conda V. Douglas's "When Thunder Walks" (where a bargain seeker, exploiting Amerindians, is monstrously inseminated by the Navajo Coyote, in retribution). A more curious case is Rivka Jacobs's "Little Maid Lost," set in Florida, where the demon Mr. Sam, the "master of half of everything," offers the fulfillment of desires to a fourteen-year-old girl (whose limited life allows her to imagine only trivial wants) before placing her in the way of death by rape and mutilation. The voodoo magic of the girl's friend, Senora Blanco, is powerless to save her.

Jacobs's story is the anthology's closest approach to the Lovecraftian notion of vast impersonal powers. *Women of Darkness* concentrates instead on individual behavior—although Melanie Tem's "Aspen Graffiti" places some modern behavior in an eerie perspective. The wife who narrates this tale observes a curious disintegration among men who remove themselves from their families, abandoning their share of parental responsibility. While the wives struggle on, the men literally fade away, and the narrator eventually stumbles upon a "gathering place," where she sees not only her husband with "the stiff bearing, the slightly gaping mouth that I had come to associate with the man I loved" but also others: "men just like him. There must have been hundreds of them: gray, almost fluid in their teeming, and absolutely silent." Women cannot prevent their fading; nor can they influence their sons' responses (whether identifying with or denying their fathers). The process is clearly beyond human control—although in the narrator's mind, her husband's disintegration is associated with her own act of carving their initials on an aspen tree, despite her husband's warning that such cuts "make a point of entry for a certain kind of fungus, and that fungus kills the tree."

A horror story that chills one reader will sometimes make another reader yawn. Several of the stories in *Women of Darkness* are ineffective for me, but the overall effect of modern malaise is a horror in itself.

—1995

WOMEN OF WONDER, EDITED BY PAMELA SARGENT

MARILYN WALTERS

Women of Wonder is an anthology of twelve stories, each one indicative of the many styles and concerns of women writers of science fiction. There is a refreshing absence of intergalactic goodies and baddies. The stories deal in some depth with varying aspects of the human psyche, observed from a uniquely feminine viewpoint. This does not mean that each story is a feminist manifesto as Sonya Dorman's introductory poem, "The Child Dreams," innocently purports to be, but rather each writer reflects in her work something of the collective female consciousness of our era; of how women view sexuality, physical appearances, atomic warfare, interpersonal relationships and prejudice.

Too often, unfortunately, the consciousness is that of woman in a man's world wherein sexual inequalities have remained dormant despite increased scientific advance. A jarring instance of this occurs in Katherine MacLean's story, "Contagion" (1950). MacLean found it necessary to explain to the reader that women can also be doctors:

> The four medicos, for June Walton was also a doctor, filed through the alien homelike forest... (p.20)

Throughout MacLean's story the presence of such a sexual double standard detracts from her central theme of the relationship between physical appearances and personal identity, which would have been otherwise far more powerful. For instance, the sociological dabbler and mechanic, Remo, is treated sympathetically in his amorous adventures:

> "This gives me a chance to study their mores." He winked wickedly. "I may not be back for several nights." (p. 36)

By contrast, "the gorgeous Sheila Davenport" is frowned upon for her flirtatiousness.

MacLean's central character, June Walton, is aware of the attraction of the other women to the colonist, Pat Mead, long before it becomes apparent to her partner Max and the males on board.

> June noticed that the female specialists were prolonging the questions more than they needed, clustering around the table laughing at his jokes, until presently Pat was almost surrounded by pretty faces, eager questions and chiming laughs. Sheila the beautiful laughed most chimingly of all. June nudged Max, and Max shrugged indifferently. It wasn't anything a man would pay attention to, perhaps. (p.32)

June Walton's own attraction to Mead is clumsily expressed to say the least:

> "You Tarzan?" she said mockingly and softly to his passing profile, and knew that he had heard. (p.37)

MacLean's weaknesses may well be stylistic rather than thematic but they leave a general impression which supports the inherent contention that men are bold, sensible and serious while women are flirtatious, frivolous and supportive; ready to take over when the men are too ill to work rather than playing any consistent decisive role in the running of the space ship, and in the meantime causing disharmony in the ranks through their capriciousness.

"That Only a Mother," by Judith Merril, is for its time (1948) a stunning insight into the horrors of atomic warfare. Following so closely on the heels of Hiroshima and Nagasaki, the startling realism of Merril's story is a timely warning to future generations—one which, unfortunately for us, has not been fully heeded. Like Maggie, the central character, we refuse to see what we do not want to see.

Chelsea Quinn Yarbro's "False Dawn" also expresses the consciousness of woman in a man's world, with horrifying clarity. Quinn Yarbro's world is the result of centuries of, presumably, male dominated aggression, senseless prejudice and territorial paranoia. In this decaying world the central character, Thea, must survive knowing that she is fair prey to a host of predators, wild dogs, pirates and deadly water spiders. Through this future world Quinn Yarbro projects the terror that all of today's women face at some stage of their lives; the ever present fear of physical, psychological and spiritual violation at the hands of men, or by the mores of a society created by them. The central character, as a mutant, represents the sub-human position of woman generally, here projected into a world totally devoid of protective social graces.

Quinn Yarbro is stylistically and thematically strong throughout apart from the curious twist towards the conclusion of the story. Thea, having survived the inevitable brutal assault of one of the males, expresses a preference for the other. I find this response decidedly strange and can only conclude that the author has allowed some wayward sexual fantasy of her own to intrude upon an otherwise convincing piece of prose. Also, by allowing Rossi/Montague to emerge as a hero in marked contrast to the villain, Lastly, Quinn Yarbro tacks a glib, traditional adventurist ending onto her story. "False Dawn," though conceptually convincing, becomes too sensational. Such detail as "He hit her in the mouth as he came" is entirely unnecessary, telling us nothing we don't already know about the character of the villain and failing to enhance the style or content of the story in any way.

In a lighter vein is Kit Reed's "Food Farm," a delightfully humorous attack upon human vanity and a sensuous dismissal of the ancient Christian ethic which brands overeating a mortal sin. It is also the poignant cry of the fat woman, one of our society's most detested mutants. Reed romps through nauseating gastronomic orgies with an almost lyrical freshness:

> Then I would lay in a new supply of cakes and rolls and baloney from the delicatessen and several cans of ready made frosting and perhaps a flitch of bacon or some ham; I would toss in a bag of oranges to ward off scurvy and a carton of handy bars for quick energy. Once I had enough I would go back to my room, concealing food here and there, rearranging my nest of pillows and comforters. I would open the first pie or the first half gallon of ice cream and then, as I began, I would plug in. (p.128)

The "fat is beautiful" equation is reinforced by the heroine's recollections of her "scrawny" parents and their lame excuses for her physique; of her mother's futile one-twoing on the living room floor; and, as heroine Nelly begins to lose weight, by the dreadful imagery of melting flesh. To complete the equation there is the rock music hero Tommy Fango's longing for a fat woman.

Skillfully interwoven with Nelly's adventures in food is the notion of "plugging in"; the adolescent addiction to popular music, a symbolic connection, via radio, to a universal pulse. Nelly shamelessly flaunts cosmetic morality to revel in what is after all an orally orientated society in which we live.

Reed's fantasy is a totally successful blend of familiar elements of everyday life: the spiritual pain of the non-compliant, the petty guilts we all experience when indulging our senses, and the institutions we have evolved to house our society's deviants; all are sensitively combined by her light, free-flowing prose style.

"Baby You Were Great" by Kate Wilhelm is an extension of today's glossy magazine image of woman, which so many women unwittingly strive to imitate, never knowing the extent to which their responses are controlled by the manufacturers of the initial image. Wilhelm shows from the inside how woman sells herself to the god of glamour, loses her own identity and freedom as a consequence, and becomes nothing more than an object of universal voyeurism.

The circle is indeed a vicious one. Once woman has allowed herself to be enticed into and manipulated by the media stereotype, the way out becomes increasingly difficult. For Kate Wilhelm's heroine the only escape is self-destruction, and even her own death is no longer solely her own choice. "Baby You Were Great" is an insight into the future possibilities of media omnipotence, and a warning to all women.

So far, the stories discussed have been set in worlds present or distant in which sexual boundaries have been for the most part what we would recognize as traditional, the latent prejudices detectable and the stereotyping intact. Other stories are concerned with either the dilemma of woman endeavoring to understand her own sexuality in worlds which are essentially asexual, or choosing to ignore questions of sexual divisions in favor of other pursuits. .

"The Wind People" by Marion Zimmer Bradley falls into the former category. The heroine, Helen, chooses to stay on an uninhabited planet with her new-born son, Robin, rather than desert him or risk his almost certain death in take-off. But as the lad grows to manhood, Helen is forced to confront herself and to examine her own rationality, her sexuality and the morality she has internalized from an earlier civilization. The tribe of Wind People remain enigmatic, their existence a possibility that Helen's rational mind will not entertain, even though her acceptance of them could mean her salvation.

Zimmer Bradley's story asks women how they would define themselves, left with only the most obvious role—that of reproduction—explicit. Have women the individual courage to initiate new modes of behavior, a new morality?

Anne McCaffrey's "The Ship Who Sang" is a curious but effective blend of the normal world of conventional sex role stereotyping and the cyborg, Helva's, asexual world. Though the central male character, Jennan, is of the sexist world, defining his preference in female companions by the color of their hair and alluding to the age old relationship between man and ship, and though Helva herself expresses sexist attitudes in her sarcasm about the attractive young nuns of Clohe, the relationship between Jennan and Helva is essentially asexual.

Thus the emphasis shifts to Helva herself. All that remains of Helva's human form is her brain, a brain that has been conditioned from infancy to perform the functions necessary to guide her spaceship body. But Helva still experiences the human emotions of hate, love, jealousy, joy, sorrow—emotions which have caused other ships to deny conditioning and to go "rogue." This is familiar ground to feminist theorists, sensitively dealt with by McCaffrey within her chosen genre. Under a heavier hand, however, the ending may have lapsed into schmaltz.

Perhaps the most complex story in the collection is Sonya Dorman's "When I Was Miss Dow." Dorman's tale revolves around an alien, asexual being who takes the form of a female human, Martha Dow. Martha becomes emotionally involved with a Terran male and the conflict between her alien free consciousness and her developing human female consciousness begins to engulf her.

> I burn with rage and jealousy, he has abandoned me to be Martha and I wish I were myself again, free in shape and single in mind. Not this sack of mud clinging to another. Yet he's teaching me that it's good to cling to another. (p.117)

The alien Martha begins to recognize a variety of human emotions and to penetrate the elaborate camouflage of human behavior:

> When the clown tumbles into the tub, I laugh. Terran history is full of tubs and clowns; at first it seems that's all there is, but you learn to see beneath the comic costumes. (p.120)

From her privileged position, floating on the line "between darkness and brightness," between human commitment and a free consciousness, Martha observes the full tragedy of the human condition

> It's what one of them called being a poet in the body of a cockroach. (p.120)

A contrast to Martha's dual consciousness is presented in the form of her pet kuta, a racing dog. Without the ability to change, the kuta is trapped within her singular shape. Now aging and crippled by a genealogical defect to which all kutas are prone, the beast lies doomed, dreaming of her former beauty and stamina. Following the death of her Terran lover, Martha returns to her alien free self, leaving the reader to ponder her penetrating observations of humanity.

Dorman's is a most accomplished handling of a far-reaching and ambitious theme.

Both Joanna Russ's "Nobody's Home" and Ursula Le Guin's "Vaster Than Empires and More Slow" fall within the latter category of the division drawn earlier. That is to say, the stories take place in worlds wherein conventional sexist attitudes are no longer dominant and developments in value structures have kept pace with scientific advance; the equality of the characters is never questioned on a sexual level.

In Joanna Russ's story, "Nobody's Home," the central conflict is between the heightened intelligence of the Komarov extended family and the animal intelligence of the newcomer, Leslie Smith. The Komarov world is a stimulating one. People are able to transport themselves instantaneously to any part of the globe and are free to engage in any activity that interests them, yet a curious phenomenon has arisen. Despite their manifold abilities, the Komarovs are becoming as bored as Leslie Smith and are titillated by the encroaching return of old practices. This is evident in their interest in the brutal duel which has taken place between the best and the second best makers of hand blown glass and articulated by Anne thus:

> "...it happens every decade or so. The children say they want to bring back cruelty, dirt, disease, glory and hell." (p.120)

Leslie Smith represents the old intelligence. Four times married, with no particular interests other than travel, Leslie is dull, but she is not stupid enough to allow herself to be exploited for very long. She is normal and can't be hidden away but instead she must be tolerated and accommodated. Leslie becomes an object of ridicule but, because she is a constant reminder of times past, she is also an object of dread.

"Vaster Than Empires and More Slow" is a masterful variation on the ancient theme of the social outcast who becomes savior, here unclouded by sexist preconceptions. Le Guin's story deals also with the concepts of empathy and extrasensory perception and the effects such special powers have upon the crew of a space vessel exploring an alien planet. The normally concealed emotions of fear, hate and pity in each of the crew members are exposed with devastating consequences.

The remaining two stories, Carol Emshwiller's "Sex and/or Mr. Morrison" and Vonda McIntyre's "Of Mist and Grass and Sand" are both charming fantasies centered upon somewhat simpler concerns, in contrast to the sophisticated searchings of Russ and Le Guin. "Sex and/or Mr. Morrison" tells of the exploits of a female peeping Tom and, for the duration of the tale at least, we may indulge ourselves in a little healthy curiosity. At the same time we are encouraged to re-examine some of our natural sensory functions and their relationship to our notions of beauty.

"Of Mist and Grass and Sand" examines the fears inherent in any clash of cultures and customs; contrasting the innocent acceptance of children with the mistrust and skepticism of adults. The story proceeds at a snake-like pace reflective of its central character, the female healer Snake, and her three reptilian associates from whom the story takes its title. This is a brilliant stylistic achievement, if at times a little dull.

What strikes me most about *Women of Wonder* is the variety of approach, of theme, of style and of achievement in the stories. Disappointing was the inability of some authors to transcend the conventional sex role stereotypes, to imagine worlds in which human relationships are somewhat more advanced on both a cerebral and a sensual level.

It would be difficult to substantiate the claim that a higher Feminist awareness correlates with a higher achievement in fiction writing. Indeed the opposite may just as easily be suggested. However, to me at least, a creative female spirit, seemingly burdened by centuries of literary archetypes, evident in the work of Le Guin and Russ, and in the imaginative penetration of existing social mores evident in the writing of Dorman, Wilhelm, Emshwiller and Reed, certainly contributes to stimulating reading.

—1977

WORDLUST AND WILD, WILD WOMYN

RUSSELL BLACKFORD

Lucy Sussex's first collection, *My Lady Tongue & Other Tales,* arrived as a handsome, well-knit trade paperback, the cover striking, provocative, the elegant pattern of Renaissance needle lace broken by a superimposed bleeding head, blood splashing yellow lace. The publishers, William Heinemann Australia, were careful not to mention that the stories are fantasy and science fiction—the blurb refers to the content of these "tales" as "the surreal, written as if realistic." In fact, some of the stories *are* surreal, notably the enigmatic and lovely "Quartet In Death Minor" in which the narrator, a dancing teacher dressed in boots and overcoat over harlequin ballet lycra, follows Death down a suburban street—Death as a skeleton twisted, origami-style, out of iron lace. But many of these stories are good straight f & sf and can be enjoyed as such.

A number of stories in *My Lady Tongue* had been published previously, including four in original Australian anthologies. It's good to see these stories together. Lucy Sussex is one of Australia's most accomplished writers of science fiction and fantasy; she's a careful and sometimes witty stylist. At its best, the Sussex approach is attention-grabbing, swift, direct. Take the opening paragraph of the title story:

> Honeycomb, my honey, sweet Honey Coombe. I love her so much I daubed her name on the biggest white wall in the ghetto and around it a two-metre heart. The paint was shocking pink and it dribbled, when I so wanted my ideogram to be perfect! She passed by that wall every day, but unfortunately so did others, and that was how the trouble started.

This is near to perfection as a story opening. The narrator rattles on, breathless, high-spirited, taken with her confessions. Slow down! But the prose is nonetheless perfectly plain, and the little narrative mysteries clear up almost immediately. They hook us into the story, but we soon understand what is going on, and the near-future world of womyn's ghettos and romantic lesbianism is depicted absolutely clearly. The beauty of "My Lady Tongue," which deservedly won the 1989 Ditmar award for best science fiction or fantasy short story, is the deadpan innocence with which it presents itself as it unfolds Raffy's fairly simple first-person love story. It tells two contrasting love stories, in fact, one, Raffy's romance with Honey, framing the other, her relationship with Benedict—all set in a world which is science fictional precisely in that a story of lesbian romance can be simply and almost childishly rattled off therein, while the embedded story of an emotionally complex heterosexual encounter is concealed as something wickedly adventurous, concealed both from other characters who had best not know, *ever*, and within the framed and folded structure of "My Lady Tongue" itself.

The only difficulty I have with the story is that Raffy's seduction of Benedict, which is described by Sussex with easy authority, is retrospectively turned into a sort of near-rape of Raffy a few pages later, when it is revealed that he had slipped her a bit of an aphrodisiac drug. Since *our* world contains no zipless aphrodisiacs, only zip-full uninhibitors, it is difficult to relate this back to any statement about male-female relationships as we actually know them. It doesn't work as a metaphor (all male-female relationships are more or less exploitative of the female) because it is too distractingly an innovation on our own social reality. In fact, a peculiar understanding of reality *will* occasionally detract from Sussex's work; "The Lipton Village Society," whose narrator is a public servant, is marred by an almost complete lack of feel for public service work culture. Nonetheless, "My Lady Tongue," taken as a whole, enacts a neat stylistic and structural subversion of traditional romances.

Sussex is stylish, deft, logophiliac; she gambols in fields of puns, jokes, verbal tricks, though all as embellishments on a basically very simple, readable, carefully paced prose style. When something exciting is happening in one of these stories, the prose jumps ahead with sudden cinematic shifts; when weird stuff is going on all around, Sussex slows the pace almost to a holding pattern in order to get a fix on the brooding or the puzzlement of a narrator or viewpoint character. To illustrate: the opening of "Quartet in Death Minor" makes both a comparison and a contrast to that of "My Lady Tongue." First, the familiar swift narratorial *coup*: "I looked out of the window and saw a skeleton walking down the moonlit street. In addition, something was wrong with the house opposite... " But then the narrative circles in on its trajectory like a plane trying to land at Sydney Airport, as the narrator describes her own introspections. Almost compulsively, she dresses and follows Death, thinks "How lovely to die." She ponders over spring blossoms and puzzles over the "ornate" shape of the skeleton: "He was like a skeleton made of flowers." Neatly, the prose interleaves the narrator's sensoria and thought processes, the whole scene paced elegantly.

Such effects are created through the careful building up of narrative structures out of very short, simple sentences and rapid dialogue which sometimes verges on stichomythia. Recurrent figures of speech and imagery create an extra layer of engagement and, usually, enjoyment. Take the story "Red Ochre," an almost pure science fiction job with currents of myth and magic. The story is set in the Queensland outback and features two aboriginal characters and a whole reserve of "Muties," genetically-deformed humans, the victims and remnants of a "DNA plague" left behind after a doomed Indonesian invasion of Australia a generation before. Also featured in the story is an animal called the "Python Plus," a genetically-engineered creature whose wheelbase is a conventional python, but with contributions from the genome of an Indian cobra, most obvious in its poisonous fangs. Throughout the story, an analogy is drawn between the aboriginal occupants of the land and the Muties, who ultimately come to see themselves as totemic animal ancestors, archetypes and progenitors who will fill the land with new life. We are told that no animals live in the wild here because (to explain at one level) aboriginal "increase magic" has ceased to be practiced at the sacred site, marked with the "red streak" of a Dreamtime serpent, clearly visible from the air; of course the failure of the land to produce game might be seen, at another explanatory level, as a function of war and plague.

Within this complex scenario, Sussex knits in fragments of idiom and makeshift figures of speech which are wittily appropriate, if sometimes distracting. When two characters glare angrily at each other, they are described, with a cheeky appropriateness to the larger story, as throwing "mental spears at each other," and three pages later one gives the narrator "a look that had knives in it." The shape of the serpent turns up not only in the form of the Python Plus, the designs in aboriginal rock painting, and in the seemingly degenerative reptilian forms of some of the Muties, but also in stray descriptions: "a snake composed of caravans and trucks came into view."

This technique can become irritating when Sussex maliciously abuses a cliché: we are told that the narrator decided to avoid the spot where the DNA virus was released—avoid it "like the plague." Worse is where brittle fragments of verbal cleverness are dropped into the viewpoint narration quite irrelevantly: "In the tautologous city of Townsville Ian had said something ..." Other aspects of Sussex's style are annoying verbal tics: many of her characters speak in an indeterminate lower-class

British-influenced dialect which has nothing to do with the stories and is too prevalent in them even to make particular characters interesting. Otherwise, they are all given a way of discoursing in oblique clever-clever locutions.

At its worst, Sussex's style is not witty or cheeky so much as simply arch. It also tends to a kind of thinness. One of the more sensoria-laden passages of "Red Ochre" reads like this:

> There was nothing human about those hills, rather something else, as pervasive as the red of the road dust, the earth between the mesh of spindly trees and the cliffs themselves. He tried to think how to describe it, and after a while gave up.

At this point of narratorial abstraction, the characters go into a set piece dialogue about how "You can't anthropomorphise the land." Of course, one of these chatty Outback Jacks then has to offer the other an explanation of the word "anthropomorphise." Meanwhile, we feel that, like her viewpoint character, Sussex has, perhaps wisely, decided to "give up."

And the endings of the stories sometimes seem like she has given up, too. One of the volume's truly powerful, funny and entertaining pieces, "God and Her Black Sense of Humour" is about a feminist journo who stumbles across a pair of marvelous and feisty female heroes—they're immortal semen vampires—they drain strength from the powerful men whom they fuck; but nothing much happens as the story winds to a close, except that the narrator wonders how Krysia and Tesia will fare under the regime of the new celibacy. She's gratified on the last page when she reads a news story about someone thieving the entire stock of the Nobel Sperm Bank. "So," the story finishes limply (dare I say?), "Krysia and Tesia had circumvented the new celibacy, just like I said they would." I'm sure they could have found a simpler way, but that would leave things dangling, wouldn't it?

—1993

SARA DOUGLASS' *BATTLEAXE* AND *ENCHANTER*

TESS WILLIAMS

[Sara Douglass was the penname of Sara Warneke, whose work was belatedly picked up by a US publisher and did very well in the marketplace. She died aged only 54, of cancer, in 2011.]

Battleaxe and *Enchanter* are the first two books of the Axis Trilogy, and I won copies of both of them as a door prize at the Festival of the Imagination, in Perth. To be honest, I viewed the books with misgivings: they have doorstop dimensions and I am much more inclined to read hard-edged sf rather than fantasy. However, on a chilly winter day, I snuggled down in front of my fire as the rain pattered on the roof and opened the first volume....

Four days later, with the rain still pattering on the roof, I was cursing HarperCollins for the six month wait I would have for the third volume and I was also wondering how Sara Douglass managed to keep me in that chair for so long. I recognized certain developments in the second book that had engaged me intellectually and personally, but what, I had to ask myself, had kept me reading *Battleaxe*?

It was hardly the basic plot line of two royal sons—one good and one not-so-good—battling for control of the kingdom of Achar and the hand of the beautiful Faraday. That is an absolute cliché. Nor was it the massing of the forces of evil in the north of Achar (led by another brother to the hero of the demon-spawn type) because Consensus Fantasy Universe Dark Lords are a further cliché. (In his Guest of Honor speech at SwanCon 18 in 1993, Terry Pratchett discussed the "Consensus Fantasy Universe" and enumerated The Dark Lord as one of its necessary inhabitants.) Nor was it the suffering of the lovely Princess Faraday, forced into a marriage she did not want by the power of a prophecy. So, again, what was the attraction in *Battleaxe*?

For me it was primarily the frequent (and sometimes quite unexpected) twists and turns of the plot and Douglass' strong cinematic style.

Timing is where she excels as a writer. In an extended and complex tale, Douglass constructs each chapter to give readers enough new information to satisfy them and enable them to resolve some question in the story-so-far, and then she adds just enough extra to throw them off balance again. The result is a long and titillating engagement with a fantasy kingdom which, while being underpinned by certain inevitable fantasy tropes, at least on some levels refuses simplistic dualism and offers some food for thought.

The food for thought lay in a certain veneer of political correctness detected in the book. In Achar two marginalized races co-exist with humans: the Avar—forest dwellers—and the Icarii—winged mountain dwellers. The three groups used to share the land and lived in harmony, but the Avar and the Icarii were driven out of the kingdom by the Seneschal, the brotherhood of the axe, a nasty bunch with all the trappings of medieval Catholicism about them. The enchanted races, however, are being given a chance to return. To make the country whole, all three groups must unite, and with the help of an even more ancient race, the Charonites, they must fight the dreaded Gorgrael and his ghastly horde of Skraelings.

As well as marginalized cultures freeing themselves from a thousand years of oppression and discrimination, ordinary human characters (many of them women) also cast off the restrictions and lies of the Seneschal and find they have latent powers and awareness which have not been recognized or encouraged by the "Way of the Plough." This is a positive feature of the book. Most contemporary literature, including genres such as fantasy, has to take certain steps away from cultural and gender stereotypes to have a chance of being popular with a young and/or enlightened audience. Douglass' attempt to recognize these imperatives (I say "attempt" because she could also have gone a lot further) in such a restrictive traditional structure is laudatory. I have to admit, however, where *Battleaxe* was a good rainy day read, *Enchanter* was more involving for me. A problem in the first book had been a dearth of complex characters: while Axis and Faraday were sympathetic and had attractive heroic proportions, neither of them showed any real evolution or substance. At best they sloughed off old conditioning, but there was definitely no sign of evolution. In the second book this pattern changes. An apparently minor female character from *Battleaxe* emerges to practically hijack the story. Her name is Azhure and there is considerable mystery about her. Earlier in the trilogy she has proved herself an able fighter, but she begins the second book as rootless and unhappy. No group seems to want to accept her, despite her beauty and the skills she begins to show.

As often happens with characters who are social outcasts, her personal dilemmas prove catalytic to the situation in Achar. Axis becomes well and truly distracted by Azhure to the point where he endangers his commitment to Faraday and the prophecy. However, Azhure is no "other woman" simply to be put back in her immoral place or to be manipulated by the writer as a vehicle for dark feminine forces. No, Azhure has a singularity about her that is remarkable. She is violent but admirable in her physical strength and war craft, she is orphaned but she attracts powerful talismans of Icarii history to her, some people suspect her of treachery but others become devoted to her as if she were born to rule. In all, she is a real puzzle in both her vulnerability and her growing power.

At the end of the book, tragedy and discord lead to the unraveling of a good part of the enigma that is her past. It was here that I really warmed to Douglass as a writer. Azhure is revealed not only as a character with magical origins and connections, but also as a character with an all too human experience of great suffering. And the metaphor Douglass uses to show us how Azhure has suffered is quite inspired. Such an image freshens understandings of the jaded issue of abuse without dragging us out of the fantasy world or forcing us to dwell too deeply in such a recreational book on the potential vileness within the human heart.

My only regret and main criticism of the books is that, to this point, the male lead has not been as significant as Azhure and has not yet achieved her stature in the story. However, more on this I will not say until I have read the final volume of the trilogy, *Starman*. That is a book I will be most happy to buy to complement my prizes. For a few dollars I will get a return trip in the magic armchair to Achar, where I will spend yet another weekend with a competent Australian writer who is rightfully taking her place on the shelves of popular genre fiction.

—1996

ADDENDUM, 2013:

This review was written a long time ago, now. *Battleaxe*, *Enchanter* and *Starman* were read many years ago and, I have to confess, never re-read. They were rainy day page-turners *par excellence*, but I never felt compelled to return to Tencendor. By the time Axis burns with his attack on the griffins, Azhure achieves her transcendental status as an Icarii enchantress and mother of Axis' strange children, and Faraday completes her Herculean task of replanting the ancient forest, I was happy to know that evil was more or less beaten and the lives of those particular characters were resolved. However, Douglass again did some special things in the final book of the trilogy—the resolution of Faraday's and Azhure's relationship was deep and respectful, refusing the clichés of jealous wife and other woman, and the twins were definitely another species, clearly moving into a very different destiny and not encumbered by their parents' limitations and abilities.

This is very much the way that Douglass' books go. While never actively seeking out her work, I have always loved her short stories and had a number of close encounters with her novels, the most recent being as a judge for the Norma K. Hemming award in 2012. Douglass' novel *The Devil's Diadem* was a joint winner of the award that year, and reading the book made me remember what a deeply pleasurable experience this author always offers when the pages are turning. Her handling of her central female characters always makes them admirable—they are usually lucky in some way by birth and ability, and unlucky in some way by fortune, but somehow they hold their complicated life stories with dignity and love. One of Douglass' gifts to fantasy writing has been the insertion of these strong, loving women into worlds where the stakes are a pitched battle between large armies of good and evil. In this cosmology, enacting a philosophy of right and wrong that is so enormous it is almost meaningless, the lives of the women bring significance as they grow a tree, grow a child, love someone, lose someone, and find they are more than they thought they were originally. The other gift that Douglass repeatedly brings to her writing is a reminder of the need to stay in tune with the natural world and, by doing that, accept the magical. For her there are more things in heaven and earth than we may know about, and respect is essential to change things for the better.

When Sara Douglass died in 2011, Australian fantasy lost an excellent writer—but she left a wonderful legacy in her many novels, a lasting tribute to the traditional genre that said something ever so quietly, but ever so well, about women and the ways they relate to each other, about children and their differences from their parents, the respect needed for the environment and the limitations of pragmatic human systems of knowledge.

DORIS LESSING: AN OVERVIEW

CAROLINE FLYNN

The trouble with Doris Lessing's science fiction is that it makes you want to believe in it. I took this feeling along with me to the 1987 World SF Convention—"Conspiracy"—in Brighton, England, at which Lessing was the chief guest writer, only to hear her say it's all a fabrication—she only made it up after reading all the great books of religion from the Old Testament through to the Koran. Lessing, a rationalist atheist, stressed the value of reading such traditional historical literature. From these sources she has constructed a new cosmology: from Sufism and Jung, the psychology of her characters.

As with other humanistic sf or speculative fiction, Lessing is operating on two levels: the fictitious, imagined cosmology or technology, and the human psychology. *The Canopus in Argos: Archives* series comprises five novels:

> 1. *Re: Colonised Planet 5; Shikasta; Personal, Psychological, Historical Documents Relating to Visit by Johor (George Sherban); Emissary (Grade 9); 87th of the Period of the Last Days*
> 2. *The Marriages Between Zones Three, Four and Five: (As Narrated by the Chroniclers of Zone* 3*)*
> 3. *The Sirian Experiments: The Report by Ambien II, of the Five*
> 4. *The Making of the Representative for Planet 8*
> 5. *Documents Relating to: The Sentimental Agents in the Volyen Empire.*

Lessing re-writes the history of Earth (Rohanda, Shikasta) and fits into the new cosmology her concerns with humanity: the physical despoliation of this planet and the psychological deterioration of its inhabitants.

Lessing is well known for her disapproval of the way literature can suffer from microscopic intellectual analysis. (She refers to a professor "whose only fault was that perhaps she had fed too long on the pieties of academia").[1] She has moved from the realistic to the sf genre and states in the introduction to *Shikasta*:

What a phenomenon it has been—science fiction, space fiction—exploding out of nowhere, unexpectedly of course, as always happens when the human mind is being forced to expand: this time starwards, galaxy-wise, and who knows where next.

Sf allows her to escape the framework of the realistic novel and its conditioned thinking. This is one of the major themes of the Canopus series and basic to Sufism, which seeks to "shake loose from logical modes of thought,"[2] never to define but to question, and to illustrate by storytelling and experience, by knowledge of the self, by transcendence of the self to the realization that the person is only part of the whole.

In her exploration of "inner space," Lessing's characters are realized according to Jungian processes which emphasize self-realization through the letting go of ego (of the "I" consciousness of her earlier realistic fiction), leading on to knowledge of collective or higher group mind; then a contrasting of stereotypes and archetypes; and death (of old attitudes of mind) and rebirth. Through the sf medium, Lessing's preoccupation with expanding consciousness is given free range, her "inner space" explorations are the microcosm, seen in the context of the universe, which is the macrocosm; "the shedding of conditioning and development of the higher working of the mind."[3]

Lessing sees humankind's major problem as one of fragmentation, alienation resulting in personal and social breakdown, war, famine and the destruction of the environment. Her characters, whether Shikastan, Canopean, Sirian or Volyen, are woven according to Sufi ideas, learning through experience or story-telling, or Jungian ideas of

> ...intuition, dreams, myth and telepathy, which open the gateway to universal perspectives absent in the fragmented "real" world.[4]

Shikasta was written, Doris Lessing says,

> ... in the belief that it would be a single self-contained book, and that when it was finished I would be done with the subject. But as I wrote I was invaded with ideas for other books, other stories, and the exhilaration that comes from being set free into a large scope, with more capacious possibilities and themes. It was clear I had made—or found—a new world for myself, a realm where the petty fates of planets, let alone individuals, are only aspects of cosmic evolution expressed in the rivalries and interactions of great galactic Empires: Canopus, Sirius, and their enemy, the Empire Puttiora, with its criminal Shammat. I feel as if I have been set free both to be as experimental as I like, and as traditional.

The scope of *Shikasta* is extraordinary, as critics attest:

> Magnificent... an astounding book that sets out to chronicle the whole world of humanity, spirit, earth, stars, soul, resources, virtue, evil, pre-Eden, forever....
>
> ...a brief history of the world, a tract against human destructiveness, an ode to the natural beauties of this earth and a hymn to the music of the spheres.[5]

David Wingrove says in *Frontier Crossings*:

> *Shikasta* derives much of its potency from our inherited ideas of Heaven and Hell, of Eden and the Fall, and of the continuous war between God and the Devil. This said, the mix is far from the traditional Christian one and includes experimentation in eugenics, the planned development of species over millennia, and a cosmic perspective that sees all process as part of the greater Whole. Canopus acts through individuals—its seemingly immortal Agents, like Johor—but such action is always carefully calculated to satisfy wider and greater criteria than individual need.[6]

The novel begins with a report from Johor on Shikasta, the "unfortunate, the broken one." A catastrophic series of stellar disasters has brought the planet—formerly Rohanda, "the fruitful, the thriving"—to the point of chaos. Johor debates the ethics of saving Shikasta from itself and from Shammat. "Invisible, unwritten, uncoded rules" forbid the abandonment of the Colony. "What these rules amount to," says Johor, "is Love."[7]

This is the essence of the Canopean philosophy. Canopus has established a Lock with Rohanda, a link with Canopus by means of the mysterious SOWF, or "substance- of-we-feeling," which is Lessing's vision of a way of excluding the cult of the unique individual... a cult which she sees as ridiculous on a planet inhabited by billions.[8]

Canopus transports a race of Giants to live in symbiosis with the native dominant species which is evolving from an ape-like animal. Eventually cities are built according to harmonic law, in various geometric patterns, arranged to extract the maximum benefit from the SOWF emanating from the lock with Canopus. A stellar shift, combined with the pirating of the Canopean emanations by Shammat, necessitates a visit from Johor. His task is to persuade the Giants to evacuate Shikasta while providing the deteriorating natives with knowledge through songs and stories for their survival through the difficult time until the Lock can be re-established.

This, then, is the state of the planet inherited by twentieth century man, the century of the three world wars. A history of Earth/Shikasta is given by the Canopean archivists. Emissaries from Canopus can enter

Shikasta by space transport or through incarnation and their visitations are for the purpose of influencing the Shikastans toward fulfilling the Canopean Necessity.

We are introduced to several characters who are Canopean in origin but are in various stages of unawareness regarding their purpose, having been seduced by Shammatan influences from their planned participation in Shikastan affairs. These characters symbolize man's "sleeping" unawareness of his spiritual self, of his part in the cosmic, harmonious whole. Only through suffering, through experience, can he transcend his external concerns and realize his higher purpose. In imitation of Hindu reincarnation, failure to realize one's purpose on Earth results in a forlorn occupation in Zone 6, a pre-birth/post-death waiting-stage for another chance.

We explore the Zones in *The Marriages Between Zones Three, Four and Five*. Whereas the tone of Shikasta is urgent, a dramatic historical document of an experiment gone tragically wrong, *The Marriages* is a fable, a legend in the Sufi tradition which asks questions rather than providing definitions or answers. The Zones are geophysical as well as metaphors for human, psychological-evolutionary states, and are inhabited. The marriages occur between the rulers of three Zones, who are instructed by the unseen Providers. Through the rulers' relationships, Lessing examines gender stereotypes and archetypes and personality.

Jung's theory of personality—the many selves, the onion-skin layers—corresponds with the Zones. Zone 6 is the lowest, a state of unawareness. The queen of Zone 5 is primitive, earthy, representing sensation, one of the four traditional psychic qualities. The major part of the novel is concerned with Ben Ata of Zone 4 and his wife, Al.Ith of Zone 3. Ben Ata's Zone is male, warlike. He is insensitive and crude, while Zone 3 represents the female qualities of nurturing. In Jungian terms, Zone 4 represents thinking, Zone 3, feeling. Zone 2 is ephemeral and stands for intuition.[9]

Ben Ata and Al.Ith unite, mate, and bear progeny. The interacting themes are complex: the war between the sexes; dominance and submission; sex, from rape to tenderness to spiritual union; the loss of self within a relationship; mutual interdependence and independence; mother-child, father-child relationships.

At a personal level, these two characters progress as individuals through the Zones. Their respective countries are stagnant, conception and birth in decline. By learning from each other and absorbing some of the other's qualities, new life and fertility return to their lands. At the Sufi level, the stagnant Zones stand for conditioned thinking. As Al.Ith and Ben Ata change and grow, moving upward towards the next

Zone, so do their subjects take in new ideas and shed old ways, acting collectively as group mind.

As the book of the Zones grew from a concept in *Shikasta*, so does *The Sirian Experiments*. The Sirian Empire is lesser in power and development than Canopus, earnest and well-meaning, advanced in technology but expressed through the character of Ambien II, one of the Five, administrators of Sirius, lacking in knowledge of the necessity, the unstated purpose towards universal harmony.

Sirius' eugenic experiments on Shikasta, with Canopus' blessing, are carried out (sometimes inhumanely) in the continents we know as Africa and South America. The experiments have limited success owing to the Sirians' mistaken belief in creating dominant and slave species which are doomed to fail because of the inability of the species to thrive and evolve, an obvious reference to the white dominance of black Africa, Lessing's homeland.

Ambien II is a bureaucrat confined by the Sirian system, but through her contact with Klorathy of Canopus she gradually becomes aware through thousands of years of work on Shikasta that there is more to know, another realm of understanding of herself and of the universe. She becomes a questioner. The tone of this novel is dry, factual, in keeping with the first person narrative by Ambien II.

Another major change of atmosphere occurs in the fourth novel, *The Making of the Representative for Planet 8*. The imminent destruction of this planet has been pre-figured in Shikasta and the following novels. Planet 8 is doomed owing to a cosmic adjustment which causes it to become gradually frozen by snow and ice. The emphasis is on storytelling, myth; the novel feels like a dream or a fable. Lessing's inspiration for this bleak novel was the dogged determination of Scott to reach his goal, the South Pole, despite terrible privations and suffering. The dominant theme of the novel is a wall, built to hold back the encroaching ice caps. In Lessing's earlier novels, a wall is a symbol of a stage of understanding to be broken through in order to pass on to a further level of understanding.

One of the characters, Doeg, the Memory Maker or Storyteller, tells of a dream, of the impossibility of conveying the atmosphere of a dream; yet feelings, emotions, and sensations are experiences all know and share; the material, sub-atomic substance of emotions such as envy or love:

> How does the material or substance of love modify that minuscule dance? How relate? For it is the physical substance of our bodies, our hearts, that breeds love or hate, or fear or hope—is that not so?—and cannot be separate from it. The wind that is love must arise somewhere

in those appalling spaces between the nub of an atom and its electrons that dissolve, like everything else, into smaller and smaller, and become a fluid or a movement—*or a door into somewhere else?*[10]

This concept harks back to the Canopean substance-of-we-feeling, that we are all innately part of each other, of a whole. A passage Lessing quotes in her first sf novel, *Briefing for a Descent into Hell*, repeats the universal message of Sufism:

> If yonder raindrop should its heart disclose Behold therein a hundred seas displayed. In every atom, if thou gaze aright, Thousands of reasoning beings are contained.
> Upon one little spot within the heart Resteth the Lord and Master of the worlds.
> Therein two worlds commingled may be seen.[11]

One last world—that of *The Sentimental Agents in the Volyen Empire*—is described on the dustjacket as "a social satire in the tradition of Voltaire and Swift." It is tongue-in-cheek, sometimes humorous, as the subverted Canopean agents on the three planets, Volyen, Volyenadna and Volyendesta succumb to the disease of Rhetoric, with its symptoms of sentiments such as fear, patriotism, greed, and so forth, which are commonly invoked by public figures and politicians. Sufferers are required to undertake the cure at the Hospital for Rhetorical Diseases by various methods of immersion or aversion therapy such as listening to the speeches of long-dead Shikastan heroes.

Klorathy appears again representing plain truth and the reality and higher purpose of Canopus. The inhabitants of Volyenadna learn to discard sentiment for such practical survival techniques as the growing of Rocknosh, the whimsically named lichen and all-purpose food, instead of arming themselves against invasion as the speech-makers would have them do with such exhortations as "We will fight them on the beaches, we will fight them on...."

The enlightened Volyenadnans triumph by mildly observing and tolerating the invasion by the Pipisauruses (fantastic birds ridden by their masters, the Makens, who feed from the bird's glandular secretions) meanwhile getting rich by supplying the Empire with the products of Rocknosh. The reader is left with a comic image, as if Doris Lessing were leaving this galactic scene with a conventional science fantasy, but the satiric message is that instead of the regulation battle, the bland population bores the Makens into leaving by their lack of resistance—a comment by Lessing on the nature of war and military rhetoric.

Doris Lessing has ventured into new worlds in her fictional speculations on the personal nature of the species of man in a cosmic perspective.

I find that her cosmology is believable because her concerns are universal. Despite her alarm at her fiction becoming the foundation for a cult of believers, she gives them some comfort:

> Yes, I do believe that it is possible, and not only for novelists, to "plug in" to an overmind, or Ur-mind, or unconscious, or what you will, and that this accounts for a great many improbabilities and "coincidences."[12]

There is another clue, to aid us in suspending our disbelief. In a passage previously quoted from the introduction to Shikasta, Lessing says she has made or found (my emphasis) a new world, intimating that perhaps Canopus has revealed itself to this novelist:

> Is the Force still with us?
> Will the Lock be re-established?
> Will we ever learn the substance-of-feeling?
> Canopus! Help!

—1991

NOTES

1. Doris Lessing, Introduction, Re: *Colonised Planet 5: Shikasta* (1979: London, Grafton, 1981).
2. Annis Pratt and L.S. Dembo, eds, *Doris Lessing: Critical Studies* (Wisconsin: University of Wisconsin Press, 1974), p.149.
3. Martin Hills, "Breaking Down Reality," in *Frontier Crossings*, ed. Robert Jackson (London: 45th World SF Convention, 1987), p.19.
4. Hills, in *Frontier Crossings*, p.19.
5. Blurbs on the back cover of *Shikasta*.
6. Wingrove, p.16.
7. *Shikasta*, p.13.
8. Doris Lessing, Introduction, *The Sirian Experiments: The Report by Ambien II, of the Five* (London, Cape, 1981).
9. Marsha Rowe, "If you mate a swan and a gander, who will ride?" in *Notebooks/Memoirs/ Archives: Reading and Rereading Doris Lessing*, ed. Jenny Taylor (Boston: Routledge and Kegan Paul, 1982), p.202.
10. Lessing, *The Making of the Representative for Planet 8*, p.68.
11. "My Secret Garden," by Sage Mahmoud Shabistri, quoted in Nancy Shields Hardin, "Doris Lessing and the Sufi Way," in Taylor's *Notebooks/Memoirs/Archives*, p.154.
12. Doris Lessing, Introduction to *Shikasta*.

THE EIGHTEENTH CENTURY AND SCIENCE FICTION: A SYMBIOSIS?

DONALD M. HASSLER

The notion that systems grow and develop through periodic crises or passages has a new currency these days, but we know the notion is at least as old as Wordsworth or Samuel Johnson, or Saint Paul for that matter. I recall vividly the first annual meeting of the American Society for Eighteenth-Century Studies in Cleveland at the same time that the wounded Apollo 13 spacecraft was carefully returning from the moon. Nine years later, the question could be asked: "Where are the new ideas about the eighteenth century?" Where indeed, perhaps, "the glory and the dream"?

When such a question is asked—either by Wordsworth, or by the eighteenth-century inventors of aesthetics and the picturesque, or by any passenger on a forties crisis—the underlying need seems to include a kind of desperation, and the question seems to require at least some bursting craziness of response. The question would not be asked if there were not a need for a new paradigm, a new leap, a new mutation (with the unspoken understanding that all new mutations seem a little crazy in the context of the established order). Some scholars would argue that there are no new ideas about the past, only tried and true methods of investigation and analysis that must be used steadily and carefully in order to uncover the continual newness of what was in the past. These positivists shuddered, I suspect, at the posed question and will shudder, I am sure, at my answer. For I proposed taking a fresh look at the eighteenth century after having read some recent science fiction and having studied the discussion of science fiction in the context of eighteenth-century studies.

For some time I had been saying that science fiction has much to learn about itself from a study of its origins in the Enlightenment, and here reverse that argument somewhat. A prime locus of origin is with the need for newness and for speculation in what Northrop Frye has labeled the "Age of Sensibility"—that period in the late eighteenth century, as I have already implied, which made particular art, the art of the picturesque, out of its own long lasting forties crisis. A favorite quotation that I like to show to science fiction readers to introduce them to an eighteenth century forerunner of their beloved speculative literature comes from the work of Erasmus Darwin, and it speaks of this need to burst out in many directions. Darwin himself is a good example of seminal newness who seeded at least two stages of new growth at the end of his century: the scientific nature poetry of Coleridge and then Shelley, and the move toward "science" in the gothic fiction of Mary Shelley. Darwin's quotation is taken from the preface to *The Botanic Garden* (1791) and speaks of speculating extravagantly:

> Extravagant theories however in those parts of philosophy, where our knowledge is yet imperfect, are not without their use; as they encourage the execution of laborious experiments, or the investigation of ingenious deductions, to confirm or refute them. And since natural objects are allied to each other by many affinities, every kind of theoretic distribution of them adds to our knowledge by developing some of their analogies.

The theoretic distribution of ideas that I want to suggest, however, is intended not to chart the growth of science fiction out of the eighteenth century Enlightenment, but rather to pinpoint a few passages in science fiction writing which may be relevant to the eighteenth century. There are many sub-topics to this symbiosis that could be developed, and most of them have already been taken up and expanded somewhat by eighteenth century scholars who were unaware of their relation to science fiction and the potential cross-fertilization from this relation. The two that interest me most have to do with the growth and development of self-consciousness about genre and with the burden of being a modern artist rather than an ancient. Provocative ideas about both of these topics can be found in the study of modern science fiction. Lawrence Lipking's book, *The Ordering of the Arts in Eighteenth-Century England* (1970), argues that as a genre matures it begins to produce histories of itself such as Johnson's *Lives of the Poets* or Charles Burney's *History Of Music*, and this thesis can be studied afresh in the growing self-consciousness of science fiction writers such as Isaac Asimov or Damon Knight. Asimov published a peculiar hybrid of a book—part reminiscence, part anthology, part literary history—which he called *Before the Golden Age: A Science Fiction Anthology of the 1930s* (1974); and to me in any case the crossings with Lipking's book are too suggestive to ignore. Perhaps working back and forth from the modern case study to the eighteenth century manifestation would be mutually beneficial. Similarly, Walter Jackson Bate's brilliant recent redevelopment of the old eighteenth century topic of the debate between the Ancients and the Moderns in his book, *The Burden of the Past and the English Poet* (1970), can be further understood by testing it against the enormous sense that science fiction writers have of their own tradition. This is a tradition that is compressed in time (going back only to 1926 in some respects) and thus exaggerated. I suggest that the exaggeration can give us ideas that will help us better understand the creative tensions in Gray or Chatterton or Cowper. Here again, a good place to start would be with the sophisticated literary reminiscence by Damon Knight entitled *The Futurians* (1977). Similarly, the relation of science fiction art to the rich visualism in the picturesque and even to the illuminated poems of Blake in the late eighteenth century is a further topic that could be recommended for study. But all this is only suggestion for further study. I cannot develop it here.

What I can discuss that will show that science fiction is more than comic books and television shows, and that will be self-contained enough to complete here more or less, are three passages—two about science fiction and one from a highly acclaimed science fiction novel. Each passage points back specifically to, and helps to illuminate, something in the eighteenth century. I must take a moment now, however, to point out a qualification—namely, the fact that I am most interested in (indeed, fascinated by) the latter part of the eighteenth century. I think of the title of a fine book on the history of science by Charles Coulston Gillispie, *The Edge of Objectivity* (1960), in which it is said that the periphery is always the cutting edge. Similarly, I am intrigued by the edge of that century, the cutting edge of the century, as it moves into what we have labeled the Romantic Movement. My apologies to the early Augustans, whom we may call the cutting edge of the late Renaissance; but nevertheless the newness of the Age of Sensibility lends itself best to the new idea I am suggesting—the idea that we look for a kind of symbiosis between science fiction and the late eighteenth century, between two artistic periods separate in time but perhaps together in spirit.

In any case, the first passage is from a discussion of British science fiction by Brian Aldiss, who incidentally was one of the first historians of science fiction to describe the importance of Erasmus Darwin in the development of early science fiction. Aldiss writes about the dystopian image of the Industrial Revolution run amok and about the need for irony:

> The Frankenstein theme of man's creation out of control is probably sf's major theme; it is a British coinage. If one characteristic of our science fiction is to be singled out, it must be continuing skepticism; above all, skepticism about man's supremacy over nature

and the benefits of unremitting technology.... With skepticism goes another frequent English usage, irony. This quality one finds also in those American writers I mentioned earlier as bridging the gulf, Philip Dick, Ursula Le Guin, and Fred Pohl. Irony is rarely found in formula writing, for obvious reasons. Formula writing's best function is reassurance, whereas irony works by questioning the reader's values. (*The Magazine of Fantasy and Science Fiction*, April 1978)

If what Aldiss says is true about the importance of irony, skepticism, and the breakdown of values in recent science fiction, and if a more sophisticated discussion is going on among critics of science fiction about these literary characteristics that sound so familiar to students of Hume, Johnson, and Gibbon (not to mention the innumerable poets of sensibility who lead to the Great Romantics), then science fiction and commentary about it may indeed be a rich location in which to study these ideas at play. In other words, if we study and understand the ironies inherent in science fiction, we may be better equipped to understand the ironies in the Age of Sensibility.

But it is not just irony. The larger notion of the breakdown of values and the acceptance of a rapid state of change as a predictable norm (and, of course, it is ironic that change should be viewed as a constant) is a key notion both for eighteenth-century studies and for science fiction. A highly respected member of the academic community described this characteristic of science fiction in a way that may be more valuable to critics and scholars than the literary journalism of a writer such as Aldiss, although one of my suggestions is that much can be learned from the science fiction writers themselves. Robert Scholes is a literary scholar whose credentials are impressive. He has written extensively on literary theory and on structuralist aesthetics. His book *Structural Fabulations: An Essay on Fiction of the Future* (1975) contains much that I would recommend to any student of Sterne, Gibbon, Hume, and all. One passage in particular will continue the notion of the acceptance of change as a prerequisite for a certain kind of art. In fact, this notion was stated very explicitly in a well- known essay by Isaac Asimov ("Social Science Fiction," 1953), in which Asimov states flatly that sf as a kind of writing about the future could never have developed until the French Revolution convinced people (for better or for worse) that dramatic changes indeed could take place within the span of a human lifetime. Scholes says it this way:

> The consciousness that history is an irreversible process led man inevitably to a new view of the future. For centuries man had thought of the future as in one sense inscrutable, except as darkly hinted at by oracles and portents, and in another sense as simply more of the

present. One might not know who would be king but one knew that there would always be one. The King is dead? Long live the King! The idea that the future might be radically different in its social or economic organization was unthinkable until some time in the seventeenth or eighteenth century, and the impact of irreversible technological change did not become apparent until the nineteenth.

Certainly these ideas are familiar to historians: the sense of history as "discovered" by French philosophes and by eighteenth-century British historians, the sense of the future as "discovered" by Godwin and Condorcet and others, and the whole sense of the impact of technology and industry that has worried us from at least the time of Mandeville (even though our worries may not have become reified until the nineteenth century). Thus, by reading modern science fiction, we can discover valuable ideas and valuable images that will help us enlighten our view of the eighteenth century. Obviously, this is because the ideas came from the eighteenth century originally; but sometimes it helps in recognizing and knowing an old friend to meet a grandchild.

The third and final lengthy quotation that I want to present comes from the work of a writer who seems to be Robert Scholes' favorite science fiction novelist. Ursula K. Le Guin has written two major science fiction novels, *The Left Hand of Darkness* (1969) and *The Dispossessed* (1974). I am interested in a particular passage from *The Left Hand of Darkness* that first struck me as an echo of the Simplon Pass passage from the sixth book of Wordsworth's *The Prelude*. It is true that Wordsworth's passage is not from the eighteenth century, but the reader must remember that Wordsworth's experience of crossing the Alps was firmly an eighteenth century experience, that the original composition of the passage occurred in the 1790s, and that the literary effects of sublimity and the preoccupation with death (although not excluded from the milieu of 1850 when the passage saw print) are also firmly related to late eighteenth-century effects. In any case, Le Guin's passage helps us to appreciate the universality of some familiar literary scholarship about Wordsworth and about the eighteenth century in general. I am referring to Donald Greene's little book, *The Age of Exuberance* (1969), in which he describes the importance of Augustinian paradox and pessimism to eighteenth century thought. Geoffrey Hartman's book, *Wordsworth's Poetry, 1787-1814* (1972) also comes to mind. The two make an odd couple, perhaps, but both describe the peculiar eighteenth century vision of the paradoxical value in death—what Hartman calls the "negative way" in Wordsworth. And now these ideas of the positive value of death and of the negative way are worked brilliantly by a science fiction writer.

In reading this passage from *The Left Hand of Darkness*, try to remember the sublime descent down the far side of the Simplon Pass, and what Wordsworth calls "that awful Power... from the mind's abyss." Le Guin's narrative is speaking about her two protagonists and a difficult and daring trip they have decided to make at a time of crisis in both of their lives:

> Ahead of us, cleared and revealed by the same vast sweep of the wind, lay twisted valleys, hundreds of feet below, full of ice and boulders. Across those valleys a great wall stood, a wall of ice, and raising our eyes up and still up to the rim of the wall we saw the ice itself, the Gobrin Glacier, blinding and horizonless to the utmost north, a white, a white the eyes could not look on.
>
> Here and there out of the valleys full of rubble and out of the cliffs and bends and masses of the great icefield's edge, black ridges rose; one great mass loomed up out of the plateau to the height of the gateway peaks we stood between, and from its side drifted heavily a mile-long wisp of smoke. Farther off there were others; peaks, pinnacles, black cindercones on the glacier. Smoke panted from fiery mouths that opened out of the ice.
>
> Estraven stood there in harness beside me looking at that magnificent and unspeakable desolation. "I'm glad I have lived to see this," he said.
>
> I felt as he did. It is good to have an end to journey towards; but it is the journey that matters, in the end. It had not rained, here on these north-facing slopes. Snowfields stretched down from the pass into the valleys of moraine. We stowed the wheels, uncapped the sledge-runners, put on our skis, and took off—down, north, onward, into that silent vastness of fire and ice that said in enormous letters of black and white DEATH, DEATH, written right across a continent. The sledge pulled like a feather, and we laughed with joy.

Obviously, all parts of our reading complement all other parts; and it is fruitful for any specialty to find broader analogies to test its own data against (as Erasmus Darwin said about speculating). Probably almost any analogies would do. But if we are looking for new ideas to enrich our study of the eighteenth century, I suggest that recent science fiction is just crazy enough to be particularly appropriate in its analogies to the craziness of the latter part of the eighteenth century. And just as both science fiction as well as the Age of Sensibility lay claim to being always receptive to new ideas, so perhaps eighteenth century studies is ready for their brand of newness.

—1979

THE ISLAND OF DOCTOR MOREAU

OR THE CASE OF DEVOLUTION

PASCALE KRUMM

Although Wells was a prolific writer, only five of his scientific romances made it into posterity, all written in the early stages of his career, within a six year span, between 1895 and 1901.[1] *The Island of Doctor Moreau* is unique among these five novels in many ways. Its original story line is much simpler and easier to understand (at least from a technical point of view) than any of the others, mainly because of the almost complete lack of scientific prose or complex explanations, but *The Island of Doctor Moreau* remains nevertheless Wells's most complex, disturbing, and morally challenging piece. Whereas the other narratives fit into the science fiction mode, this particular work is much harder to categorize. The other plots revolve around typical science fiction fare: temporal or spatial distortion (*The Time Machine*, *The Invisible Man*), spatial travel (*The First Men in the Moon*), alien invasion (*The War of the Worlds*) and such, but not so with *The Island of Doctor Moreau*, which discusses instead heady but realistic topics such as biology, physiology, and evolution. The novel can better be described not as a precursor to science fiction but to another popular genre, the late twentieth-century techno-novel *a la* Michael Crichton.[2] *The Island of Doctor Moreau* is actually a literary hybrid, a composite of many other types of novels: it contains elements of the robinsonade, the gothic, the horror, the naturalistic, and the detective story, yet its main motif rests on mythobiology, a unique combination of biology and mythology.[3]

This novel is not only complex and multi-faceted but problematic as well: it proved a difficult sell to Wells's contemporaries because of the uncommon harshness and brutality of its story line. Critics, who had praised Wells's prose before, excoriated the book. Written in 1896, the novel upset nearly everyone, with good reason, and even by hardened twentieth-century standards it remains a painful and somewhat offensive read. Not surprisingly, the novel received overwhelming negative reviews, the term "blasphemy" being used on several occasions. Chalmers Mitchell commented in the *Saturday Review* that Wells "has put out his talent to the most flagitious usury,"[4] while a reviewer for *The Guardian* wrote in a more understated and laconic manner that "we are not inclined to commend it either. It is certainly unpleasant and painful, and we cannot find it profitable."[5]

Countless other nineteenth-century British novelists from Shelley to Doyle to Stevenson had, before Wells, touched on the theme at hand: science gone awry at the hands of a brilliant but deranged scientist or maniacal doctor whose dubious experiments have deleterious consequences for himself, his surroundings, and ultimately dire implications for humankind. But none of these novelists had gone quite so far, or so the critics of the time seemed to imply, as Wells had in *The Island of Doctor Moreau*.

The premise of the novel is a familiar one, at first. Shipwrecked on a South-Pacific island, the narrator Edward Prendick, a biologist, encounters the mysterious and fearsome Doctor Moreau, a "masterful physiologist"[6] who, surrounded by frightening looking acolytes such as Montgomery "a young medical student" (p.17), rules the island with an iron fist. But soon the story takes an ominous turn; terrifying and unbearable noises come out of the doctor's laboratory, and Prendick eventually discovers the gruesome and shocking truth: Moreau operates on live animals, forcibly altering their original shape into a hybrid-human one through horribly painful skin grafts. Prendick also learns that Moreau, "a notorious vivisector" (p.36), had been forced to leave England because of the questionable and very cruel nature of his experiments. After Moreau is killed by one of his own creations, a shaken Prendick travels back to England, bearing deep psychological wounds and harboring a bleak and shattered vision of the human psyche and a dark vision of society as a whole.

The seemingly central premise of the novel, that of the human beast, is a familiar topos in literature. From Greek mythology to fairy tales, from medieval bestiaries to nineteenth-century gothic tales, the theme of man's dual nature seems deeply rooted in Western thought. The theme surfaces time and again in literature through all sorts of combinations: the character is either a wereanimal (half-human, half-beast, such as the minotaur or the werewolf), or a changeling (a human totally transformed or rather transmogrified into a beast or vice versa, like the male character in *Beauty and the Beast* or *Dracula*). In between these two scenarios a multitude of gradations, or rather degradations, can occur; sometimes the transformation from man to beast is more psychological than physical (as with Doctor Jekyll). There is however one constant:

never is the hybridization harmonious or flattering to either species, and nowhere better than in *The Island of Doctor Moreau* is this negative axiom illustrated.

While the topic of the human beast is transhistorical and transcontinental, it is especially prominent in the second half of the nineteenth century in British literature, when the motif takes on a new function.[7] As Jill Minning notes, in the nineteenth century "the fictional hybrid is more than a symbol; his existence is explained or justified by accepted scientific theory."[8] This shift from fanciful mythology to hard science is by no means coincidental but can be traced to the influence of a contemporary scientist whose new theories first revolutionized England, namely Darwin. *The Island of Doctor Moreau*, often described as a Swiftian parable,[9] is actually a very disturbing reflection on a much more contemporaneous subject closely linked with the ancient human beast theme: evolution. Darwin's theories raised disturbing (to some) new questions about the origin of mankind and the essence of humanity, and the debate soon permeated other spheres of thought, sacred and secular alike, such as the social sciences, the humanities, and particularly literature. Wells himself was not indifferent to the theory of evolution which he addressed for the second time in *The Island of Doctor Moreau*, having previously explored it in *The Time Machine*, a replay of evolution gone awry through two degenerate mutant species, the Eloi and the Morlock, living in the year 802,701, who "convey the two opposite extremes of evolutionary potential."[10]

But even though *The Island of Doctor Moreau* explores some familiar themes, Wells treats the human beast imagery in some innovative ways. In similarly-themed novels by other authors, the physical and mental alterations or rather deteriorations experienced by the hybrid characters often had a chemical (Doctor Jekyll, Professor Presbury in Doyle's "Adventure of the Creeping Man"), supernatural (Dracula), or mythical/mystical origin (Medusa).[11] In Wells's novel, though, the changes experienced by the Beast-Folk are neither genetic nor chemical but purely surgical in nature, accomplished through invasive and excruciatingly painful means.[12] Furthermore, in previous instances, the transformation originated on the human side and ended either with a beast or a human beast hybrid.[13] In *The Island of Doctor Moreau*, the reverse process occurs as animals are transformed into humans or at least into a semblance of human shape.

This last point is crucial as it raises the question of the validity and the ultimate goal of such a horrid operation. Other works dealing with the bestial/human dichotomy often served as allegorical illustrations of man's dual nature, his struggles with good (his humanity) and evil (his animality) in a universe created by God. With the emergence of Darwinism, however, the focus of man's dual nature gradually but significantly and permanently shifted from the religious and the anthropocentric to the secular and the biological realms. Darwin's *Origin of Species* (1859), and especially his *Descent of Man* (1871), brought to light man's true ancestry by scientifically confirming his non divine origins; the underlying message was alarming: man's suspected bestial and brutish origins were now, it seems, validated and confirmed by science.[14] In the public eye, Darwinism prompted the dramatic—but scientifically invalid—conclusion that man was nothing but a brutish animal, and that under the thin veneer of civilization lurks the primordial beast ready to jump out or resurface at any moment. But is this the only interpretation and conclusion stemming from *The Island of Doctor Moreau*?[15]

In fact, the answer lies deeper, and is neither as obvious nor as simple as originally thought. The complexity of meaning is already alluded to through the narrator's first impressions upon setting foot on the island, for Prendick is originally quite mistaken about the true nature of Moreau's experiments. During the entire first half of the novel Prendick unequivocally and without questions assumes that Moreau is turning men into beasts: "I was convinced now, absolutely assured, that Moreau had been vivisecting a human being." (p.57) No other scenario even occurs to the narrator, and upon discovering the veritable nature of Moreau's experiments, Prendick is even more horrified than before. If Wells's goal was to illustrate the resurgence of man's original animality, why subvert the convenient and familiar paradigm of man to beast transformation—a most logical way of symbolically showing the drastic (but erroneous) implications of evolution? In other words, why did Wells so egregiously deviate from the normative pattern set by his predecessors in presumably trying to establish the age-old conclusion of man's original bestiality?

On a simple level, one can assert that the subversion made for an original story line. But more importantly, and more cleverly, the tactic actually reinforced the new Darwinian tenet, not the common fallacy that man is descendant or evolved from animal (specifically some ape), but quite differently that man and ape actually share a common ancestry as members of two evolutionary side branches.[16] In essence, Darwinism postulates that all life forms are related and stem from the same earliest organisms, and that men and animals are equal on the evolutionary scale, rendering former concepts of "lower" or "higher" totally false and obsolete.[17] In fact, the crucial issue that arose in the wake of Darwinism was man's displaced status in Nature: he was essentially "demoted" from the highest ranking (or so it seemed) to become a mere organism among other organisms, neither higher nor lower in status.[18] This ran in total opposition with the ancient image of the Chain of Being devised by Aristotle,[19] later supplanted by the more modern ladder, which placed the amoebae at the lowest rank and man at the apex, the summum of creation. The eighteenth-century "improved" view remained however hierarchical and anti-evolutionary, and was eventually replaced a century later by an ever growing and ever changing tree with its many different side branches.[20] This new vision of evolutionary equality between man and animal is illustrated by Prendick's original mistake, which now takes on full significance. Since throughout the novel there is a constant shifting and profound uncertainty about who is human and who is animal (on the surface as well as on a deeper level), the distinction between both species really becomes impossible to ascertain. *The Island of Doctor Moreau* confuses, blurs, and even erases the long-standing dividing line between man and animal. Consequently, both species lose their differences, individualities and uniqueness (Moreau behaves like a beast, the animals possess linguistic abilities). In fact, both species melt, blend into each other (however uneasily and painfully) as Moreau is psychologically de-humanized while the animals are physically humanized and anthropomorphized. As a result, both species are quite literally equalized as man becomes beast and vice versa. In other words, Wells subverted the traditional image of man to beast transformation because his goal was not to show (as other writers did) that man was in essence as beast, but that man and beast are equal because they share a common evolutionary bond.

One has gathered by now that in order to fully understand the nature of Wells's work, it must be examined more closely in relation to biology and specifically evolution, the so-called cornerstone of biology. *The Island of Doctor Moreau* is, as we have just glimpsed, the literary outcome of Darwin's findings and a fictionalized exposition of his scientific theories. The importance of the new science of biology is most obviously shown through the novel's three main characters, Prendick, Moreau, and Montgomery, who are all practitioners of that trade. When the narrator indicates that he had studied under Thomas Henry Huxley, a real life adamant proponent of evolution, Moreau "raised his eyebrows slightly at that. 'That alters the case a little, Mr. Prendick,' he said with a trifle more respect in his manner. 'As it happens, we are biologists here. This is a biological station—of sorts.'" (p.29) Not unlike his characters, Wells had close ties to biology and evolution himself, through the influence of Huxley, his former professor of biology, a man described as more Darwinian than Darwin himself, and commonly referred to as Darwin's bulldog.[21] In fact, Wells, unlike many of his contemporary fellow writers, had a keen interest and an in-depth knowledge of Darwinism as well as a sophisticated understanding of the ethical questions and philosophical issues raised by this revolutionary concept. According to Warren Wagar, "what most forcefully engaged the mind of H.G. Wells in the early and middle 1890s was the theory of evolution and its bleak implications for the future of *Homo sapiens*."[22] Wells actually published *The Island of Doctor Moreau* the same year he wrote his essay "Human Evolution and Artificial Process" (in the October 1896 *Fortnight Review*).[23] The novel is indeed a frightening illustration of the essay, for Moreau does experiment with evolution (or his twisted interpretation of it), turning it into the cruelest of artificial processes. Moreau even mentions Darwin's theory to help him justify and rationalize his experiments in artificial evolution. He (mis)uses the theory to justify the torments he inflicts upon his unwilling subjects, and to prove to himself that pain, the main component of his research, is really a non-issue, an irrelevant and useless avatar that will, according to the laws of evolution, eventually disappear: "I never yet heard of a useless thing that was not ground out of existence by evolution sooner or later." (p.84)

But how does Darwinism (and biology in general) fare in the novel, through Moreau? In two words: not well. Although Darwin's main ideas are present in the text, Moreau constantly and systematically misinterprets and misuses them. For instance, Darwin contends that individuals do not evolve, nor devolve, but rather, that an individual interacts a certain way with his environment; furthermore, any evolutionary changes are minute and must occur over an extended period of time (these two criteria are inseparable). In other words, the principle of evolution is two-fold, first, modern life-forms are the result of descent with modification from ancestral species, and second, the mechanism of this modification (evolution) is natural selection working slowly and gradually over long stretches of time.[24] Yet, in *The Island of Doctor Moreau* this double postulate is clearly violated since the transformation of the Beast-Folk owes nothing to descent and the process at work is not a slow natural selection but on the contrary accelerated artificial selection. Another one of Moreau's evolutionary fallacies deals with devolution, a concept devoid of any scientific foundation. Moreau's newly "evolved" species, who understandably have a hard time adapting to their sudden and unnatural new status, instead of dying off (a process Darwin would call natural selection), ultimately devolve and revert back to a former atavistic state,[25] a fact Moreau himself laments: "they revert. As soon as my hand is taken from them the beast begins to creep back, begins to assert itself again...." (p.89) The process at work here, reverse evolution, or devolution, although a popular concept in nineteenth-century literature, is not scientifically viable and can never take place in real life. Species evolve, stagnate or go extinct, but they do not revert back to an exact former state, contrary to what Moreau seems to witness. In fact, Dollo's "Law of Irreversibility" explains this, stating in essence that no organism or component of an organism can return to a previous evolutionary state.[26] Furthermore, evolution is based on the premise of species reproduction, yet the Beast-Folk do not—probably cannot—reproduce.

Moreau's atrocious behavior and repellent actions are probably the most disturbing aspects of the story, but while he is cruel and sadistic, these character traits are typical in Gothic fiction. Yet, analyzed in light of Darwin's theories, and specifically his views on ethics, Moreau's behavior takes on new meaning. *The Island of Doctor Moreau* has been described as a "post-Darwinian utopia, another evolutionary novel about human society" (although the term dystopia would be more correct).[27] But how accurate is this description? Darwin was of course greatly misunderstood until the twentieth century, the greatest misconception being as Ernst Mayr (one of the world's eminent evolutionary biologists) explains, that man "is nothing but an animal."[28] According to Mayr, man is distinct from animal in two major ways: he exclusively possesses complex language as well as an ethical system, a fact clearly stated by Darwin.[29] Through the Beast-Folk and Moreau, Wells does indeed address these two distinctively human characteristics, but they are once again subverted by Moreau's actions. Darwin asserts that, of all species, man alone holds the capacity for language, yet in *The Island of Doctor Moreau* the Beast-Folk can speak, "These things—these animals *talk*!" as Prendick, utterly horrified, remarks (p.82). Similarly, Darwin maintains that only man has an ethical system, but once more, the theory is perverted and turned upside down, as Moreau is totally devoid of this so-called uniquely human value, even coolly proclaiming that "To this day I have never troubled about the ethics of the matter. The study of Nature makes a man at last as remorseless as Nature" (p.85). Moreau effectively rejects one of the two criteria that defines him as intrinsically human (ethics), while infusing the Beast-Folk with the other criterion (language).

Although Moreau claims to be a physiologist and a biologist, even an evolutionist, his interpretation of evolution is, at best, flawed. His assertion of a modern-day scientist is contradicted by his very actions and he is actually a throwback to the pre-Darwinian and pre-biological age, when Natural Theology, not Evolution Theory, ruled.[30] In fact, the early nineteenth-century landscape was still largely dominated by Natural Theology, which viewed the world order as perfect. Moreau's beliefs, then, seem to be less in tune with Darwin's and more in accord with

William Paley's (1743-1805), the eighteenth-century clergyman and famed proponent of Natural Theology. Paley came up with the argument from design and created one of the most famous and appealing metaphors in the annals of science, that of the watchmaker, to prove divine creation. His argument from design postulated that if you found a watch on the ground, its intricacy would force you to conclude that a maker designed it, and that it could not have been left there by random forces of nature. Following that same logic, living organisms similarly show evidence of complex design, therefore no chance association could have resulted in such perfection and intricateness (as that found in the human eye for example), and consequently a designer, or as Paley calls him an "artificer," must have created these organisms just as a watchmaker created the watch. Paley then concluded, "The marks of design are too strong to be got over. Design must have a designer. That designer must have been a person. That person is GOD."[31] As many after Paley have demonstrated, the argument of the watchmaker, although so well crafted that even Darwin enjoyed it, is flawed because it is based on deductive reasoning which accepts on faith God's existence and then rearranges the facts to fit the argument. If there ever was a watchmaker, the renowned Oxford scientist Richard Dawkins would later claim, he must have been a blind watchmaker.[32]

More aptly than the idea of a biologist, the notion of a watchmaker, and especially a blind watchmaker, superbly fits Moreau. He is indeed presented not as a nineteenth-century biologist, but as a divine (or rather demonic) archaic and arcane designer who intentionally created his hybrid creatures for some mysterious and arcane purpose. Even the scientist's attention to details and strive for perfection recall god-like traits: "The human shape, I can get now, almost with ease, so that it is lithe and graceful, or thick and strong" (p.88). This is made quite clear in the text, as Moreau is actually seen as a god by his creations that blindly and fearfully worship him and his Law: "Moreau, after animalizing these men, had infected their dwarfed brains with a kind of deification of himself" (p.66).[33] There is, however, one major divergence between Paley's idealized world vision and the reality of Moreau idolized world. For Paley, all living entities are ideally adapted to their environment, perfect organisms matched within a perfect world. Moreau's universe, however, is the antithesis of perfection; his world is dominated by chaos, which eventually degenerates into anarchy with the doctor's violent demise.

Curiously, Moreau's ultimate goal is perfection, an objective that he feels is within his reach: "But I will conquer yet. Each time I dip a living creature into the bath of burning pain, I say: this time I will burn out the animal, this time I will make a rational creature of my own. After all, what is ten years?" (p.89). So convincingly does Moreau proselytize, that after a while Prendick himself is almost converted as he feels overcome by a sense of complete harmony and equilibrium: "A strange persuasion came upon me that... I had here before me the whole balance of human life in miniature... in its simplest form" (p.109). But on the issue of perfection, Moreau's beliefs are again in total contradiction with Darwin, who did not see nature's design as being perfect or even striving for perfection. On the contrary, as Stephen J. Gould explains: "ideal arrangement is a lousy argument for evolution, for it mimics the postulated action of an omnipotent creator. Odd arrangements and funny solutions are the proof of evolution—paths that a sensible God would never tread but that a natural process, constrained by history, follows perforce."[34]

The notion of perfection, one of Moreau's mantras and obsessions, runs counter to evolution but brings us to another concept, that of progress. Perfection and progress are actually indivisible concepts, perfection being the end result of progress, a terminal process attained through a series of advancing steps. When Darwin presented his theory of evolution, one of the great resulting misconceptions dealt with the issue of progress, a motif that formed the core of nineteenth-century thought. Progress was the central defining concept of the time, and everything seemed to revolve around it. In the public's mind, evolution was inevitably linked with progress, and the two were seen as inseparable elements: *if you evolve, you must evolve into something better, superior*. Yet, according to Darwin, evolution is not synonymous with progress, and there is no ultimate ulterior motive or design in the evolutionary process. Once this became clear, evolution (already a difficult concept to accept since it seemed to demote man) was vehemently rejected, as it now also conflicted with the traditional view of mankind advancing towards an ultimate state of perfection.

Up to then, the worldview had been based on the Judeo-Christian doctrine of perfection, which saw humanity as moving slowly but inexorably towards perfection, a condition that would eventually be reached on Judgment Day. This was postulated early on (pre-seventeenth and eighteenth century) not only by the Church but also by naturalists like Paley who sought and saw Order in Nature as evidence of God's perfection and plenitude. But by the early nineteenth century society's focus had shifted towards a more realistic goal of progress; and by the mid nineteenth century yet another shift had occurred, negating the idea of progress and divine perfection. By ascertaining that man's origins are not divine and that humanity is not reaching for perfection (or even progress), Darwin thus deflated two major foundation concepts of that era.

But, once again, he was misrepresented. The public reasoned that since evolution was not synonymous with progress and intended design, then it must imply the opposite, regression and chaos. But what Darwin actually meant was that history is not only devoid of any metaphysical meaning, but also of meaning or direction in general, as evolution has indeed shown. Just as evolution did away with notions of high and low, so it eliminated concepts of advancement and regression. In fact—and this is shown in the theory itself—while it has made great strides in explaining the process of evolution, the theory has been incapable of explaining the reason or the purpose behind that process. These last remarks can now help us see Wells's novel in a new light.

Critics have traditionally interpreted *The Island of Doctor Moreau* as embodying a pessimistic view of evolution. Yet, this seems to go against the philosophy of evolution itself which is, as we have just noted, unencumbered by metaphysical implications or emotional biases. Since evolution is neither good nor evil, the novel then becomes a harsh criticism not of evolution, but of the misconceptions, misunderstandings and dangers associated with a false understanding of Darwin's theory, as Moreau's actions clearly demonstrate. This new interpretation of *The Island of Doctor Moreau* is supported by the way the novel introduces another major biological principle (besides evolution). *The Island of Doctor Moreau* is not only an illustration of evolution grossly misunderstood, but also of the philosophy of biology itself which, as Mayr explains, rests on proximate versus ultimate causes:

> The proximate causation is one that answers the *how* questions. Physiology, molecular biology, and developmental biology all study proximate causations of how something works. But then we have the ultimate causations, which ask the "why" questions. Evolutionary biology, much of ecology, and behavioral biology are all concerned with the why questions.[35]

In other words, biology wants to investigate, for example, how a bird sings and why it does. Since *The Island of Doctor Moreau* is an extended literary essay on biology in general and evolution in particular, the proximate and the ultimate causes figure in the novel with these two questions: *how does Moreau accomplish his experiments?* and more importantly, *why does he conduct them?* Both queries are addressed in chapter fourteen, aptly titled "Doctor Moreau Explains." The eponymous character first defines the "how," his *modus operandi*, "in the tone of a man supremely bored.... He was very simple and convincing" (p.80). He then proceeds: "For my own part I'm puzzled *why* the things I have done here have not been done before" (p.80, emphasis added), and "this extraordinary branch of knowledge has never been sought as an end... until I took it up" (p.82). Moreau conducts his experiments for the sake of "a touch of scientific curiosity" (p.82), not seemingly for any legitimate or useful and beneficial scientific end, but rather for his own pure aesthetic-scientific enjoyment. We have here a variation on the popular nineteenth-century literary motto of "art for art's sake," dear to the Symbolists and adapted to "science for science's sake." Naturally, Prendick is not satisfied with Moreau's unscientific explanations and "asked *why* he had taken the human form as a model" (emphasis added) to which Moreau "confessed that he had chosen that form by chance" (p.83). Prendick again is not satisfied and insists "Where is your justification for inflicting all this pain? The only thing that could excuse vivisection to me would be some application" (p.83). Moreau refuses to answer this new "why" but finally admits that "I wanted—it was the only thing I wanted—to find out the extreme limit of plasticity in the living shape" (p.85). This surprisingly weak and singular explanation, which would turn Moreau into a vulgar plastic surgeon, is soon contradicted by a second motif when Moreau claims that he wants to "burn out all the animal, this time I will make a rational creature of my own" (p.89).

After hearing Moreau's explanations, one realizes that, although the proximate cause is established in distressingly ample details, the ultimate cause remains unclear, as the second question, the most important one, is never really answered satisfactorily, at least from a rational scientific point of view. This again sets *The Island of Doctor Moreau* apart from the other novels mentioned earlier. In previous works dealing with the issue of humanity and bestiality, the how and the why are clearly stated and resolved and a mea culpa on the part of the guilty perpetrator is generally offered (see *Frankenstein*, *Doctor Jekyll and Mr. Hyde*, "The Adventure of the Creeping Man" and even *Dracula*).[36] In all cases, we know both how the transformation occurred and why it did. Not so in *The Island of Doctor Moreau*.

Moreau's actions, or as Prendick puts it, his "sophistry" (p.83), that is to say his fallacious way of reasoning, are an illustration of the nineteenth century's consistent false interpretation of evolution. One other consequence Darwinism had on nineteenth-century thought is the fading of certainties and dogmatism, which gave way to relativism, and Moreau is anything but a relativist, he has every trait of a dogmatist, and the dangers of such a behavior are certainly demonstrated in *The Island of Doctor Moreau*.

—2001

NOTES

1. *The Time Machine* (1895), *The Island of Doctor Moreau* (1896), *The Invisible Man* (1897), *The War of the Worlds* (1898), and *The First Men in the Moon* (1901).

2. Michael Crichton indeed also deals with the issue of evolution/devolution in such works as *Congo* (1980) for example, and to a certain extent in *Jurassic Park* (1990) and its sequel *The Lost World* (1995).

3. This is quite ironic since the novel itself revolves around creatures that are themselves hybrids.

4. *The Saturday Review* (April 11, 1896).

5. *The Guardian* (June 3, 1896).

6. H.G. Wells, *The Island of Doctor Moreau* (New York: Bantam, 1994), p.35. All subsequent references are to this edition.

7. The theme of the human beast transcends not only time but also space; the French Naturalist Emile Zola, for example, wrote an entire novel on that topic titled *La Bête humaine* (1890). In Kafka's *Metamorphosis*, the theme is taken to new extremes, symbolizing alienation and angst.

8. Jill Minning, "The Ambiguous Animal: Evolution of the Beast-Man in Scientific Creation Myths," in Olena H. Saciuk, ed., *The Shape of the Fantastic. Selected Essays from the Seventh International Conference on the Fantastic in the Arts* (New York: Greenwood Press, 1990), p.113.

9. See J.R. Hammond, "*The Island of Doctor Moreau*: A Swiftian Parable," *The Wellsian* 16 (1993), pp.30-41.

10. See D. Asker, "H.G. Wells and Regressive Evolution," *Dutch Quarterly Review of Anglo-American Letters* 12.1 (1982), pp.15-29. Quote p. 12.

11. See the chimera (goat/lion/serpent), the griffin (lion/eagle), or the hippocamp (horse/fish/serpent). For more details, see Malcolm South, ed., *Mythical and Fabulous Creatures: A Source Book and Research Guide* (New York: Greenwood Press, 1987).

12. Frankenstein's monster is also created through surgery but he is crafted from the sum of various dead human body parts, and the operation is itself painless. In *The Island of Doctor Moreau*, however, live non-sedated animals receive skin grafts through a procedure that can only be described as torture.

13. There are no examples of animals transformed into humans unless you count the fairy tale frog turning into a handsome prince.

14. To avoid controversy, Darwin did not use the term evolution in his first book until the last paragraph, speaking instead of "descent with

modification." Darwin later addressed the topic of man's ancestry in *The Descent of Man*.

15. Another message deals with Creation itself, as Moreau plays a fearful god-like creature to the animals he has operated on and enslaved. The same issue is also raised in Frankenstein.

16. Modern DNA studies would indeed prove Darwin right, as humans and chimpanzees share 99.6% of their active genes. The chimpanzee, along with the pigmy chimp, is our closest relative, and our next closest relative is the gorilla.

17. For a historical study of biology, see John A. Moore, *Science as a Way of Knowing. The Foundations of Modern Biology* (Cambridge: Harvard University Press, 1993).

18. Our own view of evolution is, once again, anthropocentric, seen only through one perspective: our own. But what happens if we examine evolution through someone else's vision, if we change the mental map? If, for example, intelligence is not the main criteria for evolution, but say speed or locomotion, then other animals such as cheetahs or birds, are much more evolved than we are.

19. For more on the chain of being, see Stephen Jay Gould, *The Flamingo's Smile: Reflections on Natural History* (New York: Norton, 1985). See particularly chapter 18, "Bound by the Great chain," pp.281-90.

20. Actually, the fixed ladder of life became in the nineteenth century a moving escalator, reflecting society's focus on progress and technology.

21. T. H. Huxley's (1824-95) fervor was notorious. Darwin's *Origin of Species* brought a lot of opposition from the Church, chiefly led by Oxford's Bishop Wilberforce. In the 1860 meeting of the British Association for the Advancement of Science, this polemic led Huxley to claim that in his opinion an ape was a more desirable ancestor than the Bishop was. For more on Huxley's views on evolution, see his *Evidence as to Man's Place in Nature* (London: Norgate, 1863).

22. W. Warren Wagar, "H.G. Wells and the Scientific Imagination," *The Virginia Quarterly Review* 65.3 (Summer 1989), pp.390-400.

23. Reprinted in Robert M. Philmus and David Y. Hughes, eds., *Wells: Early Writings in Science and Science Fiction* (University of California Press, 1975).

24. Huxley did not agree with Darwin that evolutionary change must be gradual.

25. We could explain this now: as Moreau did not alter the beast's DNA, it could revert as its own DNA took control. Wells of course did not know about DNA.

26. This is a bit ambiguous since we know that reverse mutation can occur. However, mutation and reverse mutation rates exist in an equilibrium state in which the two rates are not generally equal. Dollo's Law also states that structures that had been lost in evolution can never be re-acquired exactly the same way. See Ernst Mayr, *The Growth of Biological Thought. Diversity, Evolution and Inheritance* (Cambridge: The Bellknap Press of Harvard University Press, 1997).

27. Frank McConnell, *The Science Fiction of H.G. Wells* (Oxford: Oxford University Press, 1981), p.89.

28. See Angier, Natalie, "Ernst Mayr," *Natural History* 106.4 (May 1997), pp.8-12.

29. Technically, of course, animals possess a language of sorts.

30. Moreau is also, in one way, an ominous foreshadowing of some of the worst excesses of twentieth-century human experimentations, such as the ones performed by the Nazis.

31. William Paley, *Natural Theology: or Evidences of the Existence and Attributes of the Deity, Collected from the Appearances of Nature* (1802).

32. For a modern repudiation of the argument from design, see Richard Dawkins, *The Blind Watchmaker* (New York: Norton, 1986).

33. This episode takes place before Prendick learns that the creatures are animals, not humans.

34. Stephen J. Gould, *The Panda's Thumb: More Reflections in Natural History* (New York: Norton, 1980), pp.20-21.

35. *Natural History* (op. cit.), p.10.

36. In the case of Dracula, although he does not regret his actions, there is an implication that the vampire suffered deeply from his condition, and when he is finally annihilated "there was in the face a look of peace." Bram Stoker, *Dracula* (New York: Signet Classic, 1965), p. 380.

DEUS EX MACHINA

RED DWARF, BETTER THAN LIFE, LAST HUMAN, BY DOUG NAYLOR

MARIAN FOSTER

The thing about sf is that the narrative device known as *deus ex machina* is a valid and extremely useful aid to plot construction. The Red Dwarf television series reveals this at every turn, and *Last Human* is no exception: in *Better Than Life*, the heat-seeking missiles come out of the lift to kill the polymorph at just the right moment; in *Red Dwarf*, the god (Kryten) goes into the machine to release Lister, Rimmer and the Cat, although it takes quite a lot of the next book to get them out; in *Last Human*, the examples come thick and fast. Of course, the whole series started with its own deus: Holly—the *deus ex machina* that rules the reality of Red Dwarf (the ship), who later "performed some miracle" on Kochanski's ashes (*LH*, 35) to bring her back to life. Holly is the god from a machine in its truest sense—a god or all-powerful being who emerges from a mechanical apparatus, and by the combined percipience, knowledge, appropriateness and immediacy of his pronouncements solves the protagonist's problem.

Traditionally, the *deus ex machina* appears at the end of the action. All the Red Dwarf books finish with a surprise ending—in *Better Than Life* they are saved at the last minute by Holly, the book ending with a series of short chapters developing the theme that this particular piece of god-like knowledge introduces. In *Last Human*, the protagonists are saved by a most unexpected *deus ex machina*, who has lived, unobserved in his machine throughout the whole series, to finally emerge when most needed, and least looked-for.

In *Last Human,* Naylor reaches the ultimate form: the story is based on *deus ex machina* as an underlying premise: the Omni-zone—where rejected decisions go to—appears in *Better Than Life* as a knot of interlocking coils, hollow, twisted and undulating, spinning "in a timeless dance of beauty" (*BTL*, 155). It is the intersection of seven alternate universes, and it rules every action in *Last Human*. Time, and the choices of action, are flexible. When a particular choice leads to a particularly problematic situation, there is always an alternative reality to help out. Very occasionally, the sheer good luck of the incident verges on the improbable and introduces the negative aspect of the device: for example, when Kryten finds Rimmer a solidogram body, it is improbable enough to be jarring (*LH*, 42), and does not fit well with other aspects of the story. However, by and large, the narrative device provides the excitement and continuous action that is necessary for what was, after all, a successful TV series. It makes a very entertaining story.

It is possible that such a mechanistic and arbitrary device, when used in connection with what are, by any standards, stereotypic characters, would militate against character development. But they do develop. It is necessary, though: Lister as he appears first in *Red Dwarf* would be merely repetitiously boring if he didn't develop. The characters have changed with the series: they develop in a sequence of *deus ex machina* type incidents. This suggests interesting possibilities of plot and character interdependence: if characters are stereotypic is there consequently a stereotypic plot? And vice versa.

Lister is an English Midlands football yob with reggae inflections; Rimmer is two dimensional in the extreme; Kryten is all you ever wanted from a robot housekeeper; and Krissie is superwoman, intelligent, beautiful, competent, and sexy. Lister grows up—he does, after all, die at least once in the series, and lives an alternate life backwards from old(er) age. Even he would find it difficult not to change after living two lives. Rimmer definitely changes, helped by a doppelganger of an earlier, much less pleasant self. Krissie stays much the same—but then, there wasn't much wrong with her in the first place. She does seem to stay much the same age though—younger when she first appears, and only a few years older and wiser when she is regenerated. Kryten is not meant to change, being a robot. But he does, acquiring extra knowledge, acquiring also a human body at one point, and discovering that it has its shortcomings.

The humor in *Last Human* has toned down a little in comparison to previous books: it doesn't have the intensity of undergraduate-type hilarity found earlier—it is a case of vague amusement less than once a page versus several cases of rolling on the floor hysteria. The plot construction has improved. There is a prologue, and the sequence of the narrative is broken by interpolated scenes of parallel or explanatory incidents—like the initial appearance of McGruder—which is, again, appropriate to the theme of alternative times and realities. Perhaps this improvement is the result of a single, more experienced author. The earlier books have less complex construction.

Ultimately, all the books have been centered upon the conflict of a protagonist against his fate, that of being the last human. If such a collection of improbable episodes can be said to produce suspense, *Last Human* does so, inasmuch as it confounds the reader's expectations at every turn—surely an inherent function of speculative fiction. It becomes a struggle against reality to return Lister to Earth, as he first decided in *Red Dwarf*. But he's already been there in *Better Than Life* and it stinks and tries to kill him. In *Last Human* he tries alternative realities and they stink and try to kill him. Will he finally find some resolution to his unenviable position? Perhaps the god from the machine will rise up in a sequel to confound the apparently happy ending of *Last Human*. This now seems unlikely, though: In 1996, a fourth volume, *Backwards*, by Rob Grant alone, was released. It followed directly from *Better than Life*, ignoring Doug Naylor's *Last Human*.

—1996

ANALOGUES OF ANOMIE: LEE HARDING'S NOVELS

RUSSELL BLACKFORD

Lee Harding was both prolific and successful as a writer over a career spanning a quarter of a century. He published thirty-odd short stories (the precise number depending on how one counts the rewrites and revisions), books for children and adolescents, three important anthologies, and at least one novelty item in the form of a substantial piece of erotica. Despite all this, I'll be using six novels as the focus of this chapter; I'll be concentrating on these because they not only comprise Harding's major works of fiction but also make up almost the entirety of his fictional output during the so-called renaissance of Australian science fiction since 1975. Harding's first full-length science fiction novel, *A World of Shadows*, was published in that year, and Harding emerged as a major sf writer comparatively late in his career.

Harding's six major sf books—*A World of Shadows*, *Future Sanctuary*, *The Weeping Sky*, *Displaced Person*, *The Web of Time*, and *Waiting for the End of the World* (and the late non-sf but associated novel *Heartsease*)—are something of a disparate group, since all except, I suppose, the first two are clearly aimed at young audiences, but all seem to be pitched at different levels. Only *A World of Shadows* seems as if it is intended primarily for adult readers, though *Future Sanctuary* also has an adult protagonist and is an adult novel in that sense. Of the four books with juvenile protagonists, on the other hand, only *The Web of Time* strikes me as an unmitigated children's book, while the other three, which are possibly best described as being for young adults, are not consistent among themselves in level and tone, though they all contain varying underlying or overt qualities of fatalistic grimness. Because of this range of levels, it is difficult to trace progress (a problem compounded by questions of order of composition), or even to compare Harding novels one with the other without risking a comparison of apples with oranges.

Nonetheless, I'll be attempting to make some general observations about Harding's use of situations and images and the elements of plot, character, and language—trying to show what the six books have in common. The three Harding books which I personally consider to be his most effective are the first of those mentioned above, *A World of Shadows*, and two middle books of his *novelistic* career (late works, remember, in his *writing* career): *The Weeping Sky* and *Displaced Person*. But I also have some complimentary things to say about his latest novel—those and some less pleasant things. What I admire about three books I've listed, and which I don't find in the other three, is that Harding has created a basic situation which is original, patiently unraveled, and invested with a kind of poetic resonance. In all three cases we are left with a situation and an image which stay and suggest numerous interpretations (numerous interpretations are presented in the books as well, but these do not exhaust the possible significances of what Harding describes). I am prepared to extend high praise indeed for these books: Harding goes close to creating modern myths out of his materials. In *A World of Shadows*, the mythic potential resides in two related phenomena. First, Harding presents us with the inexplicable alien Shadows, intangible but powerful beings humanity has disturbed in its initial explorations of "second-order" space, and which invade the privacy of human minds. They are perceived as like whisperings, a non-physical coldness, a sense of shadows and oily black smoke. Second, to complicate matters and generate the movement of the story, the Shadows invade a space ship with a crew of two men, and apparently transfer the mind of one, Stephen Chandler, into the body of the other, Richard Ashby. While Chandler's mind is displaced into Ashby's body, or appears to be, Ashby's mind seems simply to disappear (no simple mind-swap to content us)—while Chandler's *body* is left seemingly mind-blanked.

The depictions of the Shadows, beings who spy on our innermost thoughts and feelings and can tamper with our minds, are effectively sinister, and the situation created is a kind of laboratory model for dealing with resolutely non-empirical questions: What is it that we mean by ascribing an identity to a person? What is it to love a particular person? The novel essays such questions of philosophy sensitively and intelligently, without losing the importance of the human relationships going on. It is largely concerned with the efforts of Chandler's wife, Laura, and his friend, Chris Nolan, a psychologist specializing in the effects of the Shadows, as both try to cope with the situation. Like the reader, they are forced to ask philosophical questions, but in the midst of their deep emotional involvement. Laura in particular has to try to discern whether the man who thinks of himself as Chandler and displays Chandler's memories and personality is "really" Chandler. Ultimately, she accepts that, even if he is not her husband, he shares the qualities she had loved in him. In itself, this would be an effective resolution of the dilemma, but Harding adds a cruel twist: the Shadows restore the "proper" personalities to each body at the crucial point, and Laura finds that she no longer loves Chandler, but rather loves the man she has lost—the man who was formed when Chandler's personality was allowed to overlay Ashby's and develop in his body: an unstable and doomed composite.

The Weeping Sky is set in an alternative medieval world in which the Child of God was martyred on the Wheel and crusades are fought in which the Saracens ally with the cultured nations of Europe against barbaric Slavs inspired by a mad prophet. The book is, however, dominated by a single powerful and ambiguous image, that of the Wall: a strange discontinuity in the sky that spreads across an isolated English valley. At various times, the Wall is interpreted as a divine miracle, as a strange natural phenomenon, as a point of intersection between dimensions of reality, and as a mocking work of the Devil. At sunset it catches the rays of the sun like a vast stained glass window, and is greeted as a miracle by gullible believers and cynical Churchmen alike. The latter are prepared to exploit its manifestation for personal gain. Conversely, the Guild of Scientists inquires after the phenomenon and studies it, in a spirit of rational inquiry: the heroes of the book are Master Roger Asquith and his bright young apprentice Conrad le Jeune, who is the main viewpoint character. These two make regular observations and precise measurements in an attempt to find a natural explanation for the Wall. A lake has appeared beneath the Wall's swelling boundary; it actually seems to "weep" water—originally pure but increasingly saline. Towards the end of the book it oozes unbearably foul sediment. Conrad devotes much of his study to marking out carefully the day-by-day growth of the lake, though by the end he becomes embroiled in more dangerous and passionate actions.

Harding skillfully shows the responses of a range of characters and groups to the Wall, and depicts the relationships which are built up among those whom it brings into contact with each other, especially Conrad and Donella de Vargas, the daughter of an old aristocrat who has been robbed and ill-treated after returning from the Crusades. Donella and Conrad fall in love, and he utters her name at the critical moment at the end of the book as he returns to cognizance of his reality after an awesome journey beyond the Wall's periphery; her name is the last word in the book. Though the Wall is seen by Donella's blind father in the moment of his death and appears to him as a sign of God, it brings disaster to the valley and its monastery, as its waters finally burst forth in a cataclysmic flood. In the end, Harding offers something like a definitive science fiction "explanation" of the Wall, but this does not detract from the many-sided, mythic quality which it gains as the book progresses.

Harding's best-known book is still *Displaced Person*, published in Australia under that title in 1979, and in the same year in the United States as *Misplaced Persons* to avoid title confusion with another book. The revised Penguin version, published in Australia in 1981, has a note: "Some minor revisions have been made..." This edition should be taken as the authoritative text, but the revisions appear to be limited to what I'd call the book's coda, a short final section after the hero, Graeme Drury has returned to the normal world following his "displacement" into a strange limbo world. The coda is meditative and speculative: Drury reflects on the experiences he has been through, and the language of the 1979 version becomes strained in an effort to cope with this. In the 1981 edition, Harding has worked on making the prose more precise and flowing. In particular, he has eliminated such clumsy expressions of introspection as "I am fascinated by..." and "So I asked myself..."; the feeling is expressed more directly and compellingly. At the same time, he has eliminated direct references to the possible existence of a "Cosmic Filing Clerk" whose mistakes have led to the displacements or misplacements of persons from one world to another. The revised ending has a lighter, surer touch in the way it makes reference to interpretations offered in the body of the book as to how the mysterious events shown are to be interpreted. Leaving aside these changes, the different versions of the novel are interchangeable.

Displaced Person describes an adolescent boy's gradual withdrawal from the reality he has known (seen in terms of school, the streets of the suburb where he lives, his family and girlfriend, local supermarkets, fast food outlets, the nearby beach and park). Initially, Graeme Drury finds that people are ceasing to notice his presence. Soon, he becomes intangible in their world, able to walk straight through walls and even other people. At the same time, color begins to leach from his environment. Ultimately he is drawn into a mysterious para-world which he shares with other people and things that have come through from normal reality. He experiences a brief friendship with a young girl from a tough background and an old man who may once have been a University teacher. A number of metaphysical explanations are offered as to the nature and meaning of the "grey world," but none is definitive. Rather, this realm seems to be more an externalization of adolescent feelings of powerlessness, doubt, cultural invisibility. But such a thematic "explanation" does not limit the capacity of the book to haunt and resonate with the reader's feelings. While the novel's attempts at metaphysical explanation are often awkward, and their patterning is very obvious (different characters *will* come out with the same explanations in the same words, independently of each other), *Displaced Person* is a real achievement. It has deservedly won the Australian Children's Book of the Year Award, and seems to be one of the books which genuinely captures the feelings and imaginations of the adolescents for whom it is written while also being intelligent and rich enough to please adults.

Although Harding's other novels are less satisfying and often more easily exhaustible than these three, they sometimes contain interesting ideas. The most recent sf book, *Waiting for the End of the World*, is perhaps Harding's most ambitious novel to date if not the most successful, and displays some of his ability to create a situation which externalizes deep-seated perceptions and fears.

Future Sanctuary is the least coherent of Harding's books. It involves a fugitive being persecuted for some nameless crime, which he fears and half-believes was one of murder, who finds escape in a mysterious realm known as "Sanctuary," which is apparently available to anyone desperate enough to find it. This novel is a psychodrama in two senses. It is revealed in the ultimate that the action as it has been described to us has taken place in the mind of Howard Landry, a mentally-disturbed poet who has been put through a futuristic psychiatric program to reintegrate his personality. As discussed by Van Ikin in his survey of Lee Harding's novels in *Science Fiction # 2*, this explanation of the action, which appears only in the final chapter, was added at the behest of the novel's publishers, Laser Books. Ikin is distressed by the change: "A novel of action and bewilderment is compelled to end in a welter of talk and sudden, enforced certainty." However, I'm not convinced that too much blame should be placed on Laser Books for the novel's failure.

The novel may not originally have been conceived as a psychodrama in such a literalist sense as it has ended up, but the movement of the novel within the novel, that is, shorn of its explanatory prologue and final chapter, remains one of the integration of an heroic personality. In this sense, it is still a symbolic psychodrama, and resembles many fantasies based upon the quest myth. In this case, though, all linkage with any "real" world has been eliminated, reducing the story of quest and integration to its bare structural bones. While the story makes sense as a kind of abstract monomyth, it is virtually meaningless in any other terms, and it may have been this which led to the publisher's demand for extra material. The option of simply explaining the symbolic movement of the psychodrama as being caused by a literal psychodramatic therapy technique within a frame story was not successful, but clearly *something* was required to attempt to save this book. The situation was made more hopeless by some horribly bad dialogue and descriptive prose for which Harding has already been taken to task by Andrew Whitmore in a caustic and hyperbolic review (*SF Commentary* # 55/56).

The Web of Time is an even slighter work, a brief novel aimed at a very young audience. In essence a staggeringly naive time-travel story, it fails where Harding's earlier books for young audiences succeeded. Once again, Harding has built upon a central image, in this book a changing model of time—which is seen first as a stream, then as a branching tree, and ultimately as a bafflingly tangled web. But the difference between this image and that of the grey world in *Displaced Person* is that, like the monomythic pattern of *Future Sanctuary*, it relates meaningfully to nothing whatsoever in our universe. The image has no existential resonance, and is at any rate as naive as the language and characterization for readers in a post-Einsteinian, post-Minkowskian world. When the central image and idea is simply irrelevant, this leaves only Harding's weaknesses, of which I shall have more to say later.

By contrast, *Waiting for the End of the World* is far more ambitious and involving. While less successful than the three novels I discussed initially, it has something of the same power to create an objective correlative for current fears and uncertainties. The title refers to the situation of the characters, whose "world" is under threat from mysterious and invincible patrols that ultimately burn the depicted landscape of forests and hills—a refuge from life in the dystopian future city. But the title also refers to *our* current situation, waiting for a nuclear flash to destroy the world we know, or, as an alternative, for civilization to break down into mechanistic urban nightmares which Harding points to. Much of this book does not work, and there is no one abiding image as powerful as that in, for example, *Displaced Person*. Some of the competing images which fail to take on this role, the longbows fashioned by the central character, and the Plantagenet ghosts which haunt him, are important only for episodes, not for the book as whole (which lacks unity). They add surprisingly little to the book's area of genuine power. Nonetheless, there *is* power in the prophetic dreams of fiery holocaust experienced by certain of the characters in the last part of the book—and the terrible, unavoidable, fulfillment of the prophecies.

One of the most notable aspects of *Waiting for the End of the World* is its fatalism: while the holocaust is dreamed in advance, and some characters act on the dream and escape it, there is a sense that nothing could have averted it. Even the title signals this—*Waiting*, yes, but not actually doing anything about what is being waited for; the word implies almost an acceptance of the evil to come. Fate prevails in all of the books I've discussed, as well as in much of Harding's shorter fiction. It seems to be a fundamental element of Harding's work that his characters act less than they are acted upon. They are often victims, almost always passive, and never dynamic free agents. As a result, the patterning of events has little to do with the choices, motives, and insights of the characters, and is more the manifestation of forces beyond their control or comprehension.

For example, the whole movement of *A World of Shadows* depends on the whims of the Shadows and it seems that the decisions of the characters have no power to alter the direction of the plot in any significant way. All the characters can do is cope as well as possible with their manipulation, "spurn" the forces which are so clearly in control of their destiny, and find love where they can, as Laura Chandler ultimately finds love with Chris Nolan, who has always loved her. The events of *Future Sanctuary* take place in the mind of Howard Landry—albeit with some creative conspiring from the psychiatric team working on his case—and the outcome supposedly flows directly from Landry's innermost motives and choices. Yet, we learn very little about Landry to make us believe in his motives and choices. An impression is created that he is wholly acted on by his environment. His psychological needs are not only externalized by the therapy; they actually seem external to him, or at least to be quite separate from the character as he is experienced in the book. So divorced is his unconscious from the thinking, planning, anxious man we see, and into whose *consciousness* we enter, that it seems like a force quite separate from him—Freudian determinism with a vengeance!

The Weeping Sky, like *A World of Shadows*, is partly a love story, and one with a happy ending of a kind. In this novel more than any other, Harding deals with a cast of characters in conflict, and to some extent the characters get their just deserts. But the book is dominated by the Wall as it goes through its transmutations, oblivious to the motives and actions of any human agency. And the Wall is itself merely an accidental outcome of vast extra-dimensional conflicts and forces which only Conrad experiences close up and survives—and over which no one has any control. Similarly, in *Displaced Person* Graeme Drury has no control over the process which draws him into the grey world, or that which then ejects him and erases all memory of the experience. He retains a tape which he fortuitously made during his "displacement," along with a note from his friend Marion whom he met in the grey world. But his own actions have contributed nothing to events: he has simply *undergone* a patterned experience which has not been shaped even ironically by his character in conflict with others or his environment. *The Web of Time* is the most light-hearted of all these books, but even here the time travelers are generally at the mercy of forces they don't properly understand and make surprisingly little contribution to their eventual salvation from being hopelessly lost in time's web.

To a greater or lesser extent, Harding's books appear to be patterned rather than plotted. The associated sense of fatalism in Harding's work is not necessarily a fault in itself, and indeed it doubtless speaks to and for the many people in his audience who find the modern world frightening, alienating, and beyond their control. In a highly favorable (and recommended) review of *The Weeping Sky* in *SF Commentary* # 55/56, Bruce Gillespie dismisses criticism of this element of the book with a simple shrug of "...that is how things are." Unlike George Turner, for example, Harding does not seem to have a message as to how the world can be grappled with and improved, but his analogues of deeply troubling aspects of his audience's situation are powerful and have been justifiably celebrated by his critical admirers.

On the other hand, I can't avoid a feeling that Harding is making things easy for himself in that he does not have to cope with the pressures of producing coherent, logical plots with meaningful resolutions. Most glaringly, *Displaced Person*, on which so much of his reputation rests, could have had its events presented in any order Harding found convenient, since the action is shaped by forces which are by definition unlimited because undefined—and whose purposes can be as close to the author's as convenient. Harding gets by here too much on pattern and image.

If we grant that Harding only *appears* to make things easy on himself in the way he plots his novels, he undeniably takes things easy in the texture of his prose. It's this which gives me the gravest misgivings about his work, especially in a writer who has had much to say about the need for a literary artist to "put his balls on the line," or to produce work with "*cojones*," as he put it in a notorious *Locus* interview.

In some cases the sheer wimpiness of Harding's style can be blamed on the fact that it is directed at a young audience. But the problem is just as apparent in his supposedly adult books, and it manifests itself as clearly in *Waiting for the End of the World*, as in the earlier work. Indeed Harding's pre-1975 stories, notably his quite ambitious efforts for *Vision of Tomorrow*, show the opposite problem, being written in a style full of extravagant, imprecise language, seeming to scream at the reader in an effort to attract attention. By contrast, *Waiting for the End of the World* depends on locutions of the following sort: "He carried the stave to a secret place hidden deep in the forest where a small stream plunged through a tangled ravine"; "Here, where all nature seemed crowded close together and the air was rich with the moist, dark smells of earth..."; "Throughout this critical period..."; "The making of the longbow demanded time, skill, and above all—patience," Perhaps it's overkill to add that these are only some of the examples freely available from just the short first page! This is typical of the whole texture of the book, and, indeed, of much of Harding's writing: a pastiche of clichés, a running adaptation of second-hand phrases that does no justice to the books' striking and precise visions, which they actually come to dominate. For it's not as if Harding simply writes in an unobtrusive, workmanlike style—as one might want to say about other Australian writers of sf, including Wynne Whiteford and David Lake; rather, the clichés in which he writes are intrusive and distracting. As often as not they are somewhat old-fashioned or bookish phrases that sound unnatural, even sententious, in modern Australian writing.

Whether Harding can be considered to have put his own literary balls on the line, as he would have it, is a matter of opinion. To some extent I believe he has in his memorable analogues of the forces of *ananke* and *anomie*. These genuinely speak to and for his chosen audience, and to all of us at some times; Harding seems to have reached deeply—and for all I know painfully—into his own psyche to bring them forth for us. But the effort is almost sabotaged by lusterless plotting, dialogue and narrative prose—and by characterization which is sometimes vivid but all too often amounts to the depiction of characters who are mere puppets. Some sharp-edged, tough-minded and exact sf writing is currently being produced in Australia, not only by our veteran writers but also by talented newcomers such as Greg Egan. The work of Lee Harding, who in many ways has been an example for the local sf community, could benefit from a similar sharpening and toughening of its dialogue and narrative prose. The tragedy is that, judging from his recent pronouncements and practice, Harding is not interested in knowing the difference.

—1990

FANTASY FICTION AND TERRY PRATCHETT'S DISCWORLD

KEVIN SMITH

Terry Pratchett was the best-selling living fiction author of the 1990s and is the second most popular living fantasy writer today. His books are constantly reprinted, and by 2011 achieved over 70 million sales. They have been translated into at least 37 other languages, and his work is so successful that his print-based fiction has inspired numerous multimedia treatments: his books are available in audio-format, computer games have been made about his fantasy world, and three of his novels have been converted into animated tales.[1] However there has been relatively little critical attention paid to his work and although it is true that popularity does not necessarily equate to quality, this essay hopes to rectify this oversight and prove that Pratchett's fiction deserves such attention.

Perhaps one of the reasons for the lack of critical interest in Pratchett's work lies in the genre to which it nominally belongs. The fantasy genre is "a form of literature that has been dismissed as being rather frivolous or foolish" (Jackson 1993: 5). Perhaps this dismissive attitude is because fantasy ignores the Aristotelian convention that art is exclusively concerned with mimesis, perhaps because of its similarity to fairy stories, which are "for children."[2] However this overlooks the genre's background in mythology, and the importance of myth in human culture.

Another possible reason for the lack of critical interest in Pratchett's work is its status as comic fiction. There is, in academic circles as in society in general, a disdain for humor as art, because it is "not serious." Symbolically, in our society actors and musicians are regarded as artists, comedians are not. This disdain for comedy in highbrow circles can be seen easily in the lack of comedic fiction nominated for awards (and even in the dearth of comedic films nominated for Oscars). Orwell's famous comment that whatever is funny is subversive may be oft quoted, but it seems that the artificial dichotomy between "serious" fiction and comedy has become ingrained in western culture, much to its own loss. However there is a strong comedic tradition within the English novel, from Fielding through Austen and Dickens and it is within this continuum that Pratchett's works operate. The social satire much admired by critics in the writings of Dickens and Austen is similarly present in Pratchett's Discworld as I shall demonstrate.

Popularity may be the final nail in the coffin for Pratchett's fiction with regard to academic interest. The twentieth century with its mass media and mass communication saw popularity become a pejorative term to "high" culture, and negative critics of popular literature often argue that the industrial method of modern publication "debases the value of art" (McCracken 1998: 24). However, as McCracken notes (1998: 20) it was not until the end of the nineteenth century that a noticeable split occurred between a self-consciously difficult and elitist high culture and the mass culture it defined itself against. Before the "self-consciously difficult" modernists there was no distinction between the popular and the artistically valuable:

> The nineteenth century novels of Charles Dickens and Elizabeth Gaskell were serialized in popular periodicals and their distribution benefited from the steam press. Yet they were consciously aimed at a family audience. Whether or not the homogeneity of the audience was real or imaginary, such novels managed to be both high literature and a part of popular culture. (McCracken 1998: 20)

I will argue that the works of Terry Pratchett are subversive, complex and artistically relevant.

FANTASY AND SCIENCE FANTASY

It is worth remembering that "all imaginary activity is fantastic, all literary works are fantasies" (Jackson [1981] 1993: 13). On a continuum between fantasy and reality, novels take up a midway point between the unreal (myth and fairy tale) and the supposedly real (history, biography). The dominant form of literary expression, realist novels, situate themselves within a social formation and ideological framework to gain verisimilitude: to appear realistic, although they are, ultimately, simply fantasies. What is it then that makes us term a particular genre "the fantastic"? Put simply, the fantastic does not attempt to portray a wholly real and realistic world, a world that we can instantly believe in because we recognize it.

It is therefore important to consider Terry Pratchett's Discworld series in light of the literary tradition of fantasy to which it belongs. As Jackson notes (1993: 14), a critical definition of fantasy is problematic due to indiscriminate usage of the term to signify any literature that does not give priority to realistic interpretation (mimesis). Jackson lists among those that are typically classified as "fantasy," "myths, legends, folk and fairy tales, utopian allegories, dream visions, surrealistic texts, science fiction, horror stories, all presenting realms 'other' than the human" (Jackson: 14). To subdivide these different but similar types of fantasy, Jackson uses three distinctions suggested by Todorov's analysis of the fantasy genre: The *marvelous* (or supernatural), *fantasy* (or unnatural) and the *uncanny* (or natural). Somewhat confusingly, the genre that is typically known as fantasy in your local bookstore would come under Jackson's subdivision of the "marvelous," whereas the definition of fantasy she adopts seems mainly concerned with the Gothic genre.

Terry Pratchett's Discworld is an example of a division of the "marvelous," what Tolkien termed a *secondary world* (Swinfen 1984: 75). The secondary world is as old as literature itself, with examples as culturally diverse as the Sumerian *Epic of Gilgamesh*, and Homer's *Odyssey*. More recent examples include Tolkien's Middle Earth and Lewis's Narnia. Creation of a secondary world gives the author a *tabula rasa* on which to craft an entirely new and imaginary world, independent from or parallel to the geography, history and possibilities of the "real" primary world. The creation of a "secondary world" forces the reader to assume a "secondary belief" (Swinfen: 5). Rather than the willing suspension of disbelief Coleridge spoke of in the *Biographia Literaria (XIV)* as essential to mimetic art, the secondary world has its own rules and conventions to which the author indoctrinates the reader. By describing the conventions and norms of the secondary world, a secondary realism is also established. We do not expect to see tanks ranging over the battlefield of Middle Earth, nor flying saucers scouting the outlands of Narnia; the author sets up a frame of reference within which they must conform in order to allow a secondary belief to go unchallenged. Swinfen explains this as follows: "Our normal experience of the primary world thus leads us to give primary belief to primary realism, while successful sub-creation induces secondary belief in the secondary realism of a secondary world" (Swinfen 1984: 5).

By denying the normal "primary" belief, the fantastic defines itself *against* what is "realistically possible." This makes fantasy a form of defamiliarization—by accepting a "secondary belief" we automatically contrast this against possibility, or our "primary belief." Creating a secondary belief allows the reader to see more easily the arbitrariness of socially constructed values that are accepted as common sense in their primary belief system.

Science fiction has much in common with the secondary world marvelous type of fantasy, leading some writers and publications to suggest a new generic classification of "science fantasy." This classification is useful because it helps to separate and further distance the marvelous types of fiction from the uncanny or Todorovian "pure fantastic"—while the fantasy genre can include examples of the uncanny such as Kafka's *Metamorphosis* or Henry James's *Turn of the Screw*, these texts would be excluded from a "science fantasy" genre because they depend on the subversion of real world physical laws rather than suggesting an entirely new set. The science fantasy genre can be seen as a result of the phenomena of "secondary belief" that Tolkien identified (Swinfen 1984: 14). Unlike the uncanny, science fantasy is not an incursion of the impossible into everyday life, but an invention of an impossible world, that incorporates its own history, laws of physics, etc.:

> Strangeness and wonder are still present, but the modern concern with precision of detail and coherent scientific data has had its effect on the creation and depiction of the secondary world. Such a world now has a precise geography, often including maps, which is quite foreign to the shadowy and imprecise journeyings of Spenser's knights in the realm of Gloriana. (Swinfen 1984: 75)

The invention of maps and countries can be seen quite clearly in Pratchett's Discworld series. In fact there are not only maps of the Disc itself, but street maps of its major cities too. The Discworld also has its own set of physical laws defined throughout the series and with the publication of *The Science of the Discworld* (1999) we can see how the Discworld series, like Niven's Ringworld, is a secondary world with its own parallel science, history, mythology, customs and metaphysics.

The secondary realism of science fantasy fits well with Brooke Rose's innovative model of fantastic/realistic fiction. By converting Todorov's linear model of fantasy into a circle she allows the categories of realism and the marvelous to touch, thereby accounting for the features of realism that she discerns in science fiction (Cornwell: 38). Cornwell notes that science fiction and certain forms of fantasy are "tangential bedfellows," provoking the remark that "it is not accidental that the Russian term for sf means 'scientific fantastic'" (Cornwell: 148).

However it is important to recognize that even though science fantasy and science fiction are tangential bedfellows, they are nevertheless different. Although science fiction is a form of fantasy, it is a form mostly concerned with technologies and societies based in the future.

Science fantasy on the other hand is a form of the marvelous, secondary world fiction that has developed its secondary world to a point where its rules and laws have become transparent to the reader.

This can be diagrammed as a circle cut into three equal portions, REALISM, UNCANNY and MARVELOUS, with further subdivisions of the latter pair showing adjacent slices, the FANTASTIC UNCANNY and the FANTASTIC MARVELOUS.

However, the rules of Science Fantasy are not inventions, but perversions of the real laws of physics. Based on Freud's claim that "the 'creative' imagination indeed is quite incapable of inventing anything; it can only combine components that are strange to one another" (Freud, Sigmund, quoted in Jackson 1993: 8), Jackson deduces that:

> Fantasy is not to do with inventing another non-human world: it is not transcendental. It has to do with inverting elements of this world, recombining its constitutive features in new relations to produce something strange, unfamiliar and *apparently* "new," absolutely "other" and different. (Jackson 1993: 8)

Hence, the physical laws of the science fantasy's secondary world are imaginable to us. A world which we could not interpret by comparing it to our own physical laws would be incomprehensible to us—for example if cause and effect had no bearing upon each other it would be hard for a reader to make sense of a story set in such an estranged imaginary universe. Similarly we can see that fantasy races likewise arise of reconstituting features of the real world into new guises; a troll is after all (in its Discworld incarnation) a mixture between human and stone, a werewolf a mix between man (or woman) and wolf. Consequently, we find parallels between fantasy lands and real ones. The Discworld country of Djelibeybe for example is a fairly obvious parody of ancient Egypt in *Pyramids* (1990) and the continent of XXXX is the Discworld Australia. Freud's theory that we can only make strange and reconstitute real world experiences also explains why fantasy can be satirical and comment upon the real world: because we can recognize, through the *ostranenie*, the derivation of the fantasy phenomena and this causes us to notice the difference between the imaginary vision and the real-world object.

Another major influence on the modern fantasy genre is the picaresque. The travels of Rincewind and his various companions are analogous to similar picaresque voyages of self-discovery. Rincewind and Twoflower form a duo, travelling the absurd world of the Disc and encountering strange cultures and phenomena in a similar way to classical picaresque heroes such as Don Quixote and Sancho Panza or

Huck Finn and Jim. The form of *The Color of Magic* (1983) and *The Light Fantastic* (1988) reconciles the exploratory, heuristic qualities of the picaresque with the mythical encounters and terminal urgency of the displaced wanderer *Odyssey* style myth. Again, this has its parallels in Tolkien's *The Hobbit*, where the tale is both an adventure and a picaresque chronicling, Bilbo Baggins's eyes being opened to the world outside the sheltered hobbit community. The use of the picaresque form in a secondary world environment is especially useful for fantasy writers, because it allows the reader and the protagonist to learn about the boundaries and systems of the fantasy world together. Strange phenomena in the secondary world are exposed as marvelous and miraculous to both the reader and the hero, so that the reader feels empathy with the character and both protagonist and reader share a sense of wonder, and of establishing new ideas of reality. This is noticed by Rabkin who "requires astonishment and recognition of this astonishment: on the part of the character in the fiction, as well of the reader" (Cornwell 1990: 13).

Often the worldly travels of the protagonists are matched by an inward journey of character growth, a fantastic *Bildungsroman*. This is certainly the case in Lewis's Narnia fantasies, or indeed the gothic fantasies of H.P Lovecraft. However, the picaresque and the *Bildungsroman* do not necessarily coexist. Although certain of Pratchett's novels (*Mort, Pyramids, Small Gods*) do equate travel and experience with character growth, certain characters retain characteristics and beliefs identical to their incarnation on the first page. Rincewind and Twoflower may travel the world (*The Color of Magic, The Light Fantastic*), but Rincewind's experiences only confirm his cynicism and reinforce his belief in running away as a means to survival.

DISCWORLD AND THE FANTASY GENRE

As the previous section illustrates, fantasy defines itself *against* the real—without realism to compare it to, a conception of fantasy would be impossible. It is for this reason that fantasy is often seen as "escapist," with the negative connotations that this term brings. By describing other worlds, we instantly contrast them with our own. Fantasy, like language, is a system of signs with no positive terms. It is for this reason that fantasy gains its subversive powers by defamiliarizing the order of things to which we have been naturalized. As Shklovsky notes in "Art as Technique," Tolstoy's use of a horse as narrator defamiliarizes naturalized but artificial concepts such as punishment, ownership, and burial. The most obvious equivalent in English literature can be seen in Swift's *Gulliver's Travels* where fantasy characters are used to satirize and question societal functions and the injustices they bring. Orwell's *Animal Farm* or *Nineteen Eighty-Four* are more recent examples of fantasy being used subversively to question naturalized institutions and concepts. However, Jackson suggests that secondary world fantasies are less subversive than examples of the uncanny or the Todorovian definition of "the fantastic":

> They [Kingsley, Lewis, Tolkien, Le Guin, Richard Adams] belong to that realm of fantasy which is more properly defined as faery or romance literature. The moral and religious allegories, parables and fables informing the stories of Kingsley and Tolkien move away from the unsettling implications which are found at the center of the purely "fantastic." Their original impulse may be similar, but they move from it, expelling their desire and frequently displacing it into religious longing and nostalgia. Thus they defuse potentially disturbing. anti-social drives and retreat from any profound confrontational with existential dis-ease.
> (Jackson 1993: 9)

Here we see how Jackson dismisses the more famous and popular secondary world fantasies of our times, citing their reliance on popular parables and fables as evidence of ideological reinforcement. Jackson fails to recognize that nostalgia is a potentially subversive force, and that the French revolution, of all things, was inspired by longing to return to an Arcadian past.[3] Even these stories of a simple mythical past force us to compare the pastoral, medieval simplicity with our own society. It is hard to shake off the impression that Jackson is in fact simply dismissing these fantasies because of their *popularity*....

Unlike Tolkien's Middle Earth, Pratchett's Discworld is not a world of clear-cut distinctions between good and evil. In Discworld we see examples of vegetarian werewolves, conscientious golems, evil elves and female dwarves. The distinct division between "good" races (Hobbits, Elves) and "bad" races (Orcs, Goblins) that exists in Tolkien is subverted completely, making Pratchett's world infinitely more complicated and variable, and therefore more representative of contemporary society than the nostalgic "clear cut" past that Jackson accuses the "secondary world" type fantasy of representing. Whereas Tolkien's work can be seen as nostalgic for a mythical golden age where good and bad and heroes and villains are easily distinguishable, Pratchett's work embraces moral relativism, and the chaotic complexity of modern life.

This chaotic complexity is reflected in the genre-mixing encountered in the many books of the Discworld series. Although the conventional picaresque fantasy is represented (and subverted), the series incorporates generic forms not usually associated with the marvelous, secondary world fiction. Although all of the books are set in the Discworld and are therefore primarily of the secondary world science fantasy genre, not all of them represent conventional fantasy narrative. For example *Jingo, Guards Guards!, Feet of Clay* and *Men at Arms* are, if anything, a combination between the seemingly incompatible genres of detective fiction and fantasy.[4] *Small Gods* is simultaneously a *Bildungsroman* and a metaphysical exposition, a representation of religious persecution featuring the Disc's version of the inquisition and an exposition of the formation of myth and belief. *Carpe Jugulum* also incorporates (embeds) the fantastic genre of the uncanny into the Disc's secondary world, providing both a parody of Stoker's *Dracula* and the myths of vampirism. The amount of genre mixing that is seen in the Discworld series makes any simplistic definition of "fantasy" seem laughably inadequate to cope with the multiple permutations of different generic mixes that these novels can take. Even the more traditional parodies of fantasy—*The Color Of Magic, The Light Fantastic*—face the problem of being simultaneously comic and fantastic. Genre classification becomes truly impossible when faced with *Carpe Jugulum* or some of Pratchett's later books: Comic Gothic Fantastic?

As Robert Silverberg (1999: 4) notes, the books of the Discworld, as at that date, can be divided into roughly four groups:

- The Rincewind series (*The Color of Magic, The Light Fantastic, Sourcery, Eric, Interesting Times, The Last Continent*)
- The Granny Weatherwax series (*Equal Rites, Wyrd Sisters, Witches Abroad, Lords and Ladies, Maskerade, Carpe Jugulum*)
- The Death series (*Mort, Reaper Man, Soul Music, The Hogfather*)
- The City Watch series (*Guards! Guards!, Men at Arms, Feet of Clay, Jingo, The Fifth Elephant*)

Additionally, there are several stand-alone novels that do not feature the major heroes (*Small Gods, Pyramids, Moving Pictures*).

Terry Pratchett's secondary world is interesting in that it discards distinctions between "serious" fantasy races and trivial ones. Tolkien would never have included, as Pratchett has, such fairy tale creatures as gnomes, fairies, bogeymen and witches into his "serious" secondary world with its genealogy and Darwinian explanations of the descent of Orcs. In fact, instead of inventing new races and species for his fantasy world, Pratchett's world thrives on utilizing collective and racial imaginations and then subverting them, making them "realistic." For example, in *The Light Fantastic*, Rincewind thinks about the life of a Gnome, after Twoflower questions why the one they encounter isn't wearing a red hat like the Gnomes in *"The Little Folks' Book of Flower Fairies"*:

Red Hats! He wondered whether to enlighten the tourist about what life was really like when a frog was a good meal, a rabbit hole a useful place to shelter out of the rain, and an owl a drifting, silent terror of the night. Moleskin trousers sounded quaint unless you personally had to remove them from their original owner when the vicious little sod was cornered in his burrow. As for red hats, anyone who went around a forest looking bright and conspicuous would only do so very, very briefly. (Pratchett, *The Light Fantastic*: 43)

As we can see, Pratchett shows the depiction of gnomes in "*The Little Folk's Book of Flower Fairies*" as unrealistic, for evolutionary reasons above all else. Gnomes are not jolly, brightly dressed creatures, but savage, brutish creatures who look like they live in a mushroom (because they do) and remain camouflaged to stay alive. This logical reappraisal of fantasy creatures and concepts and their subversion due to the unrealistic nature (by Darwinistic standards of natural selection) of folk depiction reveals the complexity of the Discworld series. Other folk beliefs are similarly incorporated, analyzed and then carried to their logical conclusions. The very concept of the world being a Disc carried on the back of a turtle is one that has been part of many cultures,[5] and Pratchett characteristically carries this concept to its logical conclusion. Of *course* the people living on the Disc would want to know the sex of the turtle, and guess at its eventual destination. The butterfly that flaps its wings and causes a hurricane on the other side of the world, that beloved metaphor of chaos theoreticians, becomes the quantum weather butterfly, a butterfly that has evolved weather controlling capabilities as a defense against predators. No metaphor, belief, or myth is safe from Pratchett's logical distortions.

As Brian McHale notes, the theories of Mikhail Bakhtin are particularly useful when examining the colliding worlds and discourses of science fantasy (McHale: 171) and postmodernism. The above examples, in fact, demonstrate the heteroglossia that is the basis of much Discworld humor. "Heteroglossia" is a translation of Bakhtin's coinage *raznorecie* that refers to the "internal differentiation or stratification of language" (Wales [1989](1997): 218). The above examples demonstrate the clashing of different varieties of language,

> "A novel is constructed," Baxtin (sic) tells us, "not on abstract differences in meaning nor on merely narrative collisions, but on concrete social speech diversity." The "concreteness" of this diversity of discourse is secured by using different repertoires of stylistic features, correlating with different repertoires of stylistic features, correlating with different situations or uses of language—what M.A.K. Halliday would call *registers*.

The interweaving of different registers in the text of a novel produces the effect of *heteroglossia*, plurality of discourse; and it is this concrete heteroglossia which serves as the vehicle for the confrontation and dialogue among world-views and ideologies in the novel, its orchestrated polyphony of voices. (McHale 1991: 166)

The standard monologic discourse[6] of a mythical romantic fantasy is subverted by the introduction of another type of discourse; in the example with the Gnome, scientific theories of natural selection, just as the scientist's metaphor is subverted by a literal fantasy interpretation in the case of the Quantum Butterfly. Indeed, it is easy to see the arguments between Rincewind and Twoflower as a dialogue between Twoflower's romantic discourse, and Rincewind's cynical discourse model of practicality.[7]

The polyphonic nature of the Discworld is always foregrounded. Witness for example the vibrant heterogeneity of the Disc's largest city of Ankh-Morpork, where trolls, humans and dwarves live side by side in a fantastic cultural melting pot. *Of course* the repercussions of this are interest groups such as the Campaign for Equal Heights (the Dwarf pressure group) or the Silicon Anti Defamation league (for Trolls) or the campaign for Dead Rights (for the undead). Of course, the city's patrician must lead a campaign of affirmative action by recruiting trolls, dwarfs, werewolves, gargoyles, golems and zombies into the police force. Fantasy settings and creatures are placed in a world recognizably modern, and real world issues of race relations and feminism are transposed into a scenario that usually represents a simple Arcadian life.

Another kind of myth that is questioned in the Discworld series is the notion of legendary figures. A selective list of figures, from fiction or from history, included in the Discworld series can be seen in the following table:

Discworld Character	Historical character	Fictional Character
Genghiz Cohen	Genghis Khan	Conan the Barbarian
Ponce da Quirm	Ponce da Leone	
Leonardo of Quirm	Leonardo da Vinci	
Laveolus		Odysseus
Hwel Shakespeare	William Shakespeare	
Alberto Mallich	Albertus Magnus	
Creosote		Schahriar[8]/ Kubla Khan / Croesus
Havelock Vetinari	Lorenzo De Medici/ Niccolo De Machiavelli	

The inclusion of historical figures into a contemporizing scenario in the Discworld resembles the dialogical form of the Menippean satire:

> The heroes of the absolute past, real-life figures from various eras of the historic past (for example, Alexander of Macedonia) and living contemporaries jostle one another in a most familiar way, to talk, even to brawl; this confrontation of times from the point of view of the present is extremely characteristic. In Menippean satire the unfettered and fantastic plots and situations all serve one goal—to put to the test and to expose ideas and ideologues. These are experimental and provocative plots. (Bakhtin, "Epic and Novel" in *The Dialogic Imagination*: 26)

As Bakhtin says of the Menippean satire, the Discworld brings epic and historical figures and places them in a real world situation, speaking in contemporary language, and acting like contemporary people:

> The "absolute past" of gods, demigods and heroes is here, in parodies and even more so in travesties, "contemporized": it is brought low, represented on a plane equal with contemporary life, in an everyday environment, in the low language of contemporaneity. (Bakhtin, "Epic and Novel" in *The Dialogic Imagination*: 21)

By intertextually including real world historical and fictional characters into the Discworld, by portraying them as "on a plane equal with contemporary life... in the low language of contemporaneity," Pratchett de-mythologizes these figures. The appearance of the characters from other fiction and history forces the reader to compare the realistic depiction of these characters to the legendary depictions that chronicle their great works or deeds. As in the treatment of myth, this is used to make the reader consider mythical interpretations or legends in a different light. Just as the inclusion of fantasy races such as Trolls and Dwarves into the multicultural heterogeneic city of Ankh-Morpork forces a reader to reconsider how the races of generic fantasy fiction would react in a modern environment,[9] the removal of epic distance from legendary characters allows us to reappraise them.

The characters, once incorporated into the Discworld plot, become more than simple archetypes or legends. The archetypal character of the "questing hero," for example, is represented in the Discworld as Cohen the Barbarian (Genghiz Cohen). First of all, the name itself is a direct allusion to both the historical figure, the archetypal barbarian, Genghiz Khan, and the muscle-headed Conan the Barbarian played in the cinema by Arnold Schwarzenegger. The double layer of parodying here is important because the fictional character of Conan is in fact partially based on the historical Genghis Khan. One of the speeches made by Conan in the film is a verbatim quote, traditionally attributed to Genghis Khan:

> "...What is good in life?"
> "To crush your enemies, drive them before you, and to hear the lamentation of their women."[10]

Again we see Pratchett applying a real world logic onto mythical concepts, as the Discworld's great hero, Ghengiz Cohen, is a very old man with a bad back and no teeth, because if a hero really was good enough to be unvanquishable, this hero *would* live to a very old age (just as, logically, gnomes with red hats would be owl-feed). Therefore, when Cohen is asked what is good in life his answer is not quite that expected of the all-conquering hero:

> ...the chieftain turned respectfully to his guest, a small figure carefully warming his chillblains by the fire, and said: "But our guest whose name is legend, must tell us truly: what are they that a man may call the greatest things in life?"
> "What shay?" he said, toothlessly.
> "I said: what are they that a man may call the greatest things in life?"
> The warriors leaned closer. This should be worth hearing.
> The guest thought long and hard and then said with deliberation: "Hot water, good dentishtry and shoft toilet paper." (Pratchett, *The Light Fantastic*: 48)

This contemporizing of the historical personage and the archetypal concept of the great champion subverts legendary ideas. Similarly Didactylos in *Small Gods* combines traits from Diogenes,[11] Archimedes,[12] Socrates[13] and Aristotle, so that the character is no longer a representation of a specific historical philosopher, but becomes a blend of legendary philosophic characteristics. By combination of recorded traits and of stereotypical conceptions of what a philosopher should be like, Pratchett creates an *archetypal* philosopher to subvert. Once again, this subversion is achieved by applying a ruthless real world logic upon a legendary or improbable concept—this great philosopher may well be the Disc equivalent of Socrates—

> Didactylos the Ephebian never achieved the respect of his fellow philosophers. They felt he wasn't philosopher material. He didn't have a bath often enough or, to put it another way, at all. And he philosophized about the wrong sorts of things. And he was *interested* in the wrong sorts of thing. Dangerous things. Other philosophers asked questions like: Is Truth Beauty and is Beauty Truth? And: Is Reality Really Created by the Observer? But Didactylos posed the famous

philosophical conundrum: "Yes, But What's It *Really* All About, Then, When You Get Right Down To It, I *Mean* Really!" (Pratchett, *Small Gods*: 167)

—but some of his other axioms are rather more down to earth:

> His philosophy was a mixture of three famous schools—the Cynics, the Stoics and the Epicureans—and summed up all three of them in his famous phrase, "You can't trust any bugger further than you can throw him, and there's nothing you can do about it, so let's have a drink. Mine's a double, if you're buying. Thank *you*. And a packet of nuts. Her left bosom is nearly uncovered, eh? Two more packets, then!" (Pratchett, *Small Gods*: 167)

Again, this satirizing of legendary figures humanizes them, and makes them seem *real*. Surely the great Greek philosophers had a sense of humor, or got drunk, or said stupid things, but these things are not recorded and are edited out of history as trivia, so legends represent abstract qualities rather than human realities. The three columned table above is not entirely accurate because historical figures often become inseparable from fictional characters as legends grow and alter. Historical figures often become nothing other than symbols in a semiotic system of beliefs, Leonardo Da Vinci for example representing genius, Machiavelli, cunning, Socrates, the ascetic search for truth. The once real people, displayed as real in the Discworld, become icons, focal points of popular belief, not personalities but arbitrary signs. Terry Pratchett manages to subvert this dehumanizing archetyping, by showing that the symbols are people and not the icons that they become through belief.

Another major feature of Pratchett's Discworld is the approximate historical era that it represents. Unlike some other modern fantasies, notably Tolkien and Lewis, the Discworld is not an entirely agrarian or pastoral society, but is nearer to a society at the beginning of the industrial revolution (of course, with this being a secondary world, the industrial revolution and the renaissance seem to be occurring simultaneously). The Disc is shown at the beginning of a turbulent process of modernization, and since the first Discworld book readers have been confronted with the Disc version of the cinema, the record, the submarine, the rifle, the camera, the computer and the theater, just to mention a few. The Disc is not a world in stasis, and the inventions that are introduced are *not* seen as abominations upon a natural way of living (as the modernization of the hobbit's barrow is in *The Lord of the Rings*) but is instead seen as part of life. Things change in the real world, and in the Discworld, but what remains constant are the people.

As noted in Section 2, the picaresque and its close relation, the *bildungsroman*, are often found in the fantasy genre. However, although the picaresque is a common form within Pratchett's work, the way in which the picaresque is used resembles closely the Bakhtinian concept of the Carnivalesque.

> The typical plot of the carnivalized narrative is that of a picaresque adventure-story in which the picaro seeks not social and economic advancement, or not only that, but answers to "ultimate questions." This philosophical pursuit of ultimate questions leads the picaro to the very limits of his world, or even beyond them. He visits heaven, hell, or other planets, and engages in "threshold dialogue" with inhabitants of these worlds. Testing the limits of human experience he experiments with extreme states of mind and body—hallucination, madness, sexual excess—and deliberately violates social norms through scandalous or criminal behavior. (McHale 1991: 172)

This definition encapsulates the picaresques of the Discworld, particularly the experiences of Rincewind in the Rincewind series (categorized above). Rincewind has been over the edge of the Disc, has visited Hell, the abode of Death, the "dungeon dimension," traveled through time, dimensions, and experienced hallucination and madness. *Witches Abroad* has a dénouement set in the midst of a carnival that takes place in the Disc equivalent of New Orleans, and parodies of official ceremonies that are "essential to popular carnival" (McHale: 174) occur in every novel in the Discworld series. Whereas traditional secondary world fantasies may utilize the picaresque (for example, *The Hobbit*), Pratchett's world is a world of the carnivalesque, once again demonstrating the heteroglossia of the Discworld.

We have seen above the ways in which Pratchett subverts the fantasy genre. However, it is equally interesting that some of the major features of the fantasy genre are still conformed to. One feature of the Discworld series is its reliance on happy endings, utilizing *deus ex machina* type interventions required to make the story conclude happily. This makes the Discworld series closer to fairy tale than myth, because as Bettelheim and Tolkien aver, fairy tales must end happily, or they are not "true" fairy tales (Bettelheim 1976: 143). And, the *deus ex machina* type of intervention is common in myth and fairy tales. Motifs such as an old woman whom the hero is kind to being a witch or god in disguise and rewarding the hero by coming to his aid are common in fairy tale, and it is this kind of symbolic exchange that is often the cause of these dramatic reversal of fortunes. For example, Rincewind rescues a frog from falling over the edge of the world in *The Color of Magic*, but as a reward for rescuing the frog, the Lady (Disc goddess of luck) allows the heroes to escape from incarceration and impending sacrifice. Like the fairy tale, the Discworld series always ends happily and always has a linear plot, it maps out a cohesive secondary world, and is narrated by an external, omniscient narrator. Pratchett conforms to traditional methods of storytelling, but what is questioned in the Discworld is the meaning of these stories, and the "truth" that stories tell.

As this brief analysis has demonstrated, the Discworld is not the nostalgic, simplistic world common to fantasy tales but a world that subverts the possibility of thinking of any world in such simplistic terms. It is this complexity that allows Pratchett to include such contradictions as a cowardly hero into his narratives. The nostalgia for "mythical" heroes is overturned completely. The secondary world of Pratchett, far from simplifying the chaos and the gray areas between good and evil, thrives on these ambiguities and brings the ambiguity of modern life into a genre that for too long has relied on simplistic allegory and myth.

THE FANTASY HERO AND THE DISC HERO

Similarities between the genre of fantasy and the fairy tale are noted above. Pratchett's Discworld, however, although incorporating folklore creatures and belief directly from fairytales, works to subvert the simplicity of the fairy tale through various means. One particularly important way in which this is achieved is through the treatment of the "hero" in the Discworld series.

The hero normally occupies a major place within the genre of fantasy; indeed certain types of fantasy are known as "heroic fantasy" due to the importance of a central character. However, in the Discworld series there is rarely a single hero—even in the Rincewind series there are usually more than three major protagonists—each of whose interaction plays a vital part in the resolution of the plot. Also, the heroes of the Disc are remarkable in their non-conformity to heroic archetypes; women on the Disc are as likely to be the ones doing the rescuing as to be the subject of the rescue. An archetype of traditional heroic concepts does not exist on the Disc without some degree of subversion. Because the Discworld is situated on a fictional level that incorporates and subverts fairy tale, mythical, and contemporary novelistic ideas of the role of the hero, the heroic archetypes subverted are derived in part from all three planes of fiction.

The role of the hero in myth or folk and fairy tales is often analyzed psychoanalytically. Joseph Campbell in *The Hero With A Thousand Faces* (1968) defines the role of the hero in myth as representing the individual's submission to his community's laws and customs. Symbolic acts such as being swallowed by a whale represent the individual subsuming any ideas of individuality for the good of the community and losing individual identity or narcissistic self concern to become truly of the community.

Bruno Bettelheim (1976: 57-58) considers the function of the hero in the fairy tale as a cipher, to be identified with by readers so that they can vicariously experience the symbolic tribulations of the fairy tale protagonist. The trials and tribulations of the fairy tale hero are psychoanalytically symbolic, and Bettelheim identifies fairy tale motifs such as the slaying of giants as vicarious identification derived from a fantasy fulfillment of the oedipal desire (the giant representing the father), affecting a catharsis of any oedipal anxiety felt by the listener and defusing these desires.

In both of these analyses little attention is paid to "heroic qualities." The hero does not have a complex personality or individual characteristics—the folklore hero has a thousand faces because the folk tale refuses to identify individuality. This is in part due to the traditional oral medium of the folk tale. Oral recitation means each folk tale is amorphous and ever-changing, every permutation is unique, and because details are never textualized or written down, there is little scope or desire for giving the hero of a folk tale individuality. The folklore hero is not an individual but a function, personality is not as important as deeds, and the lack of description allows listeners to easily identify with the role of hero. However, this kind of hero does not fit well within a written genre like the novel. It is hard to fill 200 or more pages with the exploits of a hero without this hero having *some* individuality. As Bakhtin notes in *Epic and Novel*, the novelistic hero stems from the ideology of the individual that took root during the renaissance, indicated by the increase in self-portraiture and individualistic fictional heroes typified by Shakespeare's Hamlet and Macbeth. The Discworld may be linked to the traditional fantastic worlds of myth, folk tale and legend, but the medium and society in which it is written necessitates the hero becoming more than a blank space in the text into which the readers project themselves.

Bakhtin notes that some mythical characters are individuals rather than ciphers; legendary figures like Odysseus define both the character presented, and the reader's response to that character. Bakhtin argues that we cannot empathize with such "epic heroes" because their exploits are already known by the audience and they are presented as legends rather than humans. We cannot empathize with Odysseus because we know his fate already; this is the reason why Homer is able to finish the story of the *Iliad* before its expected conclusion, the sack of Troy. Bakhtin calls this alienation "epic distance."

However, some fantasists avoid the problem of "epic distance" by the very expedient of creating a secondary world. The heroes of Tolkien's Middle Earth cycle are very much of the traditional mythical world—and yet we are able to empathize with them because we do not know their fates. We may be versed in the legends of our own world, thus distancing us from *our* world's mythical heroes, but we are ignorant about the legends of the secondary world. Tolkien is therefore able to introduce mythemes from Arthurian legend, but still avoid the empathy-killing "epic distance" that would lessen the audience response to a straight retelling of the Arthurian mythology. The heroes of Middle Earth—the Striders, the Frodos and the Gandalfs—recall nostalgically the heroic archetypes of Anglo-Saxon, Norse and Greek mythology, but avoid "epic distance" by obscuring their mythical derivation behind unfamiliar names and places.

The protagonist-heroes[14] that we encounter in the Discworld do not conform to either the mythical or fairy tale model or function. They are neither martyrs undertaking symbolic self-negating heroic acts to save their community nor ciphers with which to vicariously identify; hero characters of the Disc are all endowed with their own characteristics and individuality. They are, in fact, closer to novelistic heroes of the kind lauded by Bakhtin, and it is the refusal of Pratchett to allow his heroes to become "epic heroes" that makes identification with them possible. Pratchett refuses to allow heroic archetypes to thrive in the Discworld without being subverted, and thus we are led to the paradoxical fact that the heroes of the Discworld are rarely heroic.

The traditional heroic concept has a difficult place in contemporary fiction. In common parlance the chief protagonist of any work of fiction is described as a hero, whether they display heroic qualities or not. But due to the fantasy genre's derivation from myth and folk tale, the generic expectations of a fantasy audience are for these archetypal sword-carrying heroes. The nostalgia inherent in the fantasy genre, exemplified by Tolkien's longing for an idealized pastoral past, has meant that the "epic hero" has survived in the fantasy genre, even though it has died out in other contemporary popular genres. This idealistic concept is precisely what Pratchett successfully subverts in the Discworld series.

In the above paragraph I use the phrase "heroic qualities," but this phrase must be qualified by an explanation. Even today the epic Homeric definition of heroism seems to survive, as a term that describes characters (invariably male) excellent in the spheres of both debate and action (Rieux, E.V (trans.): 25). The *Oxford English Dictionary* neatly encapsulates this classical definition with:

> 1 a. A person noted or admired for courage, outstanding achievements, nobility etc. (Newton a hero of science) b. a great warrior. 2 the chief male character in a poem, play story, etc.

Note that definition (b) seems overwhelmingly anachronistic if we attempt to relate it to a contemporary context. Perhaps due to the horror of modern mechanized warfare, it is hard to think of a single modern "hero" who gained fame through being a "great warrior." Perhaps sometime in the 19th century, or in the fields above Europe in the air conflict during WWI where a bizarre chivalric code reigned,[15] but if one attempts to pinpoint a hero from recent conflicts, then considerable difficulty ensues. Heroes from the war in Vietnam? From Iraq or Libya? It seems, for reasons that I will elaborate later, that the definition of hero has already changed somewhat from the dictionary definition, which certainly describes the conception of heroism of the ancient Greeks.[16]

If we examine the above *OED* definition (1a), another question we have to consider is *who* it is that admires this person? The very definition of the term hero is something that is determined by a social context. Thomas Carlyle in *On Heroes and Hero Worship* delineates 6 classes of heroic types: the hero as divinity, as prophet, as poet, as priest, as man of letters and as king. This in itself indicates the subjectivity of the term hero—Carlyle betrays his historical era and societal status by precluding the possibility of a hero being a common man.

If the perception of what is heroic is determined by social context then heroes are exemplars of the thoughts and ideology of the masses. By realizing that heroism is not an eternal truth or concept but a temporary sociological construction, the interplay between a society and its heroes becomes obvious. For example, the heroes we retrospectively associate with the turbulent 1960s were rebellious and confrontational: James Dean and Marlon Brando epitomized the rebellious hero in Hollywood films, Kesey and Kerouac wrote about a similar rebellious ideal in novels and celebrities from John Lennon to Martin Luther King were admired for their desire for change. These people were not seen as heroes by the majority of people at the time of their activities, which allows us to see that the one constant that can be seen in the definition of "hero" is its very inconsistency across both geographical and temporal boundaries. In *Play up and Play the Game* (1973) Patrick Howarth describes the dominance of a particular type of hero in English fiction during the 19th and early 20th century, whom he terms "Newbolt man" after the poet, Sir Henry Newbolt:

> The ideal of this species [Newbolt man] was both happily and reverently described, appropriately enough, in a book entitled *Clifton School Days* by O.F Christie:
>
>> To be in all things decent, orderly, self-mastering; in action to follow up the coolest common sense with the most unflinching endurance; in public affairs to be devoted as a matter of course, self-sacrificing without any appearance of enthusiasm: on all social occasions—except the regular Saturnalia—to play the Horatian man of the world, the Gentleman after the high Roman fashion, making a fine art, almost a religion of Stoicism. (Howarth 1973: 14)

But this type of hero is one that was in recession in 20th century fiction as Howarth notes, "With... new fashions, new philosophies, new taboos, Newbolt man clearly faced a struggle for survival" (Howarth: 167). Changes in the hero "types" over time highlight the subjective and fluctuating definition of what is thought of as heroic, which is in turn affected by the society in which the text is produced.

Overwhelmingly aware of the subjective nature and artificiality of heroism, Pratchett subverts the fantasy genre's classicist heroic conventions most effectively and consistently with Rincewind. As noted above, most Discworld novels have an ensemble group of protagonists; for example, in the Granny Weatherwax series, although Granny Weatherwax is the major protagonist, the plot also closely follows the adventures of the other witches, and any minor protagonists instrumental to the plot. The City watch series often concentrates simultaneously on the exploits of the hero Sam Vimes, Captain Carrot, Angua, Sergeant Detritus, Corporal Nobby Nobs, Sgt. Fred Colon *and* the Patrician. The Rincewind books however are much more intensely focused on the deeds and character of Rincewind,[17] who is, if anything, a reverse hero. This seemingly oxymoronic definition is possible due to the identification of a "hero" as the main character of a narrative, rather than someone who has certain heroic codes, and also because Rincewind may be an inept coward, but he does manage to save the world several times, an act suitable for heroic status if ever there was one. He may not be the heroic "type" but his status as a hero is affirmed both by his position as protagonist and defined by his actions.

Although Rincewind does not correspond to the conventional "type," he experiences the conventional "adventures and trials" of the hero as detailed in Campbell's *The Hero with A Thousand Faces* or Propp's *Morphology of the Folk Tale*. For Propp, characters are defined by their functions, or their place in the narrative. For example, the donor and the villain are given their names by the narrative functions they perform. By examining Rincewind's actions in a similar manner, we see that Rincewind *is* a hero, by the acts he performs (saving the world is a giveaway) although his character is not of the "questing" self-subsuming stereotype. Rincewind's main characteristics are his ineptitude and cowardliness, but despite his cynicism and nihilistic belief in self-preservation, he nevertheless performs several acts of great courage. In *The Light Fantastic* he fights, bare fisted, a chthonic Lovecraftian many-tentacled demon, in *Sourcery* he attempts to fight the most powerful wizard in the universe using only a half-brick wrapped in a sock. This adds another paradoxical layer to the type of hero that Rincewind represents: he is fundamentally a coward, but a coward capable of performing extraordinary heroic acts.

Pratchett *encourages* us to parallel the reverse-heroic odyssey of Rincewind with that of Homer's Odysseus. These parallels are illustrated below, beginning with both character's "thrown-ness," they are not in control of their own destinies, and they do not choose adventure, but have it thrust upon them:

> For Homer, Odysseus is driven, helpless and against his will, during his travels.... True, he does not need to explore the Cyclops' island, but it is hardly in a spirit of objective research that he visits it (he wants guest gifts and food.) He listens to the song of the Sirens because he is going that way anyway and Circe has told him how to do it. Nor does he dismiss Aeolus' offer of a wind to take him straight home with protestations about his anthropological intents. (p.xlviii Jones, Peter V., in "Introduction": *The Odyssey* trans. E.V.Rieu)

Like Rincewind, Odysseus relies on cunning rather than brawn to succeed in his goal (staying alive). The Rincewind/Odysseus analogy is explicitly sanctioned by the author in *Eric*, where we learn that Rincewind is a direct descendant of the Discworld's equivalent of Odysseus, Laveolus. Also, in *The Color of Magic*, Rincewind is aided by one god[18] (the Lady, the Disc goddess of luck) and opposed by another (Fate) much as Odysseus is supported by Athena and opposed by Poseidon. This also leads to some interesting parallels. Fate's grudge against Rincewind and Twoflower—due to their blinding of Bel-Shamharoth, a favorite of Fate's—is equivalent to Poseidon's opposition of Odysseus due to his blinding of his son, the Cyclops Polyphemus. The Odyssey parallel is also directly included in the narration of *The Light Fantastic* where the motifs of Homer's *Iliad* and *Odyssey* are parodied:

> Mention has already been made of an attempt to inject a little honesty into reporting on the Disc, and how poets and bards were banned on pain of—well, pain—from going on about babbling brooks and rosy-fingered dawn and could only say, for example, that a face had

launched a thousand ships if they were able to produce certified dockyard accounts. (Pratchett, *The Light Fantastic: 133*)

The stereotype of the conventional hero, on the other hand, is mocked in Pratchett's work. Take as an example this conversation, involving Twoflower and Hrun the barbarian, a man Twoflower sees as a hero:

> "What happens next?" asked Twoflower.
> Hrun screwed a finger in his ear and inspected it absently.
> "Oh," he said, "I expect in a minute the door will be flung back and I'll be dragged off to some sort of temple arena where I'll fight maybe a couple of giant spiders and an eight-foot slave from the jungles of Klatch and then I'll rescue some kind of a princess from the altar and then kill off a few guards or whatever and then this girl will show me the secret passage out of the place and we'll liberate a couple of horses and escape with the treasure."
> "All that?" said Twoflower.
> "Usually." (Pratchett, *The Color of Magic:* 174)

Not only is Hrun's life seen here as a routine, much like a "regular job," but there is a complete lack of heroic motivation from a moral sense. Hrun does not rescue "some kind of a princess" because he believes in saving innocents and has no moral qualms about killing a slave or guards. The questing hero's search for adventure and reward is seen as completely immoral, in that it has become a routine and Hrun does not question the absurdity of his position in a way that Rincewind does. The archetype of heroism (the questing hero) is subverted, and if anything this reminds us that Odysseus's trials, like Rincewind's, were not voluntary, and his exile was not self-imposed as later versions (most notably Tennyson's "Ulysses") have suggested.

The subversion of the classical concept of the hero that runs through Discworld is not an isolated strand of anti-heroic thought. Like any other text, a literary fantasy is produced within, and determined by, its social context. Disenchantment with the classical concept of heroism was endemic to western society throughout the 20th century and often related to existential awareness:

> The decay of traditional Christianity as a unifying force in the life of Western man, whether it be mourned, celebrated, or merely acquiesced to, cannot be ignored. Since the death of the Genteel Tradition the theme of the exiled individual in a meaningless universe—a universe in which precepts of religious orthodoxy seem increasingly less relevant—has challenged the imagination of... writers with an almost overwhelming urgency. (Galloway 1966: 1)

It is this light in which we are invited to look at Rincewind. He is a character who is overwhelmingly aware of the absurdity of his universe, of his mortality, and of life. He is a modern hero with an existential awareness and a passion for life that Camus would have approved of—and his constant battle for life, and not for "higher" motivation, is precisely what draws a modern audience towards him. Like Yossarian in *Catch 22*, Rincewind is an everyman figure precisely because of his existential angst and awareness. The fairy tale consequence of the hero being a cipher is subverted, but so too is the epic distance and the convention that "heroes" are the only ones capable of saving the world.

I have shown how Pratchett subverts the heroic archetype by refusing to allow an archetype of heroism to exist unsubverted in the Discworld, but he also draws attention to the social construction of heroes. The reader, with privileged access to Rincewind's thoughts, knows that he is anything but a "hero"—however, he is constantly perceived as such by societies whose preconceptions have been formed by ancient legends (as in *Interesting Times*). Once again a clash of discourses and paradigms creates a misalignment between our preconceptions of what a hero should be (self subsuming, courageous, etc.) and other, incompatible discourse models (psychological realism, individuality).

Rincewind as an anti-hero highlights the social and textual construction of heroism. A hero is only a hero if a narrative is constructed around their deeds, be it in a newspaper, rumor, biography or history book. This is demonstrated in a passage in which Rincewind is faced with expulsion for impersonating a wizard:

> "...since you haven't passed any exams or performed," Ridcully raised his voice slightly, "*any services of great benefit to magic*, I'm afraid I shall have to instruct the bledlows to fetch some rope and—"
> "Er. I think I may have saved the world a couple of times," said Rincewind. "Does that help?"
> "Did anyone from the University see you do it?"
> "No, I don't think so."
> Ridcully shook his head. (Pratchett, *Interesting Times*: 43)

Rincewind is perceived as a Wizard in the Counterweight continent in *Interesting Times* precisely because of a manuscript inaccurately describing him as a great and puissant wizard circulating the country (and written by his erstwhile travelling partner, Twoflower) and because of legends that predict the coming of a great wizard. Rincewind is seen as a hero by the people of the Counterweight continent because he slots into a pre-existing narrative. But in Ankh Morpork, where wizards are common, he does not fit into a narrative of heroism and therefore is not perceived as one. After the normally sedate and academic wizards of

Unseen University nearly cause the end of the world in *Sourcery*, they later suppress any idea of Rincewind as a hero because it reminds them of their own past mistakes:

> The bursar was referring obliquely to the difficult occasion when the University had very nearly caused the end of the world, and would in fact have done so had it not been for a chain of events involving Rincewind, a magic carpet and a half-brick in a sock. (See *Sourcery*.) The whole affair was very embarrassing to wizards, as it always is to people who find out afterwards that they were on the wrong side all along, and it was remarkable how many of the University's senior staff were now adamant that at the time they had been off sick, visiting their aunt, or doing research with the door locked while humming loudly and had had no idea of what was going on outside. There had been some desultory talk about putting up a statue to Rincewind but, by the curious alchemy that tends to apply in these sensitive issues, this quickly became a plaque, then a note on the Roll of Honor, and finally a motion of censure for being improperly dressed. (Pratchett, *Eric*: 16)

These examples show the concept of heroism is one that is created through language. Heroes are created through narrative—and it is for this reason that the character of Rincewind is subversive. He highlights a clash between the two definitions of heroism that we encountered earlier; between a definition that requires a hero to be admired or to be a great warrior and the indiscriminate and universal hero as "the chief male character" by highlighting that the definition that calls the hero "the chief male character" underlies the one that needs "heroic characteristics."

The concept of the "hero with a thousand faces" is not the only concept parodied by the Discworld, and indeed the extensive use of parody within Pratchett's work helps us situate it in a postmodern context.

PRATCHETT, PARODY AND POSTMODERNISM

Pratchett makes extensive use of parody throughout the Discworld series, alerting the reader to the generic norms that are being subverted. This self-reflexive, knowing, style of writing is a hallmark of contemporary fiction, particularly of the school that is known as the postmodern:

> Parody is a perfect postmodern form, in some senses, for it paradoxically both incorporates and challenges what it challenges. It also forces a reconsideration of the idea of origin or originality that is compatible with other postmodern interrogations of liberal humanist assumptions. (Hutcheon [1988] 1999: 11)

The use of parody in a genre that is often seen as "trash fiction" is a major feature of postmodern writing:

> One of the contradictions of postmodernism... is that it does indeed "close that gap" that Leslie Fiedler (1975) saw between high and low art forms, and it does so through the ironizing of both. Think of the ironic mixtures of religious history and the detective story in *The Name of the Rose* or the war documentary and science fiction in *Slaughterhouse-Five*....
>
> Postmodernism is both academic and popular, elitist and accessible. (Hutcheon: 44)

Both observations are reflected in the Discworld series: *Wyrd Sisters* is a parodic reinterpretation of Shakespeare's *Macbeth*, *Lords and Ladies* parodies *A Midsummer Night's Dream* (itself a comic fantasy), *Eric* of *Faust, Dr. Faustus* and Dante's *Inferno*. Consider the following quotation in relation to these "reinterpretations" of highbrow canonical texts:

> ...where modernist thought of itself as a last ditch attempt to shore up, like Eliot's *Fisher King*, the ruins of western culture, postmodernists often gleefully accept its demise and plunder its remains for their artistic materials. Andy Warhol's multiple images of Marilyn Monroe and Kathy Acker's re-writing of Cervantes' *Don Quixote* are representative of the postmodernist trend toward to *bricolage*, the use of the bits and pieces of older artifacts to produce a new, if not "original," work of art, a work which blurs the traditional distinctions between the old and the new even as it blurs those between high and low art. (Keep and McLaughlin 1995)

The use of parody in the fantasy genre causes the text to become "double distanced." As I have shown earlier, fantasy *implies* the real by the absence of the real. Instead of reading marvelous texts with our everyday, realistic expectations, we assume a "secondary belief" which makes us consciously aware of the differences between fantasy and real life. Similarly, parody relies on the reader having foreknowledge of generic expectations and then sending up these conventions. For someone to "get" the joke they must recognize the generic conventions being subverted. This in itself necessitates a very self-conscious style, typified in the following extract.

> Above the noise of the river and the occasional drip of water from the ceiling they could all hear, now, the steady slosh-slosh of another craft heading towards them.
>
> "Someone's following us!" hissed Magrat.

Two pale glows appeared at the edge of the lamplight. Eventually they turned out to be the eyes of a small gray creature, vaguely froglike, paddling towards them on a log.

It reached the boat. Long clammy fingers grabbed the side, and a lugubrious face rose level with Nanny Ogg's.

" 'ullo," it said. "It'sss my birthday."

All three of them stared at if for a while. Then Granny Weatherwax picked up an oar and hit it firmly over the head. There was a splash, and a distant cursing.

"Horrible little bugger," said Granny as they rowed on. "Looked like a troublemaker to me."

"Yeah," said Nanny Ogg. "It's the slimy ones you have to watch out for."

"I wonder what he wanted?" said Magrat. (Pratchett, *Witches Abroad*: 58-59)

This extract relies on the reader's experience of the fantasy genre, namely by transporting the character Gollum from Tolkien's *The Hobbit* and *Lord of the Rings* trilogy. The reader must not only recognize Gollum by his description, trademark hissing speech and idiomatic reference to a "birthday present" (his name for the ring that forms the story of Tolkien's Rings trilogy), but also note the way that he is easily and bathetically disposed of, and compare this to Tolkien's insidious Gollum who dogs the heroes throughout the entire *Lord Of The Rings* trilogy, and is impossible to shake off. The range of parody utilized throughout the Discworld series is not confined to its fantasy predecessors. Although Tolkien, Le Guin, and Lovecraft are parodied, so is "high" culture (Chekov, Shakespeare, Coleridge, Goethe, Dante, Milton) and low or popular culture (movies, popular music, etc.). The depth and frequency of parody within the Discworld series is indeed so extensive that an online compendium of the more elusive parodic allusions exists[19]—and highlights the range and diversity of allusion in the Discworld with subjects from quantum science to ancient history, from the Bible to *Gone with the Wind*.

The use of parody is representative of the intertextuality of postmodernist fiction. By incorporating events familiar from other texts into the narrative, Pratchett highlights the dependence of the Discworld, and its humor, on the subversion and reappropriation of the texts that came before it. Like all parody, it "forces a reconsideration of the idea of origin or originality that is compatible with other postmodern interrogations of liberal humanist assumptions" (Hutcheon: 11). Consider the following extract in the light of the Barthesian view of texts as "a multi-dimensional space in which a variety of writings, none of them original, blend and clash" and Barthes' view of texts as "a tissue of quotations drawn from the innumerable centers of culture":

> All books are tenuously connected through L-Space and therefore, the content of any book ever written or *yet to be written* may, in the right circumstances, be deduced from a sufficiently close study of books already in existence. Future books exist *in potentia* as it were, in the same way that a sufficiently detailed study of a handful of primal ooze will eventually hint at the future existence of prawn crackers.
> (Pratchett, *The Last Continent*: 18)

This extract openly questions any liberal humanist assumption of fiction as a work of individual creation, and is a self-conscious comment upon Pratchett's own works, of the kind not uncommon in metafictive novels. As Eco said of *The Name of the Rose*, "I discovered what writers have always known (and have told us again and again): books always speak of other books, and every story tells a story that has already been told" (Hutcheon: 128).

Any work belonging to the genre of traditional fantasy writing would be hard pressed to find itself included in Hutcheon's definition of the postmodern, which is mostly concerned with "historiographic metafiction," or works that use and abuse the notion of a scientific, objective history. By definition there is no way that traditional fantasy literature *can* belong to this historically self-aware school, as the secondary world type of literature concerns itself with events set in other worlds or dimensions and therefore with their own histories.[20] This is unlike science fiction which, although often set in a futuristic secondary or parallel world, can use the device of time or dimensional travel to reinterpret historical events, as in Vonnegut's *Slaughterhouse Five*. The epistemological problem of the unknowability of history is a major theme of postmodern writing to be found in Swift's *Waterland* or Atwood's *The Robber Bride* and *The Handmaid's Tale*, or Salman Rushdie's *Shame* and *Midnight's Children*. This theme is also present in Pratchett's fiction, and Pratchett cleverly overcomes the barrier of a secondary world not being our own by incorporating and then subverting concepts of history that are relevant to the Disc, his secondary world. For example, in *Small Gods* the manifestation of a Disc God, Om, leads to variations between the canonical religious texts of the Omnian faith and the god's own memory of events. In *Small Gods*, Pratchett toys with ideas of a concrete, objective history in the first few pages:

> Things just happen, one after another. They don't care who knows. But *history*... ah history is different. History has to be observed. Otherwise it's not history. It's just... well, things happening one after another.
> And of course, it has to be controlled. Otherwise it might turn into anything. Because history, contrary to popular theories, *is* kings and dates and battles. And these things have to happen at the right

time. This is difficult. In a chaotic universe there are too many things to go wrong. It's too easy for a general's horse to lose a shoe at the wrong time, or for someone to mishear an order, or for the carrier of the vital message to be waylaid by some men with sticks and a cash flow problem. Then there are wild stories, parasitic growths on the tree of history, trying to bend it their way.

So history has its caretakers.

They live... well, in the nature of things they live wherever they are sent, but their spiritual home is in a hidden valley in the high Ramtops of the Discworld where the books of history are kept.

These aren't books in which the events of the past are pinned like so many butterflies to a cork. These are the books from which history is derived. There are more than twenty thousand of them; each one is ten feet high bound in lead, and the letters are so small that they have to be read with a magnifying glass.

When people say "It is written..." it is written here.

There are fewer metaphors around than people think. (Pratchett, *Small Gods* :6-7)

But the concept of a hitory that is correct, that is "written" before the event, is just as ridiculous as the idea that truth can be pinned onto the page after the event:

"Er... you know the books say that Brutha died and there was a century of terrible warfare?"

"You know my eyesight isn't what it was, Lu-Tze."

"Well... it's not entirely like that now." (Pratchett, *Small Gods*: 377)

Even the prescribed history is just another text. Likewise *Eric* posits similar objections to a "knowable" truth in several sections. For example, the Trojan horse in the Discworld is not, as history suggests, hiding a small army of warriors, but rather a distraction. As the Tsortean army wait around the horse for the army they believe to be concealed within, the Ephebian army sneak around to a rear gate. Devices such as incorporating a history to be subverted, and portraying events that are interpretable to a real world audience to mirror real world narratives of historical events, allow Pratchett's work to question history despite being on a separate plane of reality. If anything, Pratchett's works extend further than standard metafiction, questioning not only historiography but also myth, belief and the textual construction of reality.

Linda Hutcheon's assertion that "historiographic metafictions appear to privilege two modes of narration, both of which problematize the entire notion of subjectivity: multiple points of view (as in Thomas's *The White Hotel*) or an overtly controlling narrator (as in Swift's *Waterland*)"

(Hutcheon 117) would seem to problematize the third person omniscient narration common to secondary world fiction,[21] which Pratchett utilizes. However, the subjectivity that is inherent in multiple viewpoint narration would adversely affect any secondary world fiction by allowing the reader to question the reality of the secondary world itself. Because point of view is the guarantee of subjectivity in narrative (Hutcheon: 160), by avoiding the subjectivity associated with a first person narrator, the third person narration utilized by secondary world fiction allows the reader to maintain secondary belief. Although Pratchett's third person narrator is not as overtly controlling as the narrator of Swift's *Waterland*, the narrative position is nonetheless overtly controlling, often interjecting to discuss techniques that have just been utilized, or questioning descriptions, drawing attention to the textuality and fictionality of the novels. The following appears at a point in which a female mercenary is introduced into the narrative:

> Now there is a tendency at a point like this to look over one's shoulder at the cover artist and start going on at length about leather, thighboots and naked blades.
> Words like "full," "round" and even "pert" creep into the narrative, until the writer has to go and have a cold shower and lie down. (Pratchett, *The Light Fantastic*: 117)

Or discussing a narrative trope that has just been used in *Mort*:

> "You're a wizard, I think there's something you ought to know," said the Princess.
> THERE IS? Said Death.
> [That was a cinematic trick adapted for print. Death wasn't talking to the Princess. He was actually in his study, talking to Mort. But it was quite effective wasn't it? It's probably called a fast dissolve or a crosscut/zoom. Or something. An industry where a senior technician is called a Best Boy might call it anything.] (Pratchett, *Mort*: 116)

Pratchett's incorporation of recognizable historical and legendary characters resembles Menippean satire. It also highlights the fact that these characters have become texts. Legend derives etymologically from "something written down," which Pratchett doesn't hesitate to point out in *Interesting Times*:

> Mr. Saveloy rolled his eyes. "Even you, Cohen? You're all so... *dim witted*!" he snapped. "I don't know why I bother! I mean, look at you! You know what you are? You're legends!"
> The Horde stepped back. No-one had ever seen Teach lose his temper before.

> "From *Legendum,* which means 'something written down'," said Mr. Saveloy. "Books you know. Reading and writing. Which incidentally is as alien to you as the lost city of Ee—"
>
> Truckle's hand went up, a little nervously.
>
> "Actually, I once discovered the Lost City of— "
>
> "Shut up! I'm saying... what was I saying?... yes... you don't read do you? You never learned to read? Then you've wasted half your life. You could have been accumulating pearls of wisdom instead of rather shoddy gems. It's just as well people read about you and don't meet you face to face because, gentlemen, you are a big disappointment!"
>
> Rincewind watched, fascinated, waiting for Mr. Saveloy to have his head cut off. But this didn't seem about to happen. He was possibly too angry to be beheaded.
>
> "What have you actually *done*, gentlemen? And don't tell me about stolen jewels and demon lords. What have you done that's *real*?"
>
> Truckle raised a hand again.
>
> "Well I once killed all four of the—"
>
> "Yes, yes, yes," said Mr. Saveloy. "You killed *this* and you stole *that* and you defeated the giant man-eating avocados of somewhere else, but... it's all... *stuff*. It's just wallpaper, gentlemen! It never changes anything! No-one *cares*! Back in Ankh Morpork I've taught boys who think you are myths. That's what you've achieved. They don't believe you ever really existed. They think someone made you up. You're *stories*, gentlemen. When you die no-one will know, because they think you're already dead." (Pratchett, *Interesting Times* [1994] 1996:249-250)

As well as demonstrating the unknowability of history (history is after all just another text), this extract also illustrates the textual construction of reality. As Saveloy points out, Truckle constructs his identity through stories about what he has done, and his identity as a historical character (a legend) is also textually constructed. By intertextually invoking history and then questioning the validity of history itself, Pratchett also raises ontological questions, which according to McHale typify postmodernism:

> The appearance in fictional worlds of individuals who *have* existed in the real world: people such as Napoleon or Richard Nixon, places such as Paris or Dublin, ideas such as dialectical materialism or quantum mechanics. These are not *reflected* in fiction so much as *incorporated;* they constitute enclaves of ontological difference within the otherwise ontologically homogenous fictional heterocosm. (McHale 1991: 28)

McHale calls these intertextual borrowings "transworld characters" and highlights that these characters cause ontological shocks in the mind of the reader. As Alison Lee points out:

> in the nineteenth-century historical novel, "real" people, places, and events were included or alluded to in order to convince the reader of the "truth" of the fictional ones. In historiographic metafiction, however, the focus has shifted radically. Instead of historical characters and events proving the truth of the fiction they point to the indeterminacy of historical knowledge. (Lee 1990: 52)

McHale's definition of postmodernism is also helpful when interpreting Pratchett's work within a postmodernist context. McHale notes:

> Science fiction, like postmodernist fiction, is governed by the ontological dominant. Indeed, it is perhaps *the* ontological genre *par excellence*. We can think of science fictions as postmodernism's non-canonized or "low art" double, its sister-genre in the same sense that the popular detective thriller is modernist fiction's sister-genre. Darko Suvin has defined the science fiction genre as "literature of cognitive estrangement." By "estrangement" he means very nearly the Russian formalists' *ostranenie*, but a specifically ontological *ostranenie*, confronting the empirical givens of our world with something *not* given, something from outside or beyond it, "a strange newness, a *novum*." By qualifying this estrangement as "cognitive," Suvin means to eliminate purely mythopoeic projections that have no standing in a world-view founded on logic, reason, positive science. (McHale 1991: 59)

Secondary world fantasies share many common features with science fiction, and we can therefore include Pratchett's Discworld within this idea of the postmodern sister genre. The clashing of different worlds, the creation of a heterocosm where diverse discourses and ideologies clash and foreground questions of ontology, defines both science fiction and postmodernism for McHale.

However, science fiction may be the postmodern's sister genre, but that does not mean that it is as highly regarded as the postmodernist works that exist within realist genres. Linda Hutcheon's astute observation that postmodern is the "contradictory phenomenon that uses and abuses, installs and then subverts, the very concept it challenges—be it in literature, painting, sculpture, film, video, dance, television, music, philosophy, aesthetic theory, psychoanalysis, linguistics or historiography" (reprinted in Lee 1990: x) can be used partially to explain this inconsistency. By adopting the fantasy genre Pratchett is, as we have seen, able to subvert many forms of myth, fantasy and belief.

Paradoxically then, Pratchett's work—despite being a subversion of the fantasy genre—is still classifiable as a fantastic world.

Alison Lee and Niall Lucy rightly point out that postmodern fiction deliberately attempts to subvert the "realist" convention, and as we have seen Pratchett's works are, like those of Angela Carter, Salman Rushdie and Kurt Vonnegut, profoundly anti-realist. One of the reasons that the realist convention is such a major target for the postmodernists is its naturalization and its position as the dominant discourse within most fiction; its grip on television and cinema is as apparent as its grip on the novel. As Lee points out, the realist convention is as artificial in origin as any other artistic movement, and bases itself on the assumption that one can use language as a window on the world. This convention is still dominant despite years of literary criticism that destroy the basis of this position. It is also something that Pratchett works consistently to subvert. In the Discworld we become aware of the power of words—after all, magic is changing the world with words (or spells).

CONCLUSION

Silverberg's description of the Disc as a fairground mirror (1999: 3) is a particularly good analogy. The Disc is a world, and a mirror of worlds; but, like all literary representations, it is a distorting mirror. This distortion or defamiliarization is the source of the Discworld's humor and relevance. To find the distortion in fairground mirrors amusing, we must first have preconceptions of what we think we look like from normal mirrors—by showing us in a different light the fairground mirror carnivalizes us and our preconceptions, highlights the arbitrary nature of reality and "normality." The Discworld is a postmodern form of Bakhtin's carnivalesque and, as McHale notes, "Carnivalized genres such as Menippean satire are in this sense official literature's dialectical antithesis and parodic double. Postmodern fiction is the heir of Menippean satire and its most recent avatar" (McHale: 172). The Discworld is a "multi-dimensional space in which a variety of writings, none of them original, blend and clash" (Barthes: 146), and the heteroglossic and carnivalesque nature of the Disc is the basis of its humor, and of its subversive nature.

In interviews, Pratchett frequently refers to *Homo Narrans* or "Storytelling Man," suggesting the fundamental importance of storytelling to the way in which human beings understand the world around them. His work, like all Postmodern literature, is overwhelmingly concerned with the problems of ontology and epistemology and the problems of encapsulating events or "truth" into words, hence the postmodern fascination with fairy tales to be found in Graham Swift, Margaret Atwood, Angela Carter, Kate Atkinson and Salman Rushdie. Pratchett is not usually mentioned in the same breath as these illustrious and respected fabulists, but there are signs that the complexity and breadth of his work may be beginning to be noticed. The novelist, critic and historian Marina Warner notes in her hugely influential study *From the Beast to the Blonde: On Fairy Tales and their Tellers*:

> ...writers for children (and sometimes for adults, too) who draw on fairytale motifs and characters, like Terry Jones, Joan Aitken, Jane Yolen, Tove Jansson, Terry Pratchett, are conjuring up dream worlds as personally idealistic, as politically and socially contentious, and often as spiritually wary and iconoclastic, as their more apparently sophisticated precursors, Erasmus, Voltaire, and Swift. (Warner 1994: 411-412).

A collection of academic essays, *Terry Pratchett: Guilty of Literature*, was published by the Science Fiction Foundation in 2000. In July 2002 Pratchett's novel, *The Amazing Maurice and His Educated Rodents*, won the prestigious Carnegie Medal, the "top prize" for children's literature, first awarded (to Arthur Ransome) in 1936. He was knighted in 2009 "for services to literature," a mark of Pratchett's long overdue recognition. Maybe, just maybe, journalists and critics will recognize that sometimes a writer's work is popular because it is outstanding.

—2008

The author would like to acknowledge the support of Dr. Steven Earnshaw and Dr. Jill LeBihan of Sheffield Hallam University, and the Arts and Humanities Research Board.

NOTES

1. Statistics from *The Times* (London) Saturday July 13, 2002.
2. Especially after Perrault. However, prior to Perrault fairy tales were not seen as "child like" nor was their telling restricted to children. Madame d'Aulnoy's fairy tales, amongst the first to appear in print, were aimed at an intellectual adult audience, and the Grimms' philological research was not intended to become bedside reading for children.

3. See also the Thatcherist ideal of "Victorian family values" as a form of nostalgia used to subvert society, from a very high position of power. Thatcher obviously never read Dickens.

4. "Seemingly incompatible" in my opinion, because of the detective novel's use of rational deduction, and scientific method to investigate crime; as can be seen most obviously in detective fiction such as television's *Quincy* where forensic science is able to reveal hidden truths. Obviously rationalistic and scientific means go out of the window in a fantasy world.

5. Specifically in Africa, Asia, North America and Australia. (See http://www.us.lspace.org/about-terry/interviews/bookshow.html.)

6. Of course, for Bakhtin no utterance is ever entirely monologic, but is orientated towards an anticipated implied response (Wales: 123). However in the Discworld this polyphony or plurality of voices is always foregrounded. In Pratchett's world the discourses of science and fantasy clash within the pages of the novel, whereas Tolkien's scientific justification of the language and genealogy of his fantasy races is confined to the appendices.

7. Rincewind, in fact, is identified in *The Colour of Magic* as a particularly rational character to exist in a fantasy world. He dreams of chemical solutions taking the place of imps and "harnessing the lightning" to create power. Ironically, in the Discworld, Rincewind's own longing for a rational universe marks him out as a romantic dreamer.

8. This is the spelling of the name of the sultan in the Lang edition of *Arabian Nights*, the Burton edition is spelled Shahryar. (See http://www.arabiannights.org/index2.html)

9. And of course, directly mirrors our own world back though fantasy.

10. "The Annotated Pratchett File 7.0a," ed. Breebart, Leo 1996 The L-Space web 20 April 2000. http://www.us.lspace.org/books/apf/index.html

11. Living in a barrel and carrying a lantern.

12. The utterance of the legendary phrase "Gentlemen please don't disturb my circles."

13. Conjecture to life being as of shadows in a cave.

14. This definition of which type of hero we mean is important because there are often traditional type heroes in the Discworld series who act as important secondary characters, but never traditional protagonist-heroes.

15. The "Knights of the Sky" and Air Aces during World War 1 were greatly admired and earned titles much like medieval knights, an obvious example being "The Red Baron."

16. Obviously, the dictionary definition is not definitive (!). But, the semantic connotations thrown up by the word "hero" are (as this essay hopes to prove) in a constant state of change, and to measure change we must look at a fixed point and measure differences. The dictionary definition then is both an adequate marker to begin with, and useful due to the availability of its definition to the public at large.

17. The closest Pratchett comes to a narrative centered upon one character only is in *Small Gods*, where the journeys of Brutha are the main focus. Rincewind is always the centre of the Rincewind books, but there is always a subplot involving other characters. Pratchett is very interested in simultaneity, and rather than use the perspective and time-line of one character he often portrays events that happen at the same time. Again this allows us to see that the world is not saved by the actions of one "hero" but by a complex chain of events involving many people.

18. The Disc gods are simultaneously parodies of the ancient Greek gods and the fantasy fiction of H.P. Lovecraft where Ancient Gods (with unpronounceable names) play games with the lives of mortals.

19. AFP7.0a can be found at http://www.us.lspace.org/books/apf/index.html.

20. Although these histories—especially the history of the Discworld—closely parallel and represent our own.

PRATCHETT WORKS CITED

Pratchett, Terry: *Colour of Magic, The,* Corgi Books [1983] (1996).
— *Eric*, Vista [1991] (1996).
— *Equal Rites*, Corgi Books [1988] (1996).
— *Feet of Clay*, Transworld (1996).
— *Fifth Elephant, The,* Transworld (1999).
— *Guards! Guards!*, Corgi Books [1991] (1996).
— *Hogfather*, Corgi Books [1996] (1997).
— *Interesting Times*, Corgi Books [1995] (1996).
— *Jingo*, Transworld (1997).
— *Last Continent, The,* Transworld (1998).
— *Light Fantastic, The,* Corgi Books [1988] (1996).
— *Lords and Ladies*, Corgi Books [1994] (1996).
— *Maskerade*, Corgi Books [1995] (1996).
— *Men at Arms*, Corgi Books (1996.
— *Mort*, Corgi Books [1989] (1996).
— *Moving Pictures*, Corgi Books [1992] (1996).
— *Pyramids*, Corgi Books [1990] (1996).

— *Reaper Man*, Corgi Books [1992] (1996).
— *Small Gods*, Corgi Books [1995] (1996).
— *Soul Music*, Corgi Books [1994] (1996).
— *Sourcery*, Corgi Books [1989](1996).
— *Witches Abroad*, Corgi Books [1994] (1996).
— *Wyrd Sisters*, Corgi Books [1990] (1996).

CRITICAL WORKS CITED

Bakhtin, M.M.: *The Dialogic Imagination*, University of Texas Press, ed. Holquist, Michael, trans. Caryl, Emerson ([1981]1994).

Barthes, Roland: "The Death of The Author" in *Image–Music–Text* (1977) trans & ed. by Stephen Heath, Fontana (1967).

Bettelheim, Bruno: *The Uses of Enchantment: The Meaning and Importance of Fairy Tales*, Thames and Hudson (1976).

Campbell, Joseph: *The Hero with a Thousand Faces (Second Edition)*, Princeton University Press (1968).

Carlyle, Thomas: *On Heroes and Hero-worship*, Oxford University Press (1968).

Coleridge, Samuel Taylor: *Biographia Literaria* (1817).

Cornwell, Neil: *The Literary Fantastic: From Gothic to Postmodernism*, Harvester Wheatsheaf (1990).

Galloway, David D.: *The Absurd Hero in American fiction*, University of Texas Press (1966).

Howarth, Patrick: *Play Up and Play the Game: The Heroes of Popular Fiction*, Eyre Methuen (1973).

Hutcheon, Linda: *A Poetics of Postmodernism: History, Theory, Fiction*, Routledge (1999).

Jackson, Rosemary: *Fantasy: The Literature of Subversion*, Routledge (1981).

Lee, Alison: *Realism and Power: Postmodern British Fiction*, Routledge (1990).

Lucy, Niall: *Postmodern Literary Theory: An Introduction*, Blackwell (1997).

McCracken, Scott: *Pulp: Reading Popular Fiction* (Manchester University Press, 1998).

McHale, Brian: *Postmodernist Fiction*, Routledge ([1987]1991).

Pratchett, Terry, with Ian Stewart and Jack Cohen: *The Science of the Discworld* (Random House, 1999).

Silverberg, Robert (ed.): *Legends: New Works by the Masters of Modern Fantasy*, Harper Collins, London, 1999).

Swinfen, Ann: *In Defence of Fantasy: A study of the genre in English and American literature since 1945*, Routledge & Kegan Paul (1984).

Todorov, Tzvetan: *The Fantastic: A Structural Approach to a Literary Genre*, Case Western Reserve University Press (1973).

Warner, Marina: *From the Beast to the Blonde: On Fairy Tales and their Tellers*, Chatto & Windus (1994).

A CONVERSATION WITH ROGER ZELAZNY

8TH APRIL, 1978

TALKING WITH TERRY DOWLING AND KEITH CURTIS

It is a grey, overcast Saturday afternoon in April, and we are sitting downstairs in the enormous "games room" of Ron Graham's home in Sydney, directly beneath "the best science fiction library in the world," and before that splendid "bubble" window, modeled on some Heinlein story. Rain is falling in the valley beyond the glass, the tape recorder has just been turned on, and Roger Zelazny is pulling on his pipe.

We catch him midstride, discussing one of his own favorite themes—mythology, though here it is with regard to Wilson Tucker's use of Gilgamesh as an immortal character in the novels *The Time Masters* (1953) and *Time Bomb* (1955), a character who has clear parallels with his own hero of "And Call Me Conrad." We pick up the thread with mention of Tucker's present undertaking—a novel actually set back in Sumerian times, a technical point being made that Tucker does not have to force himself to write....

Dowling/Curtis: *Do you have to force yourself to write?*

Zelazny: Sometimes. I don't have any system. I've said this in the past but it's true. I try to sit down at the typewriter four times a day, even if it's only five minutes, and write three sentences. And if I feel like going on, or if something turns me on, I'll just keep writing till I'm written out. The next time I might just sit down and write the three sentences and nothing else will come. It's static, so I'll just leave it. The next time I come back I'll go through three more. This might go on for a few days, just three sentences at a time. Then suddenly, I find a part I really like and just write and write. It sort of averages out. The short pieces are different.

I usually have the entire image of the story in my head, and I'll just sit down and write it very quickly. That's pretty much the case.

What about themes? Do you find yourself coming back to a particular theme? The mythology angle, for instance?

Yeah, the mythology is kind of a pattern. I'm very taken by mythology. I read it at a very early age and kept on reading it. Before I discovered science fiction I was reading mythology. And from that I got interested in comparative religion and folklore and related subjects. And when I began writing, it was just a fertile area I could use in my stories.

I was saying at the convention in Melbourne that after a time I got typed as a writer of mythological science fiction, and at a convention I'd go to I'd invariably wind up on a panel with the title "Mythology and Science Fiction." I felt a little badly about this, I was getting considered as exclusively that sort of writer. So I intentionally tried to break away from it with things like *Doorways in the Sand* and those detective stories which came out in the book *My Name is Legion*, and other things where I tried to keep the science more central.

But I do find the mythological things are creeping in. I've worked out a book which I thought was just straight science fiction—with everything pretty much explained—and suddenly I got an idea which I thought was kind of neat for working in a mythological angle. I'm really struggling with myself. It would probably be a better book if I include it, but on the other hand I don't always like to keep reverting to it. I think what I'm going to do is vary my output, do some straight science fiction and some straight fantasy that doesn't involve mythology, and composites.

You're really into this idea of relocating the myths, re-setting the archetypes.

Yeah!

It's always seemed to me that one of the most natural areas for an American fantasy author to work in would be American Indian mythology. Or might it be a case of the opposite reaction, of avoiding the obvious? And you've got to feel the attraction of that mythology, haven't you? With your move from Baltimore to Santa Fe, have you considered doing an American Indian mythology? You're in the area.

I have thought of it, yes! I would still like to learn a lot more about it. I'm picking it up as time goes on. And things have occurred to me.

There's the fantasy possibility of the Hopi-Kachinas, for instance. No-one has ever really utilized that.

There's a mystery novel that won the Edgar a few years ago, called *Dancehall of the Dead*, by Tony Hillerman, which involves a Navaho detective working to solve a murder which occurs on the Zuñi reservation. It's run by the Navaho—pardon me—it's the Hopi. I drove through there once and stopped at Second Mesa and bought two kachinas. The Hopis' reservation land is surrounded by the Navahos', but they're very dissimilar in their religions and their personal living habits. The Hopis all live bunched together in apartment-type things, and the Navahos are spread out more. To solve this mystery, the Navaho detective has to learn things about the Hopis, about their religion, that he did not even know himself. And this murder involves the Kachinas, and the Kachinas are supposed to dance beneath this dead lake in a place called the "Dancehall of the Dead." It's a very interesting book. Tony Hillerman has done some other mystery things, but this was the one that he really did well.

Then there's Andre Norton. She is of Indian descent, and she's used this in *Lord of Thunder*. And Phil Farmer also has some Indian ancestry, and he's occasionally referred to it. But it hasn't been central to the stories I'm thinking of. It's been peripheral. The Kickaha stories, for instance....

Is there an attraction for you in American Indian mythology?

Yes, there is. It's still at that very nebulous stage, though. I'm just absorbing material. Something may come of it one day. I don't like to rush things.

How do you see your work as relating to "Literature"?

Well, I see myself as a novelist, period. I mean, the material I work with is what is classified as science fiction and fantasy, and I really don't think about these things when I'm writing. I'm just thinking about telling a story and developing my characters.

Do you ever plan publishing your poetry, aside from your short stories and your novels?

Oh, that would be fun sometime, I guess, to put together a collection.

Do you only write poetry now and again or are you constantly writing it?

Just now and again, really. I've said before, I think that shifting from a novel to a short story mode of thinking is a difficult thing. That's why I haven't written many short stories in recent years. But shifting from either of them to poetry is much more difficult for me.

You had that small volume at Discon, of course. [Poems *(Discon II, 1974)*]

Yeah, that. It has been suggested that I expand that. There are other poems that weren't included in it, and there are some that I have written since which I rather like. I suppose I could put together a small volume, and probably—yeah, I think I'd like to do that some day.

If you had your 'druthers, what would you rather write? What kind of novel?

Ah, now that's hard to say—because I never plan ahead, with the exception of the Amber books which had to proceed in sequence. But I don't really like to know what I'm going to be working on a year in advance. So I just sign blank contracts for books and whatever strikes me as a good idea is what I write about. If I had my 'druthers just writing, I think I'd like to quit doing novels for a year or two and just do short stories. I really like to do short stories, and I've done so few in recent years that I'd just like to go back to them—do a whole bunch of short stories. It may come to pass when I do a couple of books I have under contract that I do something like that for a change. I still tend to think of myself as a short story writer.

How many more Amber novels do you plan? You've got no time limit on it.

The fifth one concludes the story that began in *Nine Princes in Amber*, so that's five books in the series. I don't really have anything more planned just now. It's set up in such a manner, though, that I could come back to it someday and use the surviving characters in a variety of ways if I wanted to write more Amber books. But I'd be starting a new story. I've thought of telling the story from one of the other characters' point of view—or points of view perhaps—I still may do that. I've got the world involved pretty firmly in mind, so it wouldn't be that difficult a thing. Actually, in the series originally, I had intended to tell the different books from the different characters' points of view. It's just that I got taken by Corwin as a character and decided to stay with him. The closest I came was in that section where I had Random narrating an adventure to Corwin and friends, which is in the first person there. I was going to do a little more of that later on with some of the others as a matter of fact, but it didn't fit in with the way I finally conceived it. But the thing is, with so many characters being used in that series, I couldn't really characterize them all the way I wanted to in one book. I wanted to get each one pretty well characterized by the end of the thing, and one way which occurred to me was to shift narrative viewpoints, and I didn't do it. So I tried to draw in other ways of showing them. But it's still possible to do a book from the viewpoint of one of the others.

With so many characters being handled at the one time, how did you keep track of them? By the time you get to the fourth and fifth book, there's been a lot happening beforehand. Did you just rely on memory?

Yes! After the fourth book, I did sit down and ask myself some questions, like, what hasn't been answered so far? And I mean [laughs]—there are some things—if I get enough letters saying you never explained this or that, I suppose I'll have to write another book. But I think I thought of everything I wanted to say, and got it in.

Are you yourself pleased with the fact that it went to five books?

Yes. I would not have liked writing them all in sequence. I had to do other things in between. But yes, I have to admit I enjoyed them.

Of your books, which is your personal favorite?

Hm. Probably *Lord of Light*, if I have to name one. Just because I expended more effort on that book. And I was pleased with the result. It's more ambitious than most of them. I was happy with the way it turned out. I have a sentimental attachment to *This Immortal* because it's my first book. Of the recent ones, I like *Doorways in the Sand* because it's different from the others. I like the way it worked out also.

A lot of people have found Lord of Light *a difficult novel to get into, possibly because Hindu mythology is so formidable.*

Well, I had to edit out a lot of the stuff, of course. There was so much material and I had to be very selective in the parts I was going to use. One of the reasons I chose the Hindus was because it hadn't been done much in science fiction. It seemed that a lot of people liked the Norse and the Celtic mythologies so much. I wanted something a bit different, and I was looking for some sort of philosophical tradition that would justify the employment of some means of reincarnation and transmigration.

It was mentioned in Melbourne that you had said you were collaborating with Jack Vance.

Oh, this was a suggested project. Nothing has come of it. I haven't even spoken with Jack. There was a proposed book that would involve three authors who traded sections of it, with an artist to do books illustrating them subsequently. This was purely a proposal. It's up in the air. It was suggested last summer, and I haven't heard anything more of it since. I'm not collaborating with anyone on anything right now.

How many collaborations is that to date? Just the two? Harlan Ellison and....

Harlan Ellison—that one short story. Phil Dick—the novel. And some years ago I did a few short stories with Danny Proctor. And I suppose as a sort of mixed medium thing you can count *The Illustrated Zelazny* as a collaboration with Gray Morrow. He had his notions of the things he wanted to illustrate and a rough outline of the story, and I bodied it out some more and wrote the continuity. It worked out reasonably well.

Were you pleased with what Morrow did, and actually working with Morrow?

Yes. Actually.... Yeah, I was extremely happy with Morrow's work in the book. I didn't work directly with Morrow for that. I was working through Byron Preiss who put the project together for Baronet Books. He would get our materials from Morrow, look it over and write me a letter incorporating Morrow's suggestions, and so on, and I would respond to this with whatever I felt best and send it back to them. Then he'd talk to Gray. So it was through an intermediary we were doing this. It worked well, though.

Would you like to do more along that line?

Yes, I think I would. It was fun.

On the collaboration with Dick (Deus Irae), *was that through an intermediary or direct with him?*

That was with Phil Dick. We live in different parts of the country, so we didn't really get together to talk it over except once, and that was in '68 at the Baycon. We spent the evening talking about it. Phil had written an essay outline for the entire book. He'd also written the first fifty pages of manuscript, and all I did was I would write a section—I wrote the next section following his—and send it back to him. He looked it over and did a section himself and sent it back to me, and really it didn't seem that it required much discussion. It flowed very naturally as far as I was concerned. I'd just take his work and continue it from there and he did the same with mine. I don't think we really asked each other questions particularly. Each time I've worked with anyone like this before, it's been very different. I guess that's part of the fun of collaborating. It's not something I'd like to do all the time, but every time I've done it, I've learned something, I've learnt the way another person's mind works. My own approach, whenever I do something like this, is to try to learn how the other person thinks, so that I can anticipate him. It's a kind of Stanislavskyan method of writing, I guess [laughs].

Did it work that way with the Harlan Ellison collaboration ("Come to Me Not in Winter's White")?

That was so short that it didn't entail that much effort. It was just one basic idea. I did a section, he did a section, I did a section, and he took it and finished it and it was all over. In very brief sections. So I didn't have to become Harlan Ellison exactly [laughs].

Science fiction as Art. One of the curliest questions of all time. What do you see as the future of science fiction as a whole—as a form of literature? Do you foresee it becoming more and more incorporated into the mainstream? Or do you see a reversal of the present trend whereas they become separated?

I don't think it'll ever be completely joined up. Maybe I'm wrong. My entire experience with it for about thirty years would be of seeing it as a thing apart. It seems in other ways, in some respects, that the mainstream authors are tending to use more and more science fiction notions. But their books aren't really classified as science fiction and I suppose they're not because they're also doing other things. I personally feel that it is going to stay a thing apart, that it will undergo vogues, as it were. I think there will be periods when it's more highly regarded and then it will slip back again. It seems throughout what I've seen of its history that it's been a cyclic pattern—it rises to prominence for a time. Something will set it off briefly, like the space program or, well just recently a couple of good movies that got a lot of attention back in the States, like *Star Wars* and *Close Encounters*—and science fiction books become very popular. Then, of course, everyone will jump on the movie band-wagon and produce a crop of grade-B movies, and they'll sink, and then people will slip back to reading other things. But there's a certain residuum that remains.

I suppose the biggest single thing that's happened in the last decade has been an academic interest in science fiction in the States. I get invitations periodically to speak at different universities and such, and I've learned there are science fiction courses being taught all over. Jack Williamson has counted something like 2000 of them, so it has gotten in, and the Modern Languages Association has this special section on the Science Fiction Research Association with their periodical, *Extrapolation*, so it's got this air of academic respectability that's attached to it. I've heard it argued on both sides that this is a good thing and that this is a bad thing, and some of the arguments are against it. Newer writers may begin writing for an academic market and aiming some of their pieces at satisfying academic criticism, and lose something of its pure quality inasmuch as the writer had basically thought of it as entertainment. On the other hand, I've never felt this way personally, and I've spoken to a lot of other writers who say they never think about that sort of thing and are just writing their stories.

The only thing that would bother me is if anyone were to be forced to read something I had written. That would go against my grain. If you're taking a course and you've got to read Zelazny by Thursday! I sold stories to people who were putting together textbooks involved in science fiction, and I've looked through them to see my stories, and I get to the end and they have a series of questions about what the author is trying to do, and what symbolism it involves, and such, and some of the questions I couldn't answer myself [laughs], and I wrote the stories!

Do you read much outside of your own field? Do you read criticism?

No. Not too much. I've never been that interested in critical appraisals of my work. Most of my reading is outside of science fiction actually. I read about six or seven books at a time, and I read something of each of them every day to keep them all moving. But most of them are non-fiction. I keep one on the physical sciences, one on the life sciences, a history book, other things of the sort. I keep one science fiction book going at all times just to keep abreast of the new things that are happening, and to catch up on some classics that I've missed out on. One work of general fiction....

Do you have favorite science fiction writers?

Ah. Not really. It varies. I mean, I like a lot of the new ones who are coming along. Of the older ones, my tastes are probably pretty much the same as most people who have been reading it for a long time now. Phil Farmer is a favorite of mine. I read most of Heinlein at a fairly early age. And I like Ray Bradbury. Of the newer ones—Ed Bryant, Tom Monteleone, Michael Bishop, George R.R. Martin....

It sounds a bit churlish, but Farmer's Tiers novels—were they in your mind at all when Amber was being written?

Yes! Yes, they were.

Which means that you had to consciously avoid any kind of similarity?

Well I didn't really have to try to avoid that. I couldn't do it quite that way. But one of the things that had occurred to me about the Tiers novels was that I liked the fact that Farmer had these nearly immortal Lords who tested one another, and I was thinking that the family relationships involved with something like that would have been more fun to explore. That's why I dedicated one of the Amber books to Phil Farmer—I told him about it—and possibly why he dedicated the last *World of Tiers* novel to me. There is a relationship, but I was trying to do different things with it. Yes, I'm a great admirer of Farmer's. A very fertile imagination. A fine writer!

Do you ever see yourself as being anything other than a writer?

No. I can't conceive of doing anything else the way I do writing. I can see myself doing something else along with writing. I don't have to write. There are plenty of things to spend my time with.

Were you a science fiction fan before becoming a writer, or vice versa?

I was a fan before I was a writer. I had a few things in fanzines in the early '50s actually. But I'd been reading science fiction before that, and reading fanzines. The first convention I attended was in 1955—the Worldcon in Cleveland. I didn't attend another one for eleven years. We lived too far away.

Did you ever do any fanzine work?

I was assistant editor of a very brief-running fanzine in the early '50s. That's '52 and '53.

How do you feel about the film of Damnation Alley? *No?*

No!

A bad subject?

I was not happy.... I wasn't connected with the production so I don't feel it's a personal failure.

Did they give you a chance to be involved with it?

Not really. They let me read the script a couple of years before it came out. But it was a different script, and it went through numerous revisions after that and I didn't see the final version of it. I think they could have done a better job.

Have there been other approaches made about doing films of your work?

I've got some other options. There's the short story, "The Keys to December." *The Dream Master* is under some option. All of the *Amber* books, there's a possibility there might be an *Amber* movie.

How do you feel about that? Do you think it loses by being a film?

I don't know. The guy had an interesting approach. He thought he might do it the way George MacDonald Fraser did *The Three Musketeers/The Four Musketeers*. You have the one long script for the story, shoot about eight hours, and then edit it down into two or three movies. I'd like to do this.

Would you like to be involved with that? Is that the way your mind goes?

I don't like to get involved with scripts. Unless I had to agree for the contract. And if we did that, used all five *Amber* stories, and they shot the entire thing, made a few movies, and they were successful—if they wanted to do another one, then I would work on a sequel to the existing *Amber* books and work on the script. But I wouldn't really like to do scripts as I understand the process right now.

Other than films, have you been approached to do the Amber *stories in any other medium? Like comics?*

Marvel Comics was interested at one time. But my agent didn't like the agreement and the approach, and they apparently didn't like the alternatives. Nothing ever came of it.

The Morrow-illustrated book can't exactly be called a comic, because it's more than that. Yet, do you yourself want to work in a comic medium?

I wouldn't mind doing that as much as I would movies. With the one I did in mind, I can see that it's not as restrictive as I think film scripts would be. But talking so much with Harlan about how much your work would have changed between composition and its actual appearance, I just don't like to think of my stuff going that route. But a comic is okay. There's just one other person involved and you can work things out with him to your mutual satisfaction.

—1978

(The preceding interview has been presented exactly as it took place—the substantial part of a longer and more relaxed conversation. Editing has been kept to a minimum, used mainly to standardize a three-way exchange into a simple question-and-answer format. The question sequence is as it occurred, determined, alas, by the length of the tape.)

ROGER ZELAZNY'S FORM AND CHAOS PHILOSOPHY

CARL P. YOKE

Roger Zelazny is a writer of such stature that he needs little introduction to science fiction readers. Since the publication of his first story in 1962, he has won three Hugo and three Nebula Awards, received more than twenty nominations for these prizes, won the French Prix Apollo, and been nominated for both the Gandalf and Ditmar Awards. He has published approximately seventy-five stories, articles, and poems, and more than twenty novels. He has been anthologized and re-printed so many times that even he has lost track. His popularity is assured, his place in science fiction history secure.

His work is generally regarded as highly mythic, heavily symbolic, erudite, poetic, and difficult. His themes are immortality, guilt, love, vanity, sacrifice, revenge, power, and suicide. Though his principal characters are almost always near-gods, they are psychologically credible. His plots are often complicated and clever. His Amber novels illustrate this perfectly. As the story unravels, the reader is turned around and around by its revelations.

Certainly this has contributed to his success, as has his ability to create what Theodore Sturgeon called truly memorable characters in his "Introduction" to the short story collection *Four for Tomorrow*. But part of that success is also due to a well conceived philosophical position which encompasses his view of the human condition and provides the conceptual sub-structure for his stories. Zelazny, himself, has labeled it his "form and chaos" philosophy.

In general, this philosophy poses two equal but opposite forces at work in the universe. They interact dynamically and forever, and are reflected in all life-forms. One force is called form, the other, chaos.

Form is best defined as the creative urge, the desire to shape, the compulsion to synthesize. It is the process which takes diverse and disconnected raw materials and moulds them into a new product. It is reflected in all life-forms, in the arts, and in the evolution of ideas and systems. A specific example of form is anabolism, the metabolic process whereby simple substances are synthesized into the complex materials of living tissue. Another is the arrangement of individual sounds to create music.

Chaos is the opposite force. It is the process of tearing down, of analysis, of breaking down complex materials, ideas, or systems, into their simplest components. It is destruction. It is erosion, decay, and aging. A specific example of chaos is catabolism, the metabolic process whereby complex tissues are reduced to their simplest substances. Another is the erosion of rock by wind or water.

Form and chaos underlie all concepts and things of the universe. Everywhere new products are being formed and old ones destroyed. The forces are mutually supportive. Together, they create never-ending cycles of creation and destruction. The decay of a fallen tree, for example, breaks the wood down into simple, microscopic materials which are themselves combined in the creation of new trees and plants. All things reflect this process, and in living things form and chaos operate simultaneously.

Form and chaos exist without any absolute moral value. They are not, in other words, synonymous with good and evil respectively. Those are the judgments of intelligent beings and may be attached to either force, depending upon the point of view and circumstances of the assessor. The destruction of the deicrat system in *Lord of Light*, for example, while good from Sam's point of view is not from the view of the existing gods. Form and chaos are simply two forces at work to avoid stasis, the one intolerable condition in Zelazny's philosophy. By preventing stasis, they create change, and change is an immutable law in Zelazny's universe.

At any particular time in any particular location, one of the forces will be dominant even though both may be operating simultaneously. Though it may appear that a stasis exists, because the balance between them is so equal, it is only that the rate of action has slowed to such a point that determining which force is dominant is impossible. The breadth of interaction or its subtlety may also prevent detection. Free from manipulation by intelligent beings, form and chaos will maintain a rhythm, swinging back and forth endlessly between extremes, but it is clear in Zelazny's work that intelligent beings can influence the duration, degree, and direction of the interaction.

The cycles of creation, destruction, and re-creation are spiral. If one could witness a place where a creation had taken place, see it destroyed, and then recreated, the reformation would be different from the original no matter what measures had been taken to restore the previous condition. Though it might appear identical, subtle differences would exist, which would make it unique. I believe that Zelazny would even agree that a clone would be unique because even though it duplicates the pattern of the original, the materials which comprise it are not the same. Though the pattern might indicate that a molecule of carbon be used at a particular point in the construction of a tissue, the specific molecule used will not be the same one as that of the original. Whether or not this is a significant difference would depend upon particular circumstances.

The rhythm created by the interaction of form and chaos is quite literally universal. Though Zelazny arrived at this idea at an early age, probably as an outgrowth of his own thinking about the relationship between good and evil, his later reading of Havelock Ellis probably helped shape the concept as it eventually appears in "A Rose for Ecclesiastes." Zelazny even alludes to Ellis in his now famous novelette:

> Well now, the dance was the highest art, according to Locar, not to mention Havelock Ellis, and I was about to see how their centuries-dead philosopher felt it should be conducted.[1]

Ellis' thinking about the relationship between rhythm and the dance is best expressed in the following passage from his *The Dance of Life*:

> So it is today. We, too, witness a classico-mathematical Renaissance. It is bringing us a new vision of the universe, but also a new vision of human life. That is why it is necessary to insist upon life as a dance. This is not a mere metaphor. The dance is the rule of number and of rhythm and of measure and of order, of the controlling influence of form, of the subordination of the parts to the whole. This is what a dance is. And these same properties also make up the classic spirit, not only in life, but, still more clearly and definitely in the universe itself. We are strictly correct when we regard not only life but the universe as a dance. For the universe is made up of a certain number of elements, less than a hundred, and the "periodic law" of these elements is metrical. They are ranged, that is to say, not haphazardly, not in groups, but by number, and those of like quality appear at fixed and regular intervals. Thus our world is, even fundamentally, a dance, a single metrical stanza in a poem which will be hidden forever from us, except in so far as the philosophers, who are today even here applying the methods of mathematics, may believe that they have imparted to it the character of objective knowledge.[2]

To Ellis' general idea, Zelazny adds concepts drawn from Rilke. The great German poet agonized for years over his inability to reconcile the antinomies he saw in life before he hit upon the symbols of the rose and the dance as evidence that they sprang from a common source.³ In the dance, he saw not only a symbol of transformation but also a symbol of the rhythm of the universe as generated by the tension created by its eternal oppositions. Peters makes this point clearly in his analysis of Orpheus in "The Sonnets to Orpheus":

> In Orpheus, the "singing god" of the double kingdom [that is, either the light and dark or upper and nether worlds] he [Rilke] had found the symbol for the continuous transformation of the world into rhythmic vibrations; and in the figure of the dancer, both an illustration of that process and the assurance that at the highest level the dichotomy between art and life is resolved.⁴

This revelation led Rilke eventually to the idea that an individual must pursue the course of self-fulfillment rather than self-surrender and that this can best be accomplished by fully achieving one's identity rather than by losing it. He comes to praise the uniqueness of the individual and to value it. Finally, he seeks transcendence-of-self in immanence. For him,

> The figure of the dancer is an illustration of this paradox, for during the ecstasy of the dance the dancer attains both complete self-expression and complete self-surrender. Hence, like Orpheus, the dancer is a mediator; he is an artist who thrusts figures into space and a mystic who experiences pure being. Dancing is both an art and a cult.⁵

Zelazny follows Rilke's lead. For him, the dance becomes the symbol of the rhythm of the universe and the dancer an illustration of complete self-fulfillment within the framework of universal antinomies, represented collectively for him by form and chaos.

As the dancer lives in the closest possible relationship with universal rhythm, Zelazny believes that all men should do likewise. Form and chaos are reflected in man as well as the rhythm they create, and his instinct and intuition will reveal it if he will but trust them. If man can live in harmony with that rhythm, he will achieve self-realization, which will, in turn, bring peace and happiness. Carlton Davits achieves such self-realization in "The Doors of His Face, the Lamps of His Mouth." If man does not, then psychological complexes build up in him which obscure his insight. This is often the case with Zelazny's heroes, and in particular, they suffer from a bad case of vanity. Davits, Charles Render, and Gallinger, all reveal this blockage.

Zelazny also recognizes a kind of conservation of form law in his philosophy. Simply stated, all things once formed, tend to try to preserve themselves by resisting chaos. Examples of this in the natural world are:

the new growth of plants, the continuous generation of certain human tissues such as blood, the regeneration of some animal parts, and plastic memory. Plastic memory is the tendency of plastic products to want to return to their first forms if slightly heated and re-shaped. This idea agrees with a similar concept from Ellis:

> ...I have never seen the same world twice. That, indeed, is but to repeat the Heraclitean saying... that no man bathes twice in the same stream. Yet—and this opposing fact is fully as significant—we really have to accept a continuous stream as constituted in our minds; it flows in the same direction; it coheres in what is more or less the same shape. Much the same may be said of the ever-changing bather whom the stream receives. So that, after all, there is not only variety but also unity. The diversity of the Many is balanced by the stability of the One. That is why life must always be a dance, for that is what a dance is: the perpetual slightly varied movements which are yet always held true to the shape of the whole.[6]

These then are some of the concepts which make up Roger Zelazny's form and chaos philosophy, as well as some of their sources. Though this philosophy underlies all of Zelazny's fiction, it is more explicit in some works than in others. An analysis of how it affects three of his better known pieces of fiction follows.

§

Zelazny's earliest published novelette, "A Rose for Ecclesiastes," establishes what will become a familiar pattern to science fiction readers: mythic quality, an abundance of simile and metaphor, ever-present and often frustrating allusions, Biblical references; the themes of vanity, fertility, and love, and the symbols of the rose and the dance. Under close analysis, it also reveals the form and chaos philosophy as its conceptual sub-structure.

The Martians, individually and collectively, are examples of form carried to the extreme, in fact to the point where they are prevented from saving themselves even when offered a solution.

Betty, another linguist in the party, first makes Gallinger aware of the Martians' highly evolved sense of form when she introduces him to M'Cwyie, matriarch of the society.

> "Uh—" She paused, "Do not forget their Eleven Forms of Politeness and Degree. They take matters of form quite seriously...."

and

"She [M'Cwyie] expects you to observe certain rituals in handling them [the Martian sacred documents], like repeating the sacred words when you turn pages—she will teach you the system."[7]

Gallinger's initial impression of their concern with form is reinforced later when he learns that there are two thousand, two hundred and twenty-four dances of Locar, that each is highly structured, and that Braxa, the story's heroine, knows them all. Still later, the strength of Martian conviction is dramatically illustrated when Braxa, now pregnant, shocks him by announcing her own death:

> "You have read the Book of Locar.... Death was decided, voted upon, and passed, shortly after it appeared in this form. But long before, the followers of Locar knew. They decided it long ago. 'We have done all things,' they said, 'we have seen all things, we have heard and felt all things. The dance was good. Now let it end.'"[8]

Gallinger had just explained that if their child were born normal, it would prove that the Martians could intermarry with Earthmen and that this would save their race by countering the problem of Martian male sterility.

Both Braxa and the unborn child have been condemned to death, however, by the Temple Mothers because the sacred books say that there can be nothing new, that all things have been said, seen, and done. So strong is the Martian pessimism and so tightly controlled is their thinking that it prevents them from growing, from developing, from seizing the solution to their problem.

Neither form nor chaos is permitted to dominate indefinitely in Zelazny's philosophy, however. Sooner or later, the subordinate force will take control, and it is the breaking down of old forms that becomes the essence of the novelette.

As mentioned earlier, typical Zelazny characters reflect both form and chaos since the rhythm of the universe is intimately a part of their make-up. They may be alternately creators or destroyers, or they may be creating in one area while simultaneously destroying in another. Such is the case with both Gallinger and Braxa. Both are creating in the course of the story, but both are also instruments for destroying old forms.

Gallinger is the ultimate force for destroying Martian society, and in this respect he mirrors Sam of *Lord of Light*. He destroys their pessimism by showing them something new, a hydroponically-grown rose. The Martians had never seen a flower before. He mocks the words of Locar, their highest god, by restoring their fertility. Moreover, he shows them a way that their race can avoid imminent doom.

After the chaos that will inevitably come from the destruction of their current values, there will also come re-formation. And once they learn to grow plants, the Martian landscape will burst forth with new life. Thus, while in the very process of destroying, Gallinger is also presenting mechanisms for re-creation.

Braxa, too, possesses both capabilities. By bearing Gallinger's child, she presents the first tangible evidence of the new creation, but she is also the mechanism for the destruction of Gallinger's personality as it exists at the outset of the story.

When he first falls in love with her, Gallinger is extremely vain, choosing to hold himself above his colleagues. When he later finds out that Braxa does not love him, that she never has loved him, that she has only conceived their child out of some misconstrued sense of duty, he is shattered. Because of her actions, however, he learns humility, and that newly-acquired humility will permit him to grow as an individual once the trauma has ended.

Zelazny believes that preoccupation with materialistic or egoistic concerns stunts an individual's healthy mental development, and Gallinger is a specific example of this belief. Because of his pride, he is as static as the Martians. He is bound by the warped "form" of his personality. Like the Martians, the blockage must be removed before healthy growth can begin. For the specific dynamics of his psychology, Zelazny is heavily indebted to Carl Jung.

The central irony of the story emerges from the relationship between Braxa and Gallinger. While both of them produce vast destruction by their actions, that very destruction lays the foundation for an even vaster and more significant creation.

§

In Zelazny's Amber series (*Nine Princes in Amber*, *The Guns of Avalon*, *The Hand of Oberon*, *The Sign of the Unicorn* and *The Courts of Chaos*), he takes us even deeper into the form and chaos philosophy. Not only does it provide the conceptual basis for the novels, it also becomes part of the physical world created for them. More specifically, the universe of the story is a metaphor for the philosophy. Geographically, the limits of that universe are Amber, representing form, and Chaos, representing chaos. They are drawn initially as if they were the opposite poles of a continuum, with the forces which they represent vying for control of the shadowlands that lie between them. But that relationship does not speak to the genesis of order or to the ultimate possibilities that exist for the universe.

These questions are addressed by the Amber novels. Two comments in *The Courts of Chaos* provide part of the answer. The first is made by Dara, daughter of Corwin's brother Benedict, and Lintra, leader of the hellmaids, when she explains why the lords of Chaos were willing to make a pact with Brand, another of Corwin's brothers and arch-villain of the story, despite the possibility of dire consequences:

> Brand was given what he wanted... but he was not trusted. It was feared that once he possessed the power to shape the world as he would, he would not stop with ruling over a revised Amber. He would attempt to extend his dominion over Chaos as well. A weaker Amber was what we desired, so that Chaos would be stronger than it is now—the striking of a new balance, giving us more control over the shadowlands that lie between our two realms. It was realized long ago that the two kingdoms can never be merged, or one destroyed, without also disrupting all the processes that lie in flux between us. Total stasis or complete chaos would be the result. Yet, though it was seen what Brand had in mind, our leaders came to terms with him. It was the best opportunity to present itself in ages.[9]

The second is made by Corwin as he wends his way to Chaos:

> The fact that it was easier for us to take a straight course does not make it the only way. We all pursue it so much of the time, though, that we tend to forget that one can also make progress by going in circles...[10]

It is clear from these statements that short of destroying the universe completely, form and chaos must remain forever opposed and that change will be the product of their interaction because stasis cannot be permitted. It is also clear that the pattern of their interaction is a rhythmic one with a period of form followed by one of chaos, and that followed by a re-creation, and so on. This is what Corwin means by "going in circles," though for Zelazny the proper terminology might be "upward spirals."

As mentioned earlier, however, the Amber novels go one step further than any of Zelazny's other works in amplifying the form and chaos philosophy. Specifically, they pose the ultimate source of all things in the knowable universe as chaos itself. In this belief, Zelazny mirrors both Mesopotamian and Egyptian cosmology.[11] Zelazny does acknowledge that something exists beyond the Amber universe.

Corwin's creation of a parallel universe when he inscribes a new primal pattern near the end of *The Courts of Chaos* and his comment about Oberon going to the "Old Country" (a place defined as being beyond both Amber and Chaos) while he watches his father's funeral procession, make it clear that Zelazny believes that the absolute source of all things, for that matter all possibility, lies beyond human understanding. Zelazny has pushed the philosophical basis of the story back to the "first cause," and in doing so, he recognizes the limits of man's ability to comprehend. Whether that "first cause" proves someday to be a white hole or some other yet-to-be-defined singularity, man will always be locked in by his own limitations.

Though Zelazny makes no attempt to go further, he would agree that the "first cause," whatever it is, contains the seeds for all the possibilities of the universe within it and spews these forth in its initial gush. In terms of the Amber novels, this means that though all things spring from chaos, the possibilities for form pre-exist in them.

Dworkin, mad dwarf, artist, inscriber of the original Pattern, and grandfather of the Amber clan, confirms the nature of things in a prolonged discussion with Corwin, whom he believes to be Oberon. It should be noted that Dworkin's error is a logical one since Oberon is a "shapeshifter" and therefore capable of assuming other forms. He does, in fact, deceive Corwin for quite a long time by pretending to be Ganelon. Dworkin argues that the Primal Pattern ought to be destroyed and the whole process begun again, while Oberon has argued that it ought to be repaired. (The Pattern defines all order in the universe.) Dworkin says:

> "Destroy the Pattern and we destroy Amber—and all of the shadows in polar array about it. Give me leave to destroy myself in the midst of the Pattern and we will obliterate it. Give me leave by giving your word that you will then take the Jewel which contains the essence of order and use it to create a new Pattern, bright and pure, untainted, drawing upon the stuff of your own being while the legions of chaos attempt to distract you on every side. Promise me that and let me end it, for broken as I, am, I would rather die for order than live for it."[12]

This statement supports several axioms that are implemented in the novels:

    1) that form and chaos must remain forever opposed;
    2) that form is created from chaos;
    3) that the conditions for form pre-exist in chaos;
    4) that the possibilities for form exist within the Jewel of Judgment;
    5) that man is one of the devices for implementing form (in this case, it is first Dworkin and then Corwin);
    6) that the oscillation between the two forces is a universal constant.

As far as man himself is concerned, the novels show that he reflects form and chaos because they are part of his basic nature and that he may bring form from chaos by means of will and discipline. In another statement, Dworkin confirms this:

> "I do not know which of your children shed our blood on this spot, if this is what you mean. It was done. Let it go at that. Our darker natures come forth strongly in them. It must be that they are too close to the chaos from which we sprang, growing without the exercises of will we endured in defeating it. I had thought that the ritual of traveling the Pattern might suffice for them. I can think of nothing stronger. Yet it failed. They strike out against everything. They seek to destroy the Pattern itself."[13]

When Corwin creates a parallel universe by inscribing a new primal Pattern, the task is significantly taxing to him, drawing upon all of his will power, all of his discipline, and leaving him so exhausted when the act is completed that Brand can simply walk up to him and take the Jewel of Judgment from him. This is as it should be.

But it must be remembered that Corwin's life, from the moment he woke up on the shadow-Earth until the inscription, has been an exercise designed by his father, Oberon, to prepare him for the Kingship of Amber. Though he eventually decides against it, the mental toughness he developed is that which he needs to inscribe the new Pattern.

Corwin does change in the course of the novels. One of the things he must learn on his journey to maturity is the dual nature of man and how to deal with it. That he successfully accomplishes this task is revealed in a comment he makes on his way to Chaos to deliver the Jewel before the final storm destroys everything. He has encountered a strange girl, very similar to the fairy of "La Belle Dame Sans Merci," who tries to delay him by enchantment. Recognizing and then reflecting on her nature, he compares her to yet another strange enchantress he met earlier when he left Avalon:

> "Yet, I thought of the woman-thing which had trapped me on the black road as I was leaving Avalon. I had gone at first to aid her, succumbed quickly to her unnatural charms—then, when her mask was removed, saw that there was nothing at all behind it.... Still, I have met people who have impressed me favorably at first, people whom I came to hate when I learned what they were like underneath. And sometimes they were like that woman-thing—with nothing really much there. I have found that the mask is often far more acceptable than the alternative. So ... this girl I held to me might really be a monster inside. Probably was. Aren't most of us? I could think of worse ways to go if I wanted to give up at this point. I liked her."[14]

There are, of course, more graphic examples of the monster characteristics in man scattered throughout the novels. Dara and Dworkin both reveal their darker natures. In a scene near the end of *The Guns of Avalon*, Corwin is shocked at Dara's appearance. He has caught up with her just as she is completing her first tracing of the Pattern. He describes his reaction:

> "Yes, it was Dara! Tall and magnificent now. Both beautiful and somehow horrible at the same time. The sight of her tore at the fabric of my mind. Her arms were raised in exultation and an inhuman laughter flowed from her lips. I wanted to look away, yet I could not move. Had I truly held, caressed, made love to—*that*? I was mightily repelled and simultaneously attracted as I had never been before. I could not understand this overwhelming ambivalence."[15]

And in the scene near the beginning of *The Hand of Oberon* where Dworkin mistakes Corwin for Oberon, the conversation breaks off when the mad artist suddenly starts to revert to something from Chaos, "... his features began to flow like melting wax and he somehow seemed larger and longer-limbed than he had been."[16]

The monster exists in all of us, of course, and when Corwin recognizes it in himself he truly begins to achieve maturity. Such self-awareness is displayed in *The Courts of Chaos*. Two comments will illustrate. The first is made to Oberon when Corwin turns down his father's offer of the throne. "My own hands are not clean," he says. The second is made to his sister, Fiona, as Corwin lies exhausted on the battlefield waiting to see if Random can stem the oncoming storm with the Jewel of Judgment. "I have tricked people and I have killed them. I have calculated and I have lost."

In Zelazny's work, in general, men change dramatically under the impact of their experience. This is exactly what happens to Corwin, and in the process of maturation he learns many valuable lessons about human nature. One of them is that good and evil are not nearly as neatly defined as he would have them be, and another is that the basic nature of man is ambiguous. He also learns that good and evil are not synonymous with form and chaos.

To the contrary, Zelazny is very careful to separate one set of ideas from the other by the symbolism of the novels. An examination of two major symbol clusters will clarify this point. The first, representing good, is attached to the unicorn, which is itself identified strongly with Christ. The second, representing evil, is attached to Brand and the devil. There is overwhelming evidence in the novels to support these interpretations.

Without discussing the extensive and complicated evolution of the unicorn symbol, it is sufficient to say that it finally came to be associated with Christ and good.[17] That Zelazny intends for the unicorn to be used in its extrinsic sense is indicated by the fact that he uses that description of it which became associated with Christianity: a pure white animal, slightly smaller than a horse, with goat's beard, cloven hooves, and spiraled horn.[18]

Moreover, there is other evidence to support the contention that Amber's unicorn symbolizes good and, at least vaguely, suggests Christ. Two of its primary characteristics, water-conning and snake-eating, define its role in battling evil. Water-conning is the characteristic of dipping its horn into poisoned water to detoxify it so that other animals may drink,[19] and its penchant for eating snakes certainly implies a role in battling evil since snakes are traditional Christian symbols for the devil. The good versus evil relationship is further supported by the traditional graphics of the "Wheel of Fortune" Tarot card, one of several Major Arcana cards which are represented in various ways in the novels. It is usually drawn with Typhon, the Egyptian God of Evil, in the form of a serpent on one side and Hermes-Anubis, representing good and intelligence, on the other.[20]

Another unicorn characteristic that is found in many of the legends about it is that it has a ruby growing at the base of its horn. On at least one occasion, there is a specific reference to that ruby being used as a medicine to cure the wound of an ailing "King of the Grail."[21] Moreover, the elements of the Grail legend, as identified by Jessie Weston in *From Ritual to Romance*, are used in part to shape the Amber novels. Another connection with good is thus established since the Grail legend is specifically associated with Christ.

Two allusions, in particular, reinforce the impression of Corwin as an agent of good. First is a reference to "Archangel Corwin" in *The Courts of Chaos*, by a dark stranger he encounters in a cave where he temporarily seeks refuge from the storm that is sweeping towards Chaos and destroying all before it. The reference is probably to Archangel Michael, who is known for repelling Lucifer with a band of loyal angels. Second, Corwin is wounded in the side, just like Lancelot du Lac, whom he saves in *The Guns of Avalon*. This wounding echoes that of Christ.

This is not to say that Zelazny is identifying Corwin with Christ, but rather that they are parallel figures. The images, allusions, and symbols are suggestive, not specific.

As with good, evil is focused through Brand and not necessarily through Chaos. A cluster of images and symbols leads to this conclusion. For example, Brand is described as having flaming red hair and his very name can imply fire. Further, red and fire are traditionally associated with the devil. He is an agent of chaos, and he tempts Corwin in the final book by promising to share power with him in his reconstructed universe. Not only is this temptation analogous with that of the Bible, it is also analogous with that of the Fool by the Devil in the Tarot. (Tarot symbolism permeates the Amber books.) Eden Gray writes that the Fool "has been shown all the secrets of life and how to use them, yet is tempted by the Devil... to use his newfound power to create a life of selfish gain and material pleasure."[22] Significantly, Corwin's temptation occurs just after he has learned to use the Jewel of Judgment, the universe's most powerful creative tool.

There is much other evidence to suggest that Brand represents evil. For example, like Lucifer he wants to overthrow the existing order, and when he is finally killed it is with a silver-tipped arrow made especially for that purpose. The power of silver over supernatural evil is well known in connection with werewolves, and it exhibits a similar power in the Amber novels. It is no coincidence that silver is one of Corwin's colors.

Evil is eventually defeated and good triumphs. In the process, Corwin learns that form and chaos must exist forever in a "living" universe. It is inevitable if the patterns which create universes are spun from the personalities of beings who themselves reflect these powers.

§

Lord of Light, probably Zelazny's best novel to date and winner of the 1968 Hugo award, also reflects the form and chaos doctrine in its philosophical structure. Moreover, its Buddhist and Hindu source materials prove to be highly analogous.

In the historical relationship between Hinduism and Buddhism, Zelazny found an excellent metaphor for the dynamic relationship between form and chaos. The parallels between the two are unmistakable. Buddha found the Hindu system to be static and corrupt, weighed down by meaningless and dead ritual, insensitive to the common man, and too complex to be understood by him.[23] Sam, the novel's hero, finds deicratism the same.

Buddha's mission on Earth was to reform an old religion, not to start a new one,[24] and Sam's mission in the novel is identical—to reform deicratism by means of accelerationism. Both Buddha and Sam become instruments of change. Hinduism becomes the model for deicratism, and Buddhism for accelerationism. Thus, philosophically, *Lord of Light* is broadly structured by the relationship between the two great religions and the form and chaos doctrine.

In the dynamics of form and chaos, systems (which are forms) tend to become more rigid and complex as they age. They also tend to increase in inertia and restriction. Eventually this process reaches a point where the forces of form and of chaos are nearly in balance, or a near stasis has been created. The rate of change is practically zero.

The effects on a culture and individuals in it are devastating. Intelligent beings can become neurotic, even psychotic, under these conditions. And so can the society.

As the system is warped farther and farther from the natural rhythm of the universe, intelligent beings intuitively sense it (some more than others of course) and move to rectify the situation. Intelligent beings then become instruments of chaos by attempting to destroy the nearly static system or by drastically modifying it to bring it into phase.

In *Lord of Light*, this is exactly the situation with deicratism, a religious system. It has become so encumbered with rules, rituals, gods, and ceremonies that it has become unresponsive to the common man. It must therefore be destroyed or drastically changed. Sam senses this and moves to accomplish it.

In the Hindu "Trimurti," Zelazny found an even more specific metaphor for the relationship between form and chaos. Because it is couched in human terms, its adaptation to the novel was easy. The traditional understanding of the meaning of the three gods was perfect. Brahma represents the creative force of the universe, Siva the destructive, and Vishnu preserves the conditions of the universe so that the other two forces can interact. Brahma and Siva are drawn from Vishnu, and the other gods of the Indian pantheon are drawn from the three. Vishnu himself came from the Absolute.[25] In short, the "Trimurti" sets the form-making and form-destroying functions against one another while ensuring that the conditions for their interaction are maintained.

Zelazny follows this general pattern in the development of *Lord of Light*, even though he makes no attempt to duplicate the traditional mythology attached to the "Trimurti" gods. He lets the story run its course within the limitations and possibilities he has posed in the world of the novel. Body shifting, for example, permits different individuals to assume a particular god's identity. Two different people, first Madeline and then Kali, function as Brahma, for instance, during the story. Regardless of the shifting identities, someone always functions as form-maker, or creator, while someone else functions as form-destroyer up to the very end of the novel.

It is no coincidence that at that point, Brahma and Siva (traditional creator and destroyer respectively) are themselves destroyed and that Vishnu (the traditional preserver) rules in heaven. These facts symbolize the end of the current age, or yuga, and the beginning of a new creation. Other story data support this interpretation. Sam appears, for example, just prior to the battle of Khaipur (the final battle of the novel) riding a white horse. He has been previously known as Lord Kalkin, and he has been identified at the beginning of section vii with "Maitreya, Lord of Light."

Hinduism specifies that the end of the current age, the Kali Yuga, will be signaled by the appearance of the god Kalki, the tenth avatar of Vishnu, riding a white horse and wielding a sword that will blaze like a comet to create, renew, and restore purity to the Earth.[26] In Buddhism, Maitreya is the Buddha of the Future. He will save mankind through his love by bringing each individual to a state of illumination, in the sense of self-realization.[27] The parallels are unmistakable.

The character of Sam is also the product of the form and chaos doctrine. Like all of Zelazny's major characters, and like man in general, Sam reflects both functions. In one of his early identities he is Lord Kalkin, binder of energy and form-maker. He, and others of the First, create a new Earthlike civilization on Urath by tearing control of it from its native inhabitants. Ironically, but typical of Zelazny's view of man, Sam is destroying form in the very process of creating it. It is important to remember, however, that form-making is his general function and that the sheer scope of the creations outweighs the destruction.

Later, as Mahasamatman, he switches general functions. He becomes the un-binder, the liberator, the destroyer of forms, systems, and patterns. He frees the demons he originally bound in Hellwell, he attacks the gods both physically and psychologically, and he destroys the dominant political system and religion.

Even guilt is attributable to the form and chaos philosophy. In a moving scene from the novel, Taraka, a demon and once a creature of pure, clear flame, describes his first feelings of guilt:

> My pleasures diminish by the day! Do you know why this is, Siddhartha? [Yet another of Sam's identities.] Can you tell me why strange feelings now come over me, dampening my strongest moments, weakening me and casting me down when I should be elated, when I should be filled with joy? Is this the curse of the Buddha?[28]

Seizing an opportunity when Sam's defenses are down, Taraka had invaded Sam's body, partly as revenge for being bound in Hellwell for several centuries by him and partly to experience those fleshly pleasures which were denied to him otherwise. While in Sam's body, however, Taraka learns about guilt, and in an ironic twist he now finds himself more tightly bound than when he was physically confined. His pure nature has been changed in the symbiotic relationship.

Sam explains what has happened to Taraka:

> ...all men have within them both that which is dark and that which is light. A man is a thing of many divisions, not a pure, clear flame such as you once were. His intellect often wars with his emotions, his will with his desires... his ideals are at odds with his environment, and if he follows them, he knows keenly the loss of that which was old—but if he does not follow them, he feels the pain of having forsaken a new and noble dream. Whatever he does represents both a gain and a loss, an arrival and a departure. Always he mourns that which is gone and fears some part of that which is new. Reason opposes tradition. Emotions oppose the restrictions his fellow men lay upon him. Always, from the friction of these things, there arises the thing you called the curse of man and mocked—guilt.[29]

This description is consonant with Zelazny's general picture of man as a creature embodying both form and chaos and usually being out-of-phase with the rhythm created by these two forces. Guilt is the product of the lack of synchronization.

Though the natural rhythm of the universe flows through man, because he is a part of nature himself, he usually blocks off his awareness of it by fixing on earthly and physical pleasures. He feels the lack of harmony as guilt but remains unconscious of its origin.

Man is not eternally condemned to this state, however. If he were to learn to trust his intuition, he would eventually raise his level of awareness and promote his own growth towards higher and higher levels of consciousness. Finally, he would achieve a state of illumination, which would bring him a complete understanding of the great plan of the universe and of how each piece of man's activity fits into it. This is the Buddhist concept of illumination, or enlightenment, and the goal of every individual. With its achievement comes perfect harmony because the soul becomes part of the "Absolute."

This is, in fact, the very trip that Sam makes during the novel.

Because all dichotomies are ultimately traceable to the opposition that exists between form and chaos, it is no surprise to find *Lord of Light* loaded with polar images and symbols. By doing this, Zelazny accomplishes two important objectives: he supports the concept that form and chaos underlie all things, and he metaphorically represents their relationship throughout the novel.

Several examples will illustrate the pervasiveness of this imagery. Perhaps the most obvious antinomies are light and dark, life and death, and creation and destruction. They are represented initially by the opposition of hero to enemy, or Sam to Yama. Eventually they become allies, though, to destroy the static system of deicratism. This is a perfect reflection of the dynamics of form and chaos, which also combine briefly when confronted by stasis.

There is also the polarity of the Celestial City. Created by Vishnu, it is a perfect balance of form and chaos. He designed it so that the metropolitan area would be offset by the wilderness of the Kaniburrah Forest. Both exist under the same dome.

> While wilderness can exist independent of cities, that which dwells within a city requires more than the tamed plants of a pleasance. If the world were all city, he [Vishnu] had reasoned, the dwellers within it would turn a portion of it into a wilderness, for there is that within them all which desires that somewhere there be an end to order and a beginning to chaos.[30]

Another polar image is found in the opposition of Accelerationism and Deicratism, the two political philosophies, systems, and religions of the humans of Urath. The first represents progress, self-development, and discovery. The second, paternal control, ignorance, and exploitation. Sam opposes the latter because it has become static and corrupt.

In addition to these polarities, the novel also displays polarities in style and structure. The exotic and sublime of Hinduism and Buddhism, for example, are set against the mechanism and technology of the First. In explaining the abstract concepts of nirvana and reincarnation technologically, Zelazny is highly ingenious.

These are then but a few examples of the polar imagery in *Lord of Light*. They were selected to represent the nature and extent of the imagery and not as an inventory of it. They are extremely appropriate to the novel, not only because of the nature of form and chaos but also because the very basis of Hinduism, and therefore Buddhism, is found in eternal opposition. In explaining the confusion most scholars find in Hindu mythology, J. Herbert writes:

> ...the achievement up to this point is the mobilization both of the basic eternal principles and of creative, divine will, which governs the forces involved. The subsequent development is that in which dualities-polarities appear....
>
> Once this duality—or rather polarity—of god and the devil in the world appeared, multiplicity proper can manifest itself—not as yet the multiplicity of objects, beings, and individualized movements, but that of secondary principles that will enable the rest to come to life.[31]

§

In addition to the stories discussed here, the form and chaos philosophy is prominent in many of Zelazny's early works. *This Immortal, The Dream Master, Creatures of Light and Darkness,* and *Jack of Shadows,* show heavy indebtedness to it. In others, it may not be so obvious. Whether it is or not, the form and chaos doctrine is fundamental to Zelazny's thinking and therefore instrumental in shaping his fiction.

—1979

NOTES

1. Roger Zelazny, "A Rose for Ecclesiastes," *Four for Tomorrow* (Ace Books, New York, 1973), p.182.
2. Havelock Ellis, *The Dance of Life* (Constable, London, 1923), pp.x-xi.
3. B.F. Peters, Rainer Maria Rilke: *Masks and the Man* (University of Washington Press, Seattle Washington, 1960), p.187.
4. Rainer Maria Rilke, p.165.
5. Rainer Maria Rilke, p.171.
6. *The Dance of Life,* p.vii.
7. *Four for Tomorrow,* p.174.
8. *Four for Tomorrow,* p.207.
9. Roger Zelazny, *The Courts of Chaos* (Doubleday, Garden City, New York, 1978), pp.15-16.
10. *The Courts of Chaos,* p.54.
11. Eugene S. Schwartz, *Overskill* (Ballantine, New York, 1971), pp.15-16.
12. Roger Zelazny, *The Hand of Oberon* (Doubleday, Garden City, New York, 1976), p.60.
13. *The Hand of Oberon,* p.64.
14. *The Courts of Chaos,* p.84,
15. Roger Zelazny, *The Guns of Avalon* (Doubleday, Garden City, New York, 1972), p.179.
16. *The Hand of Oberon,* p.68.
17. Odell Shepard, *The Lore of the Unicorn* (Barnes and Noble, New York, 1967), p.81.
18. *The Lore of the Unicorn,* p.71.
19. *The Lore of the Unicorn,* pp.150-154.
20. Eden Gray, *A Complete Guide to the Tarot* (Crown Publishers, New York, 1970), P.32.
21. *The Lore of the Unicorn,* p.82.

22. *A Complete Guide to the Tarot*, p.150.

23. Joseph Politella, *Seven Religions* (Kent State University, Kent, Ohio, 1958), p.66.

24. *Seven Religions*, p.67.

25. Pierre Grimal (ed.), *Larousse World Mythology* (Hamlyn, London, 1969), p.211.

26. *Seven Religions*, pp.29-30.

27. W.Y. Evans-Wentz (trans.), *The Tibetan Book of the Dead* (Causeway Books, New York, 1973), p.108.

28. Roger Zelazny, *Lord of Light* (Doubleday, Garden City, New York, 1967), p.161.

29. *Lord of Light*, pp.161-162.

30. *Lord of Light*, p.191.

31. *Larousse World Mythology*, p.210.

"WAKE UP, YOU LOT!"

JOHN FOYSTER AS SF CRITIC

BRUCE GILLESPIE

I

At the end of the 1960s, the Australian sf fan John Foyster (who died of cancer in 2003, aged 62) was known throughout the science fiction world as one of its best critics, yet today it is hard to find evidence of his work. *Exploring Cordwainer Smith*, a booklet of criticism and interviews based on Foyster's investigations, is still mentioned in bibliographies of works about Smith, yet Foyster's most extensive body of writing dealt with the work of Samuel R. Delany and J. G. Ballard. Only readers who have access to both series of *Australian Science Fiction Review* (1966–70 and 1986–92) and several other publications of the late sixties and early seventies (especially *SF Commentary*, *Science Fiction Review* and *Speculation*) can gain an insight into Foyster's contribution to sf criticism.

Foyster's approach would now be regarded as old-fashioned because he expected science fiction writers to write well-made stories and interesting prose and readers to be able to judge whether or not a story was much good. Foyster didn't think most sf writers were much good at writing, and he said so. Because of his refusal to "run a line"—to back any particular theory of literary criticism—his work could not be categorized. It does not fit within today's world of grand theories that reduce writing to merely a type of "cultural signs." His heirs are rare, but fortunately one of them, David Langford (especially in *Up Through an Empty House of Stars: Reviews and Essays 1980–2002*, Cosmos Books, 2003), is still writing vigorously.

Foyster's work is hardly likely to be kept alive by the writers whose works he wrote about. Foyster pulled no punches, and was as severe on the writing of his friends (especially Lee Harding, Damien Broderick and John Baxter) as on unmet persons from overseas. Harry Warner's protest that writers are "delicate organisms" only strengthened Foyster's skepticism.

By 1966, writers and other critics believed that critics should be polite; John Foyster, in print at least, was never polite. He had before him the example of James Blish, whose collected criticism as "William Atheling Jr." was issued in 1966 in *The Issue at Hand*. In 1967, the collected essays of Damon Knight, an even more impolite critic, were collected and issued as *In Search of Wonder*. A similar collection of Foyster's work issued in the early 1970s would no doubt have secured his reputation, but unfortunately no such publication occurred.

Not only was Foyster impolite, but he did his best not to make generalizations about science fiction. As the 1970s proceeded, the practice of the new breed of academic critics was to crush a vast butterfly collection of sf books under the steamroller of critical theory. As sf works suffered under the armies of categorizers and theoreticians, it became increasingly difficult to work out which books were worth reading. Foyster, by contrast, concentrated his critical mind on particular works and authors, leaving one in no doubt as to which were worth reading, and which were not. George Turner, who made his own splash as an sf critic in 1967, called this "technical criticism," and was proud of writing it. Foyster didn't give a name to his own method; he just invited people to read books carefully.

I'm writing this essay to make people aware of what they might find if they locate and read Foyster's work. Also, I'm expressing a debt of gratitude. Not that John Foyster ever took me aside and said, "Listen, Gillespie, you really should write this or that way." Lee Harding, who was better at explaining John Foyster to people than Foyster ever was, once said to me: "Listen, Bruce, why don't you stop writing academic-style criticism? Look at John Foyster's writing; he says more than you do, says it better, and never uses any academic jargon." Lo! I looked, and saw that Lee Harding was correct, and that it was possible to explain what you want about a work of fiction without using any academic jargon. Not that my work resembles that of John Foyster, but it quickly cured me of writing English III essays for fanzines.

II

John Foyster's writing for fanzines falls into two main categories: "fannish" writing (about fan activities and personal concerns), and reviews and criticism of science fiction magazines, stories and books. The first category makes up most of Foyster's non-professional writing. The second category, sf criticism, occupies two relatively short periods: (a) from 1966 to 1970, in *Australian Science Fiction Review* (the original series) and *exploding madonna/The Journal of Omphalistic Epistemology (JOE)*, and (b) from 1986 to 1991, in the second series of *Australian Science Fiction Review*. Yet those periods of intense activity provide a rich lode of material for the discerning reader.

Australian Science Fiction Review began as a result of a discussion at the science fiction convention in Melbourne during Easter 1966. There had been no such convention in Australia since 1958. It was felt that the enthusiasm generated during that convention could best be kept alive by the production of a nationally focused "small circulation magazine devoted to the discussion of science fiction." Pressed to become editor of such a magazine, Lee Harding nominated John Bangsund. With John as editor, Lee Harding and John Foyster became the staff of the new magazine, *Australian Science Fiction Review (ASFR)*. The first issue appeared in June 1966.

Rereading my copies of *ASFR* nearly forty years later, I get the impression that at first John Foyster did not expect to write a large number of reviews for the magazine. It was obvious that the staff hoped that most of its contributors would be writers such as Brian Aldiss, Michael Moorcock, Langdon Jones and John Baxter, the headline acts in No. 1.

Lee Harding writes a fair number of the pages in No. 1 (including the delicious article "Communist Chulpex Raped My Wife!", a long review of Avram Davidson's *Masters of the Maze*), and John Foyster opens his account with a review of Philip K. Dick's *The Three Stigmata of Palmer Eldritch*, which had just been published in a British edition. John does not so much review the book as review the other reviewers, a practice startlingly different from reviews to be found in the overseas professional sf magazines (prozines). As a fanatical Philip K. Dick admirer, I was not much taken with Foyster's dismissal of the book itself (including his assertion that Jack Vance used the drug-reality theme more effectively in 1958 in a story called "The Men Return"), but was amused to find him wiping the floor with P. Schuyler Miller's review in *Analog*, Judith Merril's review in *F&SF* and Algis Budrys's review in *Galaxy*. It was this sort of skepticism that was completely absent in the prozines. At last! I thought, I've found intelligent people who write about science fiction.

In *ASFR* 2, August 1966, a reviewing format for the magazine began to take shape. Between them, John Foyster and Lee Harding wrote 10 of the 36 pages, with four more pages written by "K. U. F. Widdershins" (later revealed to be John Foyster) and "Alan Reynard" (later revealed to be Lee Harding). Foyster's main piece was a lengthy discussion of four short novels by an author I had never heard of: Dwight V. Swain. My reaction: why bother?

On page 26, K. U. F. Widdershins reviewed Harry Harrison's *Bill, the Galactic Hero*, which has just been released in British hardback. It is not clear whether or not Mr. Widdershins liked the book, since the final lines of the review are: "All in all, this novel must be extremely highly rated, for its entertainment value is 'tops.' I recommend it strongly to all readers." This is the tone adopted by reviewers in the prozines of the time. Even the Bruce Gillespie of 1966 could detect some insincerity in the recommendation. John Bangsund writes as a footnote: "Some readers have complained about Dr. Widdershins's reviews, on the grounds 'that he obviously doesn't like sf.' I trust the above review will put their minds, so to speak, to rest."

As the letters of comment, somewhat delayed by the six weeks it took to reach anywhere on the other side of the world, began to pour into *ASFR*, it became clear that the salvo fired constantly at Widdershins and Foyster would be that they didn't like science fiction very much. Playing with that concept became the hallmark of the Foyster/Widdershins persona.

In *ASFR* 5, Widdershins reviewed what would eventually become Keith Roberts' novel *Pavane*. It was appearing as separate stories in the British magazine *Impulse* (the revamped *Science Fantasy*):

> The... stories... [each] deal with an episode in the history of Roberts's England. They cover a couple of generations, and each of them suffers the fault of appearing to be truncated; for each the resolution is unsatisfactory... As the series now stands, many questions are unanswered: who are the "people"? Is Brother John the same man as Sir John the seneschal? (And if not, why not?) We may never discover now the secrets of Cordwainer Smith's world, but let us hope that Keith Roberts will reveal, in time, just what makes his delightful world tick.

In his letter of comment published in *ASFR* 9, April 1967, Keith Roberts writes, among other things:

> I've just got to take exception to the Widdershins report, or review, or whatever he calls it, of *Pavane* in issue five. Whoever is lurking behind that noxious pseudonym really should have his head immersed in a vat of treacle, or sheepdip, or whatever bizarre fluid comes most readily to hand Down There. I've read bad reports of my work and I've read downright vindictive ones but I've never come across such an absolute masterpiece of misunderstanding; I'm well aware that widdershins traditionally go backwards but this is really too much... Mr.

Ditherspin successfully confuses the whole issue, with I must admit great skill and economy, before moving on to What I Have To Say...

To which Widdershins replies:

> So that's how Keith Roberts reacts to a review fairly oozing with praise! May I construct the essence of the review? I suggested that the *Pavane* stories were the best things to come out from *Impulse*. That all the stories were worthy of expansion, and that I looked forward to this. And that I look forward, in general, to seeing more of the same. I did complain that the stories almost seemed cut off in the middle... I am, of course, quite shaken by this. I feel, and felt then, that my review was straightforward unabashed praise. I admit no other interpretation. Roberts has, almost paranoically, misinterpreted and confused what I wrote.

Had Roberts known it, he would be one of the last correspondents to receive a contrite reply from Widdershins or Foyster.

ASFR correspondents, especially well-known sf writers, reacted more and more strongly to reviews by the *ASFR* team (which, after No. 10, included George Turner). John Foyster began to think about reviewing science fiction in a quite different environment, which led him, a year later, to the secret publication of *exploding madonna*.

III

The task of reviewing the sf books that flooded into the *ASFR* offices had deflected Foyster from his true path—writing full-length criticism. The first evidence of the true Foyster can be found in Issue No. 4, October 1966. An etching of Don Quixote bestrides the cover. In that issue, Foyster devotes 19 pages to "The Editorials of John Campbell."

To say that I was dismayed when I received that issue is an understatement. But I did for the first time glimpse the possibility offered by the serious fanzine—as a forum for long detailed articles about single subjects.

I was dismayed, then more than now, at Foyster's taking the sf magazines seriously. True, in 1966 the prozines were still the only sources of short fiction in the field, but they were all at such a low ebb, in the quality of both their fiction and non-fiction, that *ASFR* seemed a mighty bolt of inspiration by comparison. John Campbell's *Analog* consisted of little but very boring technologically based stories and dreary right-wing diatribes by the editor or his writers. Production values were high, and *Analog* was the only magazine paying 10 cents a word to authors. But by the mid 1960s, it seemed unlikely that any ambitious writer would send his or her work to Campbell, except for the money.

However, Foyster wrote:

> I think this article does make clear my admiration for the man who has edited the best science fiction magazine for almost thirty years. And in his own writings we can see just why his work has been so outstanding.
>
> Campbell is a maverick: he just won't conform to any mould. The result is that somewhere, sometime, he must offend everyone. But he is always interesting, always challenging. One may think that a given article is meaningless twaddle, but one must always admit that it is well-written, interesting twaddle.

I had long since given up on Campbell's editorials as boring twaddle that pandered to his right-wing audience and challenged nobody. The value of Foyster's long article lies in that giveaway line: "Campbell is a maverick: he just won't conform to any mould. The result is that somewhere, sometime, he must offend everyone." Did Foyster ever more accurately summarize his own writing career?

IV

Through the end of 1966 and into 1967, I found that I disagreed with Foyster and/or Widdershins most of the time, but also found that his work, and that of other *ASFR* writers, shone as the only light in the murky wood of 1960s science fiction. In particular, I couldn't agree with Foyster's admiration for the works of Samuel R. Delany, an author whose earliest short stories had left me spluttering with exasperation, and whose novels proved unreadable beyond the first page.

Nevertheless, the Foyster–Delany correspondence is one of the most satisfactory aspects of these years, especially as Delany steadfastly refused to be offended by Foyster's taunts and jibes.

Foyster's review of *Babel-17* (*ASFR* 10, June 1967) falls into two parts, a review of the book itself, and a critique of some of Delany's earliest published opinions about sf criticism. Says Foyster of *Babel-17*:

> Delany harks back to the old days of sf, when ideas were a dime a dozen and a decent author was not afraid to spend a penny. By comparison with many modern writers, Delany is a positive spendthrift; the material in this novel would provide eight or ten novels for other writers.
>
> It has. Delany's ideas are not new, at least in the sense that they are familiar to readers of sf. At the same time there is a certain freshness about the way they have been handled, as though the author had a deep

regard for the stories in which the concepts first appeared. This is not say that Delany has copied, but rather that he has taken several old strands of ideas and used them to weave a new yarn. As a result, there are strong pieces and weak pieces...

Whichever way you slice it, though, *Babel-17* is good reading, as sf. Delany has more than average control over his writing, though a few novels published in *Startling* would have sharpened up a few remaining weaknesses in his writing: a tendency to verbosity, a mild desire to show off, and very occasionally, definite fuzziness around the edges... The tendency towards using as many words as possible is understandable when one is paid by the word, but that is not how I understand Ace's method of payment. Nevertheless, no matter how good the author's work (and Delany writes very well), in a story which is basically an adventure yarn, too many words can get in the way. Too many words can slow the action, or at least throw the reader off the track. I may like what you are writing, Jack, but I've forgotten who is training the ray-gun on the Saturnian grulzak.

And when I say that Delany tends to show off, I really mean that sometimes there's a little too much embroidery, too much cuteness. This, too, one can take in small doses. It may well be that my tolerance is low.

Delany replies in *ASFR* 14, February 1968:

I've never put any hard-science into a tale without checking on it. The "science" section in *Babel-17* that John Foyster got so upset about a few issues back was merely a dramatization of Fredrick Kantor's rather brilliant solution to what was considered a classically insoluble problem—up until 1965: the totally internal determination of location from within a free-falling system. It's a problem that classical relativity maintains is impossible...the Kantor solution was hot news at the time. But that was '65....

Foyster replies:

You may imagine my chagrin at not having heard about Dr. Kantor's wonderful discovery. This was tempered by the further discovery that neither *Physics Abstracts* nor *Mathematical Reviews* had heard of this "hot news." None of the 20 or so other journals in the area (aerospace, astronomy, mathematics and physics) which I consulted for a couple of hours seemed to have heard of it, either. So if Mr. Delany can tell us where we can read all about it...

An author took his chances if he patted himself on the back in the presence of John Foyster. However, Delany did *not* reply to the much weightier comment from Foyster, that his prose shows "too much cuteness."

In the second part of his review of *Babel-17*, Foyster takes on an editorial by Delany in *New Worlds* 172, which appeared at about the time that Michael Moorcock decided that Delany was actually a New Wave writer, and Delany was pleased to be so anointed.

> The editorial presents, one presumes, Delany's views on sf. He draws comparisons between music in general and fiction in general, perhaps unwisely, compares forms of music as an analogy with the forms of fiction, i.e. sf and mainstream. The unwisdom comes, perhaps, in suggesting that the quartet might stand for sf and the symphony for mainstream. The objection—and I regard it as an insurmountable one—is that while one composer may write quartets and symphonies, there has been, as far as I can see, only one sf writer who has also written in the other field—Cordwainer Smith.
>
> This general assumption, then, seems untenable to me. But there are specific points in Delany's article which further suggest his intense concern with the oneness of sf and mainstream. He wants a critical vocabulary for sf and claims that no one has yet been able to build the bridge between sf and mainstream. I would submit that the need is not for a bridge, but a ladder. I further suggest that the inability of critics to examine sf in the way Delany wants is due to the absence of the kind of sf he supposes to exist...

This is almost the first general discussion about the relative merits of sf and "mainstream" into which John Foyster was ever drawn, and occurs in the same issue in which George Turner published his first article, which protested about the "double standard" in sf. As Foyster later confessed to Turner, he was rather in favor of the "double standard"—that is, he thought it difficult to compare works of sf and the best works of literature.

Delany and Foyster continued to argue about such matters during the next couple of years, culminating in a long letter–article that Delany sent to *exploding madonna* in 1968. In reply to this nine-page letter (*em* 5, January 1969), much of it in defense of the New Wave, Foyster replies, in part:

> Consider the critical performance of *New Worlds* this year. Sladek's review of Barthelme failed to get much across to me. Sallis's review of *Hump* is an example of the worst kind of one-upmanship (the sort of thing to which *New Worlds* is much given, in fact). Sallis reviewing (?) poetry (No. 181) is simply laughable, while Shackleton/ Aldiss does a fair job on Hillegas. Notice that it is clapped-out, nearly orthodox Aldiss who does most nearly approach a decent job. The rest can be wiped, with no loss at all.
>
> There is so much in both literature and science that it isn't really possible for any one person to get a good hold on the lot. I don't know

that I entirely approve of your approach to literature (dig the critics), but in science things are really tough. I suppose that a full-time reader could keep a broad grasp of the situation, but scarcely enough to claim genuine familiarity.

While you write about the invention of a spaceship (as an example) you forget that science fiction is written as wish-fulfillment for juveniles. This was then and will remain for some time the basic selling point of science fiction: it is simply unfortunate for older readers that they happen to like it too. Whether they have failed to grow up, or do have Broad Mental Horizons, is something on which I'm not prepared to cast judgment. But that's why I find it hard to take seriously the claims of sf as literature—it's basically written as adventure stories, and people like yourself who try to make sf "mature" are voices crying in the wilderness. I also find it hard to forget Mike Moorcock's origins as an editor, for example.

V

So why—as those *ASFR* letter writers complained—did John Foyster read science fiction, let alone write about it?

One short answer is that he *didn't* read a lot of current science fiction, except when reviewing books for both series of *Australian Science Fiction Review*. I gained the impression that he often riffled back through his collection of the sf magazines of the 1940s and 1950s (which led to his writing an interminable "Long View" series of articles for *ASFR*, Second Series).

The other short answer is: for enjoyment. What appeared to annoy John Foyster was the constant scurrying by sf writers and critics to find pedestals to climb on in the hope that somebody would worship them while they were standing there.

In his introduction to the *SF Commentary* 19, January 1971, which brings together six issues of *exploding madonna* and three of *JOE*, Foyster writes:

> The trouble with writing about science fiction is that one becomes serious about it... One way or another, people get serious about science fiction, the most frivolous form of entertainment yet devised...
>
> However... I might remark that you are receiving this fanzine because, unwittingly and perhaps unwillingly, you have given me the impression, to quote Widdershins, that you discuss science fiction seriously... If a couple of you are interested, let us stagger into the darkness together. You are, by the way, Mr. Brian Aldiss, Mr. James Blish, Mr. Red Boggs, Mr. Algis Budrys, Mr. Sten Dahlskog, Mr. Samuel Delany, Mr. Damon Knight, Mr. Franz Rottensteiner and Mr. Harry Warner...

I do not agree with Mr. Warner entirely when he writes: "A writer is a delicate organism; equally automatically, a reader may be as neurotic as a writer; his criticisms, though mere personal fads, may harm the delicate mechanism" (*Horizons* 113, page 2204)... Writers are *not* really delicate organisms, in general... While many science fiction writers are interested in discussing what is going on in the world of science fiction, there are also quite a few whose epistolatory endeavors are directed solely towards the extraction of egoboo: in a word, you gotta have a proper respeck. I don't, comrades.

Which brings us back to Widdershins' initial clash with Keith Roberts, as well as many other writers. Having found through two and a half years of writing for *ASFR* that, above all, writers want their "proper respeck," Foyster decided to speak only to fellow critics, who, except for Franz Rottensteiner, in the end proved as prickly as the fiction writers. This so exasperated Foyster that, in January 1969 he wrote to the recipients of *exploding madonna*:

> *Wake up you lot!* Here I am with my critical faculties hanging out in the cold and I haven't interested a single soul in talking about the *way* stf should be approached. Not one. Probably no one cares: it certainly *looks* that way.

Which, in turn, might explain why, not too many months later, Foyster turned over the whole lot to me. (I had by then, with a few other people, begged my way onto the mailing list). I reprinted *exploding madonna* and *JOE* as a 132-page issue of *SF Commentary*, and by early 1971 Foyster returned to publishing (with Leigh Edmonds) fannish fanzines with such ringing titles as *Boys' Own Fanzine*, *Norstrilian News* and *Chunder!*

EPILOGUE

John Foyster was (and still may be) famous for his admiration of the works of Cordwainer Smith (Dr. Paul Anthony Myron Linebarger, who died in 1966 at the age of 53). Foyster at his best can be found in the special issue of *ASFR* about the work of Smith/Linebarger. It was always my impression that John Foyster discovered who Cordwainer Smith was, using various detective skills and travelling to Canberra to meet the people who had known Linebarger. However, not long before he died Foyster sent me the enigmatic message that "it was Damien Broderick who did the detective pilgrimage regarding Cordwainer Smith," not Foyster. This was the first hint that Damien Broderick had ever had anything to do with the Cordwainer Smith project. Through Yvonne Rousseau (Foyster's widow), Damien sent an email clarifying the situation:

> Towards the end of 1965, I read *Space Lords* shortly after it arrived in Oz. There I learned that Smith lived in Canberra, attended the Anglican church (or something; this is from memory), and his broker was Mr. Greenish, whom readers might approach to discuss Smith's credit rating (or whatever; some whimsy). I wished to apply for the Stanford Writing Fellowship, a year's well-paid stint in the States (something both Rory Barnes and Jean Bedford [Broderick's house mates in 1965] won in subsequent years); I had *A Man Returned* in my hand, nasty little squib that it was, and felt I might impress the judges if I could get a note from Mr. Smith endorsing my cause (I was a naive child). So I flew to Canberra on a venture and a prop jet, located Mr. Greenish's office, had a flea put in my ear, wandered disconsolately to the ANU [Australian National University], came upon Bob Brissenden via Dorothy Green's daughter Harriet (whom I'd known at Monash [University]); Bob told me that oh yes, this must be Paul Linebarger, but he was currently in the Pacific islands doing research. I stayed at Dorothy's house overnight... then I went home *and forgot Linebarger's name*. This is almost incomprehensible, but I was a pragmatic child; the plan had come unstuck, I'd used up all my money fruitlessly, so why clutter my mind with such stuff? When I told John Foyster this tale he was, perhaps, and understandably, a little indignant. So he subsequently went forth and repeated some of these evolutions, or at any rate his own version of them, and thus encountered Arthur Burns, and presumably *wrote the name down*, and the secret was out.

Except for John Bangsund's original introduction, the Cordwainer Smith material has been reprinted several times, first by Andrew Porter as a leaflet called *Exploring Cordwainer Smith*, then as the last issue of Peter Weston's famous British fanzine *Speculation*, and then in the second series of *Australian Science Fiction Review*, No. 21, Spring 1989.

In the Cordwainer Smith special issue of *ASFR*, Foyster wrote a critical essay on "Cordwainer Smith," and extracted an article from Dr. Arthur Burns about Linebarger, and also interviewed him. Foyster's and Burns's approach to Smith was so original at the time that it influenced, perhaps even warped, all later discussion of Smith.

Foyster quotes Robert Silverberg, June 1965, summarizing my own feeling about the Cordwainer Smith stories:

> "I think that Cordwainer Smith is a visitor from some remote period of the future, living among us perhaps as an exile from his own era or perhaps just as a tourist, and amusing himself by casting some of his knowledge of historical events into the form of science fiction."

Foyster's own view of Smith is very different:

> If we examine the stories a little more closely we find that Smith was very much a man of our time, and that his feelings and thoughts were very much those of his contemporaries.
>
> In "The Dead Lady of Clown Town," "The Ballad of Lost C'mell" and "A Planet Named Shayol," to choose only three stories from his collection *Space Lords*, he writes strongly and with great feeling of the racial problems which surrounded him in his own land. His love of Australia is revealed in the Rod McBan stories. It isn't fair to Silverberg, but there is one way at least in which Smith shows himself very much tied to his time. His story "On the Storm Planet" deals with an attempt by Casher O'Neill to assassinate the turtle girl, T'ruth. If one turns to page 38 in the February 1965 *Galaxy* or to page 69 in *Quest of Three Worlds*, one finds, despite the interference of both editors, the acrostic KENNEDY SHOT. Several pages later a second acrostic appears: OSWALD SHOT TOO. (Mr. Arthur Burns, who had it from the author, is responsible for this information.)

This revelation, with many other examples provided in the Arthur Burns interview, set off the Cordwainer Smith industry, best characterized by the work of John J. Pierce, and which led eventually to the publication of the *Cordwainer Smith Concordance* by NESFA Press. Unfortunately, this has given the impression that Smith is mainly interesting for the number of hidden references he could pack into each story.

Foyster has a much wider view of Smith than Pierce and most other commentators:

> Cordwainer Smith was the first writer to write science fiction which could possibly be accepted as "Literature."
>
> I do not make this claim for him. His work does it for me, and for anyone who chooses to look...
>
> Smith's approach to the revelation of the future is almost unique. Most sf writers have difficulty in convincing readers of the reality of the future they create. Some ignore the problem, and hope the reader can accept their ideas. Others attempt to make them credible by explaining what is occurring, as it happens... Smith reveals the workings of his world in a natural manner. In "Scanners Live in Vain," for instance, the nature of the scanners and the habermen is made plain to the reader by the recitation of a ritual or catechism which is vital both to the character Martel and to the plot. It is not something tacked on "to make it all seem real."
>
> Robert Silverberg writes of Smith's world as being "so tiresomely familiar to him that he does not see the need to spell out the details." This is not quite true. The details of Smith's future are only made clear as this becomes necessary, and those who have read the bulk of his work will realize that it is filled with cross-references which help to

give the whole a remarkable unity... Thus any given story by Smith may seem to contain things not seen, not explained. To see, to understand, one must refer to another, perhaps remote, story.

This is one of the first Foyster essays in which he concentrates on the style of the author as well as the structure of his or her stories:

> And what of the general style of the stories?... He is talking to children; in his stories he is producing history as fairy tales. This is explicit in one story, "The Lady who Sailed 'The Soul,'" where the familiar old story is told by a mother to her daughter. But it is implicit in many of his verbal mannerisms, in other stories. This is not to demean, in any way, the intelligence or maturity of his readers; myths and legends have always been told in simple language, by father to son, and to do otherwise would spoil much of their magic.

Because of the casual approach to the opening of a story, and because of the child-like language used, Smith's technique could easily fail; in writing thus he walks on one side of the narrow gap between beauty and fatuity. But his foot is sure. As an indication of his masterly control—indeed, to use the two sentences by which I would be prepared to let his reputation stand or fall, I will quote the ending of a story sometimes forgotten: "The Burning of the Brain":

> Magno Taliano had risen from his chair and was being led from the room by his wife and consort, Dolores Oh. He had the amiable smile of an idiot, and his face for the first time in more than a hundred years trembled with shy and silly love.

Assuming that any other sf writer had written the story, it would have ended with the word "idiot." Go further; try to find any writer who would have finished the sentence more or less in that way. It would not be the same. For the words "and silly" are unique with Smith. In these words, these two words, he transcends the petty world of science fiction and reaches out into the world of reality.

Foyster also quotes my own favorite Smith sentence, the first sentence of "The Dead Lady of Clown Town":

> You already know the end—the immense drama of the Lord Jestocost, seventh of his line, and how the cat-girl C'mell initiated the vast conspiracy.

This still gives me goose bumps—the suggestion in the first line that we are sitting there at the end of the time listening to a storyteller retell a legend that has already been around for thousands of years.

—2003

CHAPTER SOURCES IN CHRONOLOGICAL ORDER

Marilyn Walters: Pamela Sargent's *Women of Wonder*, *Science Fiction* #1 1:1 (1977)

Terry Dowling and Keith Curtis: In Conversation with Roger Zelazny, *Science Fiction* #2 1:2 (1978)

Donald M. Hassler: The Eighteenth Century and Science Fiction, *Science Fiction* #4 2:1 (1979)

Carl Yoke: Roger Zelazny's Form and Chaos Philosophy, *Science Fiction* #5 2:2 (1979)

Terry Dowling and George Mannix: An Interview with Peter Weir, Master of Unease, *Science Fiction* #7 3:1 (1981)

Anne Brewster: An Interview with Stanislaw Lem, *Science Fiction* #10 4:1 (1982)

Russell Blackford: Analogues of Anomie: Lee Harding's Novels, *Science Fiction* #30 10:3 (1990)

Caroline Flynn: Doris Lessing, An Overview, *Science Fiction* #32 11:2 (1991)

Hal Colebatch: Patterns of Epic: The Re-Affirmation of Western Values in *Star Wars* and *The Lord of The Rings*, *Science Fiction* #33 11:3 (1992)

Russell Blackford: Wordlust and Wild, Wild Womyn, *Science Fiction* #34 12:1 (1993)

Yvonne Rousseau: Kathryn Ptacek's *Women of Darkness*, *Science Fiction* #37 13:1 (1996)

Tess Williams: *Battleaxe* and *Enchanter*, by Sara Douglass, *Science Fiction* #38 13:2 (1996)

Marian Foster: Deus ex Machina: *Red Dwarf, Better Than Life, Last Human*, *Science Fiction* #38 13:2 (1996)

Pascale Krumm: *The Island of Doctor Moreau*, or the Case of Devolution, *Science Fiction* #43 16:1 (2001)

Jacob George C: Gaia in the *Foundation* Novels: Ecological Hypothesis as Fictional Terminus, *Science Fiction* #44 16:2 (2002)

Kevin Smith: Fantasy Fiction and Terry Pratchett's Discworld, *Science Fiction* #45 17:1 (2008)

Bruce Gillespie: "Wake Up, You Lot!": John Foyster as SF Critic, *Science Fiction* #46 17:2 (2009)

CONTRIBUTORS

RUSSELL BLACKFORD is a philosopher and critic. He is known especially as an outspoken defender of secularism and individual rights. He has published three novels set in the Terminator universe, among others, and holds a law degree and a pair of PhDs. He and writer Jenny Blackford live in Newcastle, New South Wales.

ANNE BREWSTER, with a PhD from Flinders University, is an Associate Professor in the School of the Arts and Media at the University of New South Wales. She is a leading specialist in fictocriticism and author of such books as *Literary Formations: Postcoloniality, Nationalism, Globalism*.

DAMIEN BRODERICK holds a PhD from Deakin University, and has published more than 50 novels, scholarly and popular science books on literature, the paranormal, the technological singularity, the prospect of radical life extension, and the very far future. In 2010 he was runner-up for the Theodore Sturgeon short fiction award, and received the A. Bertram Chandler Award. These days he lives in San Antonio, Texas.

JACOB GEORGE C holds a PhD in English and teaches at Department of English, Union Christian College, Kerala, India, and worked in the Middle East for nearly a decade. "C" stands for "Cheruvathoor," which is used only on his passport.

HAL COLEBATCH has five degrees including a PhD in Political Science. In 2003 he was awarded an Australian Centenary Medal for services to poetry, writing, law and political commentary. He has published a number of volumes of poetry, several sf novels, and numerous stories set in Larry Niven's Known Worlds.

KEITH CURTIS, a Norfolk expatriate educated in Wymondham College, is a bibliomane, book dealer, poet, and former sf convention auctioneer whose residences are always overflowing with his stock in trade. Curtis edited the A. Bertram Chandler 1990 collection *From Sea To Shining Star*. In 1980 he was flown to the World SF Convention in

Boston as winner of the Down Under Fan fund. He lives these days in seclusion in Hobart, Tasmania, not far from the Royal Botanical Gardens.

TERRY DOWLING holds a PhD in Creative Writing from the University of Western Australia, and has published many awarded and anthologized stories in all fantastika genres: science fiction (notably his Tom Rynosseros sequence), horror and fantasy. He has created several computer games, and his debut novel *Clowns at Midnight* appeared from PS Publishing in 2010.

CAROLINE FLYNN was born in Sydney before WWII, married at 18, and raised five sons. Hearing that Doris Lessing was to be the main guest at the 1987 Worldcon in Brighton, she instantly decided to go, and met briefly with Lessing. Back in Australia, Caroline completed undergraduate study at (now) Charles Sturt University (Bathurst, NSW) and studied Speculative Fiction, with Doris Lessing and the language of science fiction as major interests. She spent eight years teaching conversational English in Japan: "an alternative reality."

MARIAN FOSTER moved to Western Australia in the late 1960s from England, after living in South Africa and New Zealand for short periods. She holds a PhD in English, a TAFE diploma in management, and studied commerce, mathematics and computing (statistics and information technology). Introduced to sf as a teenager through her father's library books, she later preferred fantasy to science fiction, reading Anne McCaffrey, Barbara Hambly and Julian May, among others, and is interested in the particular voice of Australian speculative writing.

BRUCE GILLESPIE, one of Australia's most celebrated sf fanzine editors, in 1969 founded *Science Fiction Commentary* which has been nominated three times for a Hugo. His early writings on the work of Philip K. Dick drew attention to an author comparatively neglected at the time. He published translations into English of Stanislaw Lem's essays. He gained the 2007 A. Bertram Chandler Award, and lives in Melbourne, Victoria, with Elaine Cochrane, surrounded by immense numbers of books, cats and CDs.

DONALD M. HASSLER has been Professor of English since 1977 at Kent State University. He received the Eaton Award for the best critical book on science fiction published in 1991 for his book on Isaac Asimov, and edited the journal *Extrapolation*.

VAN IKIN, winner of the inaugural A. Bertram Chandler Award in 1992, is a professor of English at the University of Western Australia, and gained his PhD from Sydney University. He is co-author (with Russell Blackford and Sean McMullen) of *Strange Constellations* and editor of three anthologies of Australian sf (including *Mortal Fire: Best Australian SF*—the first-ever Australian *Best of* collection, co-edited with Terry Dowling in 1993). He has edited and published *Science Fiction* since 1977.

PASCALE KRUMM, originally from Strasbourg, France, holds a PhD in French literature from the University of Virginia. She was a college professor in the US for 10 years. Her specialties were 19th century French and British literature. In 2000, she left academia for a career in public health at the US Centers for Disease Control and Prevention (CDC) in Atlanta, Georgia. She is currently the speechwriter for the CDC Director.

GEORGE MANNIX was an editorial adviser on *Science Fiction* when it was first established. He was, then, a director and producer at PACT Theatre in Sydney. He went on to work in film, acted as locations scout on *Mad Max III*, and now works for Parramatta City Council in a public events capacity.

YVONNE ROUSSEAU lives quietly in Adelaide, South Australia in the large book-crammed house she shared with her late husband John Foyster, reading prodigiously and writing wittily but publishing far too little.

KEVIN P. SMITH was associated with Sheffield Hallam University in the UK when his paper on Pratchett was submitted to *Science Fiction*, but has proved impossible to trace since then.

MARILYN WALTERS, PhD, is a practicing artist based in Sydney. She taught at Sydney University Art Workshop and the School of Philosophy, Sydney University in the 1970s, and recently concluded a 20 year teaching career at the University of Western Sydney to become a full time painter.

TESS WILLIAMS, self-described cyborg and Hydra, is author of the novels *Map of Power* and *Sea as Mirror* as well as several sf stories and articles on feminist sf. She is co-editor of *Women of Other Worlds: Excursions through Science Fiction and Feminism* (with Helen Merrick, 1999) and wrote her PhD on *Shared Metaphors of Change in "Post Neo-Darwinian" Evolutionary Theory and Feminist Science Fiction*. These days she works in academe as Research Development Officer at the University of Western Australia.

CARL YOKE was Associate Professor of English, and Assistant to the Associate Vice President of the Extended University, Kent State University. He was a childhood school friend of Roger Zelazny, and has written extensively on Zelazny's work.

INDEX

A

Absurd Hero in American fiction, The, 150
Acker, Kathy, 139
Adams, Richard, 122
Adventure of the Creeping Man, 92, 100
Age of Exuberance, The, 88
Aldiss, Brian W., 86-87, 184, 190-91
Alien, 18, 34-36
Amazing Maurice and His Educated Rodents, The, 147
Amber (Zelazny fantasy series), 155, 159-63, 169-75
Ambiguous Animal, The, 101
Analog, 184, 186
And Call Me Conrad, 152
Angier, Natalie, 103
Animal Farm, 122
Apartment, The, 20
Arabian Nights, 148
Aristotle, 94
Arrabal, Fernando, 19
Art as Technique, 121
Art of Star Wars, The, 45
ASFR, Second Series, 191
Asimov, Isaac, 8, 17, 51-57, 85, 87
Asimov's Galaxy, 57
Asker, D., 101
Aspen Graffiti, 61
Atwood, Margaret, 141, 147
Austen, Jane, 117
Australian Film Institute, 22
Australian Science Fiction Review, 9, 182, 184, 191, 193

B

Babel-17, 187-89
Baby, 60
Baby You Were Great, 65
Bakhtin, M.M., 124, 126, 131-32, 146, 148, 150
Baku, The, 60
Ballad of Lost C'mell, The, 194
Ballard, J.G., 17, 30, 182
Barnes, Rory, 180, 193
Barthes, Roland, 140, 146, 150
Bate, Walter Jackson, 86
Battleaxe, 73-74
Baxter, John, 183-84
Bedford, Jean, 193
Before the Golden Age, 85
Berberick, Nancy Varian, 60
Beresford, Bruce, 19
Bergman, Ingmar, 27
Bettelheim, Bruno, 129, 131, 150
Better Than Life, 104-06
Bill, the Galactic Hero, 185
Biographia Literaria, 118, 150
Bishop, Michael, 159
Blackford, Russell, 9, 69, 107
Blind Watchmaker, The, 103
Blish, James, 183, 191
Botanic Garden, The, 85
Boys' Own Fanzine, 192
Bradbury, Ray, 159
Bradley, Marion Zimmer, 65
Breaking Down Reality, 83
Brennan, Dick, 19
Brewster, Anne, 12
Briefing for a Descent into Hell, 82
Brissenden, Bob, 193
Broderick, Damien, 7, 183, 192-93
Brooke Rose, Christine, 119
Bryant, Ed, 159
Budrys, Algis, 184, 191
Burden of the Past and the English Poet, The, 86
Burke, Edmund, 42-43
Burney, Charles, 85
Burning of the Brain, The, 195
Burns, Arthur, 193-94

C

Campbell, John W., 18, 186-87
Campbell, Joseph, 130, 134, 150
Cannibal Cats Come Out Tonight, 59
Canopus in Argos Archives series, 77
Carey, Peter, 9
Carlyle, Thomas, 133, 150
Carpe Jugulum, 123
Carpenter, Humphrey, 50
Carpenter, John, 18
Cars That Ate Paris, The, 15, 24, 30-31
Carter, Angela, 146
Catch 22, 137
Chamberlain, Richard, 24
Chaplin, Charles, 22
Child Dreams, The, 62
Chirico, Giorgio de, 21
Christ, 173, 174
Christie, O.F, 134
Chunder, 192
Cinema Papers, 15, 25
Clarke, Arthur C., 8
Clarke, I.F., 50
Cleese, John, 35
Clifton School Days, 134
Cloning of Joanna May, The, 60
Close Encounters of the Third Kind, 36, 158
Clute, John, 7, 11
Cohen, Jack, 143, 150
Colebatch, Hal, 10, 37, 50
Coleridge, Samuel Taylor, 85, 118, 150
Color of Magic, The, 121, 123, 129, 135-36, 148, 149
Come to Me Not in Winter's White, 158
Communist Chulpex Raped My Wife!, 184
Complete Guide to the Tarot, A, 180, 181
Congo, 101
Consensus Fantasy Universe, 73
Contagion, 62
Conversation with Isaac Asimov, A, 55
Cordwainer Smith, 185, 189, 192-94
Cordwainer Smith Concordance, 194
Cornwell, Neil, 119, 121, 150
Courts of Chaos, The, 169-74, 180
Cox, Wennicke Eide, 59, 60
Creatures of Light and Darkness, 180
Crichton, Michael, 90, 101
Curtis, Keith, 10, 1, 152

D

D'Aulnoy, Madam, 147
Dali, Salvador, 20
Damnation Alley, 160
Dance of Life, The, 165, 180
Dancehall of the Dead, 154
Dark Star, 18
Darwin, 92-102
Darwin, Erasmus, 85-86, 89
Darwinism, 93, 95, 100
Davidson, Avram, 184
Dawkins, Richard, 97, 103
Dead Lady of Clown Town, The, 194, 195
Death of The Author, The, 150
Delany, Samuel R., 182, 187-91
Dembo, L.S., 83
Descent of Man, The, 93, 102
Deus Irae, 157
Devil's Rose, The, 58, 59
Dialogic Imagination, The, 126, 150
Dick, Philip K., 17, 87, 157, 184
Dickens, Charles, 18, 44, 117, 148
Displaced Person, 107-14
Dispossessed, The, 88
Doctor Jekyll and Mr. Hyde, 100
Doors of His Face, the Lamps of His Mouth, The, 166
Doorways in the Sand, 153, 156
Doris Lessing Critical Studies, 83
Dorman, Sonya, 62, 66, 68
Douglas, Conda V., 61
Douglass, Sara, 73, 74, 75
Dowling, Terry, 9, 10-11, 15, 152
Doyle, Arthur Conan, 91-92
Dr. Strangelove, 35
Dracula, 92, 100, 103, 123
Dream Master, The, 161, 180
Dutch Quarterly Review of Anglo-American Letters, 101

E

Eden Gray, 175, 180
Edge of Objectivity, The, 86
Edmonds, Leigh, 192
Eisenstein, Sergei, 24
Eliot, T.S., 139
Ellis, Havelock, 165, 167, 180
Ellison, Harlan, 157, 158, 161
Empire Strikes Back, The, 47-48
Emshwiller, Carol, 67-68
Enchanter, 73, 74
Encyclopedia of Science Fiction, 15
Epperson, Sharon, 60
Equal Rites, 123, 149
Eric, 123, 135, 138-39, 142, 149
Evans-Wentz, W.Y., 181

Evidence as to Man's Place in Nature, 102
exploding madonna, 184, 186, 190-92
Exploring Cordwainer Smith, 182, 193
Extrapolation, 159

F

fairy tales, 13, 91, 118, 129-30, 147, 195
False Dawn, 63-64
Fando and Lis, 19
Fantastic, The, 151
Fantastika, 7, 11
Fantastika in the World Storm, 7
Fantasy: The Literature of Subversion, 150
Farmer, Philip Jose, 154, 159-60
Fawlty Towers, 35
Feet of Clay, 123, 149
Fiedler, Leslie, 139
Fielding, Henry, 117
Fifth Elephant, The, 149
First Men in the Moon, The, 90, 101
Fitzgerald, F. Scott, 18
Flamingo's Smile, The, 102
Flash Gordon, 17
Flynn, Caroline, 77
Fog, The, 18
Food Farm, 64
Fortnight Review, 95
Foster, Marian, 104
Foundation, 8, 51-57
Foundation and Earth, 55-57
Foundation and Empire, 52, 55, 57
Foundation's Edge, 53, 55-57
Four for Tomorrow, 163, 180
Foyster, John, 9, 182-195
Frankenstein, 86, 100-02
Fraser, George MacDonald, 161
Frazer, Sir James, 44
Freud, Sigmund, 120
From Ritual to Romance, 174
From the Beast to the Blonde, 147, 151
Frontier Crossings, 79, 83
Future Sanctuary, 107, 111, 112, 113
Futurians, The, 86

G

Gaia, 8, 51-57
Gallipoli, 32-33
Galloway, David D., 136, 150
Gaskell, Elizabeth, 117
George C., Jacob, 51
Giger, 19
Gillespie, Bruce, 114, 182-85

Gillispie, Charles Coulston, 86
Glass Reptile Breakout, 9
God and Her Black Sense of Humour, 72
Golden Bough, The, 44
Gould, Stephen Jay, 98, 102-03
Grahame Bond, 20, 35
Grant, Rob, 106
Green, Dorothy, 193
Green, Guy, 15
Green, Harriet, 193
Greene, Donald, 88
Greenish, Mr., 193
Greer, Germaine, 19
Grimal, Pierre, 181
Growth of Biological Thought, The, 103
Guardian, The, 91, 101
Guards! Guards!, 123, 149
Gulliver's Travels, 121
Guns of Avalon, The, 169, 173-74, 180

H

H. G. Wells and Regressive Evolution, 101
H.G. Wells and the Scientific Imagination, 102
Haber, Karen, 60
Hall, Melissa Mia, 59
Halliday, M.A.K., 124
Halloween, 18
Hammond, J.R., 101
Hand of Oberon, The, 169, 173, 180
Handmaid's Tale, The, 141
Hanging Rock, 24
Hardin, Nancy Shields, 83
Harding, Lee, 11, 107-15, 183-85
Harrison, Harry, 185
Hartman, Geoffrey, 88
Hassler, Donald M., 84
Hawks, Howard, 18, 22
Hawthorne, Nathaniel, 57
Heartsease, 107
Heinlein, Robert, 8, 152, 159
Hero With a Thousand Faces, The, 130, 134, 150
Hiller, Arthur, 33
Hillerman, Tony, 154
Hills, Martin, 83
History Of Music, 85
Hitchcock, Alfred, 16, 18, 21-25, 35
Hobbit, The, 121, 129, 140
Hogfather, 123, 149
Holder, Nancy, 59
Homer, 118, 131, 135

Homesdale, 15, 24, 31
Hooked on Buzzer, 59
Horizons, 191, 192
Howarth, Patrick, 133-34, 150
Hughes, David Y., 102
Human Evolution and Artificial Process, 95
Hutcheon, Linda, 138-45, 150
Huxley, Aldous, 18
Huxley, T.H., 94, 102

I

Ikin, Van, 7, 9, 111
Image–Music–Text, 150
Impulse, 185-86
In Defence of Fantasy, 151
In Search of Wonder, 183
In the Shadows of My Fear, 60
Ingersoll, Earl G., 57
Interesting Times, 123, 137, 143-44, 149
Invincible, The, 12
Invisible Man, The, 90, 101
Island of Doctor Moreau, The, 90-101

J

Jack of Shadows, 180
Jackson, Robert, 83
Jackson, Rosemary, 116-22, 150
Jacobs, Rivka, 61
James, Henry, 119
Jingo, 123, 149
JOE, 184, 191-92
Jones, Langdon, 184
Jones, Peter V., 135
Journal of Omphalistic Epistemology, The (JOE), 184
Jung, Carl, 21, 26, 77, 80, 169
Jurassic Park, 101

K

Kafka, Franz, 101, 119
Kantor, Fredrick, 189
Keep, Christopher, 139
Keys to December, The, 161
Knight, Damon, 85-86, 183, 191
Koch, Christopher, 32
Koch, Phillip, 32
Krumm, Pascale, 90
Kubrick, Stanley, 18, 21, 24, 35, 36
Kurosawa, Akira, 22

L

La Bête humaine, 101

La conquete de l'air et la paix universelle, 50
Lady who Sailed "The Soul," 195
Langford, David, 182
Larousse World Mythology, 181
Last Battle, The, 48
Last Continent, The, 123, 141, 149
Last Human, 104-06
Last Wave, The, 15, 19, 21-22, 31,-32, 35
Le Guin, Ursula K., 66-68, 87-89, 122, 140
Lee, Alison, 107, 111, 115, 145-46, 150, 183
Lee, Tanith, 58-59
Left Hand of Darkness, The, 88-89
Legends: New Works by the Masters of Modern Fantasy, 150
Lem, Stanislaw, 12
Lessing, Doris, 8, 77-83
Lewis, C.S., 44, 48, 118, 128
Light Fantastic, The, 121-24, 127, 135-36, 143, 149
Linebarger, Paul Anthony Myron (Cordwainer Smith), 192-93
Lipking, Lawrence, 85
Lipton Village Society, The, 70
Literary Fantastic, The, 150
Little Folks' Book of Flower Fairies, The, 123
Little Maid Lost, 61
Lives of the Poets, 85
Long View, The, 191
Lord of Light, 156, 164, 168, 175-81
Lord of the Rings, 8, 128, 140
Lord of The Rings, 37-49
Lord of Thunder, 154
Lords and Ladies, 123, 139, 149
Lore of the Unicorn, The, 180
Lost World, The, 101
Love Story, 33
Lovecraft, H.P, 121, 140
Lovelock, James E., 53-57
Lucy, Niall, 146, 150

M

Macbeth, 131, 139
MacLean, Katherine, 62-63
Magus, The, 15
Making of the Representative for Planet 8, 77, 81, 83
Mallet, Francois, 50
Man Returned, A, 193
Mannix, George, 10, 15

Marriages Between Zones Three, Four and Five, 77, 80
Martin, George R.R. 159
Maskerade, 123, 149
Masks and the Man, 180
Massie, Elizabeth, 59
Masters of the Maze, 184
Mayr, Ernst, 96, 99, 103
McCaffrey, Anne, 65-66
McConnell, Frank, 103
McCracken, Scott, 117, 150
McElroy, Jim, 31, 33
McFarlane, Brian, 25
McHale, Brian, 124-25, 129, 144-46, 150
McIntyre, Vonda, 67
McLaughlin, Tim, 139
McMullen, Sean, 9
Memoirs Found in a Bathtub, 12
Memories, Dreams, Reflections, 21
Men at Arms, 123, 149
Men Return, The, 184
Merril, Judith, 63, 184
Metamorphosis, The, 101, 119
Midnight Madness, 61
Midnight's Children, 141
Midsummer Night's Dream, A, 139
Miller, P. Schuyler, 184
Minning, Jill, 92, 101
Misplaced Persons, 110
Mitchell, Chalmers, 91
Monster McGill, 60
Monteleone, Tom, 159
Moorcock, Michael, 184, 189, 191
Moore, John A., 102
Morphology of the Folk Tale, 134
Morrow, Gray, 157, 161
Mort, 121, 123, 143, 149
Mortal Fire, 9
Mother Calls But I Do Not Answer, 59
Moving Pictures, 123, 149
My Lady Tongue, 70
My Lady Tongue & Other Tales, 69
My Name is Legion, 153
My Secret Garden, 83
Mythical and Fabulous Creatures, 101

N

Name of the Rose, The, 139-41
Natural History, 102-03
Natural Theology, 103
Naylor, Doug, 104, 106
New Worlds, 189-90
Newbolt, Sir Henry, 133-34

Nicholls, Peter, 15
Nine Princes in Amber, 155, 169
Nineteen Eighty-Four, 122
Nobody Lives There Now. Nothing Happens, 59
Nobody's Home, 66-67
Norstrilian News, 192
Norton, Andre, 102-03, 154
Notebooks/Memoirs/ Archives: Reading and Rereading Doris Lessing, 83

O

Of Mist and Grass and Sand, 67
On Heroes and Hero Worship, 133, 150
On the Storm Planet, 194
Ordering of the Arts in Eighteenth-Century England, The, 85
Orgelm, Sandra, 58
Origin of Species, The, 93, 102
Orlock, Carol, 59
Orwell, George, 116, 122
Osborne, Cary G., 60
Overskill, 180

P

Paley, William, 97-98, 103
Panda's Thumb, The, 103
Pavane, 185, 186
Payes, Rachel Cosgrove, 59
Perfect Vacuum, A, 12
Perrault, 147
Peters, B.F., 166, 180
Philmus, Robert M., 102
Picnic, 30
Picnic at Hanging Rock, 15, 29, 31
Pierce, John J., 194
Planet Named Shayol, A, 194
Play Up and Play the Game, 133, 150
Plumber, The, 15, 24, 29-33
Poetics of Postmodernism, A, 150
Pohl, Fred, 87
Polanski, Roman, 15
Politella, Joseph, 181
Pollard, Geoff, 10
Porter, Andrew, 193
Postmodern Literary Theory, 150
Postmodernist Fiction, 150
Pratchett, Terry, 8, 73, 116,-50
Pratt, Annis, 83
Prelude, The, 88
Propp, Vladimir, 134
Ptacek, Kathryn, 58
Pulp Reading Popular Fiction, 150

Putten, Joan Vander, 60
Pyramids, 120-23, 149

Q

Quartet in Death Minor, 70
Quest of Three Worlds, 194
Quincy, 148

R

Rabkin, Eric, 121
Ransom Cowl Walks the Road, 60
Realism and Power, 150
Reaper Man, 123, 150
Red Dwarf, 104-06
Red Ochre, 71-72
Reed, Kit, 60, 64, 68
Renoir, Pierre-Auguste, 22
Return of the Heroes, 50
Return of the Jedi, 41
Reynard, Alan (Lee Harding), 184
Rieux, E.V, 133
Rilke, Rainer Maria, 165, 166, 180
Robber Bride, The, 141
Roberts, Keith, 185-86, 192
Rottensteiner, Franz, 191-92
Rousseau, J-J, 42
Rousseau, Yvonne, 58, 193
Rowe, Marsha, 83
Rushdie, Salman, 141, 146-47
Russ, Joanna, 66-68
Russo, Patricia, 60

S

Saciuk, Olena H., 101
Sallis, James, 190
Sambo Sentado, 60
Sargent, Pamela, 62
Saturday Review, The, 91, 101
Scanners Live in Vain, 194
Scarlet Letter, The, 57
Scholes, Robert, 87-88
Schwartz, Eugene S., 180
Science as a Way of Knowing, 102
Science Fantasy, 117, 120, 185
Science Fiction of H.G. Wells, 103
Science Fiction Review, 182
Science of the Discworld, The, 119, 150
Science-Fiction Studies, 57
Scott, Ridley, 19, 36
Second Foundation, 53, 57
Sentimental Agents in the Volyen Empire, The, 77, 82
Seven Religions, 181

Sex and/or Mr. Morrison, 67
SF Commentary, 112, 182, 191-92
Shabistri, Sage Mahmoud, 83
Shakespeare, William, 47, 131, 139
Shape of the Fantastic, The, 101
Shelley, Mary, 85, 91
Shepard, Odell, 180
Shikasta, 77- 83
Ship Who Sang, The, 65
Shklovsky, Victor, 121
Sign of the Unicorn, The, 169
Silverberg, Robert, 123, 146, 150, 193-94
Sirian Experiments, The, 77, 81, 83
Sister, 59, 60
Sladek, John, 190
Slaughterhouse-Five, 139-41
Slide Number Seven, 60
Small Gods, 121-23, 127-28, 141-42, 150
Smith, Kevin, 116
Social Science Fiction, 87
Sonnets to Orpheus, The, 166
Soul Music, 123, 150
Sourcery, 123, 135, 138, 150
South, Malcolm, 101
Space Lords, 193-94
Speculation, 182, 193
Star Diaries, The, 12
Star Wars, 8, 18, 37, 40-49, 158
Starman, 75
Stevenson, R.L.,91
Stewart, Ian, 150
Stoker, Bram, 103, 123
Structural Fabulations, 87
Sturgeon, Theodore, 163
Sussex, Lucy, 69-72
Swain, Dwight V., 185
Swift, Graham, 147
Swinfen, Ann, 118-19, 151

T

Taylor, Jenny, 83
Taylor, Lucy, 60
Tem, Melanie, 61
Tenant, The, 15
That Only a Mother, 63
Thatcher, Margaret, 148
Thing, The, 18
This Immortal, 156, 180
Thoms, Albie, 19
Thorn Birds, The, 32, 33
Three Stigmata of Palmer Eldritch, The, 184
Time Bomb, 152

Time Machine, The, 90, 92, 101
Time Masters, The, 152
Todorov, Tzvetan, 118-19, 151
Tolkien, J. R. R., 8, 13, 39, 41, 43, 48, 50, 118-29, 132, 140, 148
Troilus and Cressida, 47
True Love, 60
Tucker, Wilson, 152
Turn of the Screw, The, 119
Turner, George, 114, 183, 186, 190
Tuttle, Lisa, 58-59
Twilight Zone, 15
2001, 17, 24, 101
Two Towers, The, 43, 48

U

Up Through an Empty House of Stars, 182
Uses of Enchantment, The, 150

V

van Vogt, A. E., 8
Vance, Jack, 156, 184
Vaster Than Empires and More Slow, 66, 67
Vian, Boris, 20
Virginia Quarterly Review, 102
Vonnegut, Kurt, 141, 146

W

Wagar, W. Warren, 95, 102
Waiting for the End of the World, 107, 111-14
Walters, Marilyn, 62
War of the Worlds, The, 90, 101
Warhol, Andy, 20, 139
Warneke, Sara (Sara Douglass), 73
Warner, Harry, 183, 191-92
Warner, Marina, 33, 147, 151
Warriors of the Tao, 9
Waterland, 141-42
Web of Time, The, 107, 112, 114
Webb, Wendy, 61
Weeping Sky, The, 107-09, 113-14
Weir, Peter, 15, 27, 30
Weldon, Fay, 60

Wells, H.G., 11, 44, 90-96, 99-102
Wells: Early Writings in Science and Science Fiction, 102
Wellsian, The, 44, 101
Weston, Jessie, 174
Weston, Peter, 193
When I Was Miss Dow, 66
When Thunder Walks, 61
White Hotel, The, 142
Who Goes There?, 18
Widdershins, K. U. F. (John Foyster), 184-87, 191-92
Wilhelm, Kate, 65, 68
Williams, Tess, 73
Williamson, David, 32-33
Williamson, Jack, 158
Wind People, The, 65
Wingrove, David, 79, 83
Witches Abroad, 123, 129, 140, 150
Women of Darkness: Original Horror and Dark Fantasy by Contemporary Women Writers, 58-61
Women of Wonder, 62, 68
Wordsworth, William, 84, 88-89
Wordsworth's Poetry, 1787-1814, 88
World of Shadows, A, 107-08, 113
World of Tiers series (P.J. Farmer), 160
Wynne, Bradley, 10
Wyrd Sisters, 123, 139, 150

X

Xeno Fiction, 9

Y

Yarbro, Chelsea Quinn, 63-64
Year of Living Dangerously, The, 26, 32, 33
Yoke, Carl P., 11, 163
you mate a swan and a gander, who will ride?, 83

Z

Zelazny, Roger, 8, 11, 152-81
Zola, Emile, 101

www.ingramcontent.com/pod-product-compliance
Lightning Source LLC
LaVergne TN
LVHW041617070426
835507LV00008B/290